A-Z
of
Plant & Machinery

2018-19 Edition

Ray Chidell & Jake Iles

© Claritax Books Ltd (July 2018)

Disclaimer

This publication is sold with the understanding that neither the publishers nor the authors, with regard to this publication, are engaged in providing legal or professional services.

The material contained in this publication does not constitute tax advice and readers are advised that they should always obtain such professional advice before acting, or refraining from acting, on any information contained in this book. Readers are also advised that UK tax law is subject to frequent and unpredictable change.

Every effort has been taken to compile the contents of this book accurately and carefully. However, neither the publisher nor the author can accept any responsibility or liability to any person, whether a purchaser of this book or not, in respect of anything done or omitted to be done by any such person in reliance, partly or wholly, on any part or on the whole of the contents of this book.

Claritax Books is a trading name of Claritax Books Ltd.

Claritax Books Ltd
6 Grosvenor Park Road
Chester
CH1 1QQ

Company number 07658388
VAT number 114 9371 20

Law date

The text is based on the tax law as at 15 June 2018.

First edition August 2012
Second edition August 2013
Third edition August 2014
Fourth edition September 2015
Fifth edition August 2016
Sixth edition August 2017
This seventh edition July 2018

A-Z
of
Plant & Machinery

2018-19 Edition

Ray Chidell & Jake Iles

Published by:

Claritax Books Ltd
6 Grosvenor Park Road
Chester, CH1 1QQ

www.claritaxbooks.com

ISBN: 978-1-912386-06-2

Other titles from Claritax Books

Other tax titles from Claritax Books include:

- Advising British Expats
- Capital Allowances (companion volume to this book)
- Capital Allowances for Commercial Property
- Construction Industry Scheme
- Discovery Assessments
- Employee Benefits & Expenses
- Employment Status
- Enterprise Investment Scheme
- Entrepreneurs' Relief
- Financial Planning with Trusts
- Furnished Holiday Lettings
- Main Residence Relief
- Pension Tax Guide
- Research and Development
- Residence: The Definition in Practice
- Stamp Duty Land Tax
- Tax Chamber Hearings
- Tax Losses
- VAT Registration

See www.claritaxbooks.com for details of these and of our other forthcoming titles.

About the authors

Ray Chidell, MA (Cantab), CTA (Fellow)

Ray has worked as a tax specialist for around 30 years and is recognised as one of the UK's leading authorities on capital allowances. Ray originally qualified as a tax inspector but switched to the accounting profession in 1989, working for Baker Tilly and later Mazars, the latter role including six years as a tax partner.

Ray is now a technical director of Six Forward Capital Allowances, supporting the provision of a full capital allowances service to accountants and their clients.

Ray has written about capital allowances matters for more than two decades. After working as a senior technical author for other publishers for eight years, he launched Claritax Books in 2011, a role he continues to enjoy alongside his technical capital allowances work.

Ray can be contacted by phone on 01244 342179, or by email to raychidell@claritax.co.uk.

Jake Iles MBA, MCMI

Jake has worked as a capital allowances specialist for the last 12 years, having originally qualified as a mechanical and electrical engineer. In 1997 he moved into senior programme management on an unrivalled multinational collaborative project. His responsibilities on that project included, among other things, the life cycle cost, funding, improvements and environmental issues facing the construction and management of buildings and facilities in four European countries.

Jake has been the managing director of Six Forward Capital Allowances for eight years and, along with his multi-skilled team, is responsible for the provision of a full capital allowances service, that includes in-house survey and valuation, to more than 250 UK accountants and their clients, analysing expenditure of over £1 billion per year.

Jake has written capital allowances articles for the accounting institutions and is a regular presenter and speaker, sometimes with Ray, to tax specialists, accountants and solicitors.

Jake can be contacted on 0800 0787 964 or by email to jiles@sixforward.com.

Abbreviations

AIA	Annual investment allowance
Art.	Article
BIM	Business Income Manual
BTC	British Tax Cases
CA	Capital Allowances (manual)
CAA 2001	Capital Allowances Act 2001
CG	Capital Gains (manual)
CGT	capital gains tax
Ch.	Chapter
CIR	Commissioners of Inland Revenue
CPSE	Commercial property standard enquiries
CT	Corporation tax
CTA	Corporation Tax Act
ECAs	Enhanced capital allowances
EEA	European Economic Area
EIM	Employment Income Manual
ESC	Extra statutory concession
EU	European Union
FA	Finance Act
FHL	Furnished holiday letting
FYA	First-year allowance
GAAP	Generally accepted accounting principles
HMRC	HM Revenue & Customs
HVAC	Heating, ventilation and air conditioning
IBA	Industrial buildings allowances
ITA 2007	Income Tax Act 2007
ITEPA 2003	Income Tax (Earnings and Pensions) Act 2003
ITTOIA 2005	Income Tax (Trading and Other Income) Act 2005
OT	Oil Taxation Manual
P&M	Plant and machinery
PMAs	Plant and machinery allowances
Pt.	Part
Reg.	Regulation
S.	Section
Sch.	Schedule
SDLT	Stamp duty land tax

SI	Statutory instrument
TCGA 1992	The Taxation of Capital Gains Act 1992
TIIN	Tax information and impact note
TMA 1970	Taxes Management Act 1970
UKFTT	United Kingdom First-tier Tribunal
UKHL	United Kingdom House of Lords
UKUT	United Kingdom Upper Tribunal
WDA	Writing-down allowance

Table of contents

Appendices

Preface

As this 2018-19 edition is published, there is a question mark over the future (or at least the future direction) of capital allowances, pending the outcome of a review by the Office of Tax Simplification.

That review had the stated purpose of simplifying the capital allowances system by addressing "issues of uncertainty as regards boundaries and policy objective". The review also suggested that "broader and more radical approaches" might be considered, including even the replacement of capital allowances by accounts depreciation. The report did warn, however, that the impacts of such a change would need careful consideration.

For now, at least, capital allowances remain firmly in place, and they continue to offer one of the most important (and wholly legitimate) forms of tax relief for businesses of all sizes.

Since publication of the previous edition, I have continued to work closely with Jake Iles and his team in my capacity as a (part-time) technical director with Six Forward Capital Allowances. Even though I have worked in the field of capital allowances for some 30 years, this work continues to provide day-to-day insights into the practical aspects of capital allowances claims.

This book continues to reflect Jake's practical experience and suggestions, and I am grateful to him and to all the team at Six Forward for their feedback and suggestions for new content.

Ray Chidell
June 2018

Introduction

The first goal of this *A to Z of Plant and Machinery* is to help readers, in a very practical way, to determine whether (or when) particular assets are likely to qualify as plant or machinery for capital allowance purposes. The book also serves as a practical guide to the claiming of first-year allowances under the somewhat complex rules for energy-saving and water-saving assets.

The book is written to complement *Capital Allowances* 2018-19, by the same authors and also available from Claritax Books.

This 2018-19 edition includes the following new material.

- additional HMRC example re distinction between repairs and capital expenditure (with commentary re distinction between fixtures and non-fixtures) (**3.4**);

- updated coverage re air-to-air energy recovery devices (**A6**).

- expanded coverage of battery technology (**B4**).

- removal of ECAs for localised rapid steam generators (**B8**).

- new section on costs of cabling (**C1**).

- updated coverage of allowances for cars (**C11**).

- updated coverage of charging points for electric vehicles (**C15 and F11**).

- expanded coverage of the treatment of doors, including the caveat regarding assets with a principal purpose of enclosing the interior of a building (**D13**).

- new category giving amended rules for first-year tax credits (**F12**).

- extension of first-year allowances for gas refuelling equipment (**G2**).

- expanded coverage of the treatment of gates, regarding assets with a principal purpose of enclosing the interior of a building (**G4**).

- new category of green technology, detailing different capital allowances treatments (**G10**).

- new category re hearses and funeral vehicles (**H6**).
- new sub-category re evaporative air coolers (**H8**).
- expanded commentary re inspection pits (**I3**).
- additional categories of lighting controls qualifying for enhanced capital allowances (**L7**).
- detail provided for efficient white lighting units (**L7**).
- removal of high efficiency lighting units from categories qualifying for enhanced capital allowances (**L7**).
- new category re line markings in a car park (**L9**).
- important development in HMRC attitude towards definition of "machinery" (**M1**).
- expanded coverage of the treatment of partition walls, regarding assets with a principal purpose of enclosing the interior of a building (**P3**).
- removal of ECAs for biomass fired warm air heaters (**R1**).
- expanded coverage of distinction between drainage and sewerage systems (**S6**).
- considerable expansion of the commentary on artificial sports surfaces, especially the *Anchor International* decision (**S29**).
- updated coverage of waste heat to electricity conversion equipment (**W6**).
- extension of first-year allowances for zero-emission goods vehicles (**Z1**).
- caveat about application of the *Football League* letter to current circumstances (**Appendix 2 (introduction)**).
- enactment of the *Capital Allowances (Energy-saving Plant and Machinery) Order* 2018 (SI 2018/268) (**A5, A6, A18, B8, C24, C26, E5, H1, H7, H8, M11, R1, R6, S24, U2**).

The details of enhanced capital allowances have once more been reviewed and the commentary has been updated as necessary to reflect appropriate changes.

The structure of the book is simple. After the introductory chapters, the main A to Z section provides analyses of more than 300 categories of expenditure. These various categories may be the subject of particular statutory references, or of a useful case law interpretation. HMRC may have given guidance on how they would intend to apply the law in relation to the expenditure in question. But the categories are also those that come up in practice all the time. Anyone who has ever had to analyse expenditure on a new property, for example, will have found it necessary to consider the correct treatment of hot and cold water systems, of general lighting, of associated professional fees, and so on.

The HMRC guidance is typically found in the *Capital Allowances Manual*, but the HMRC perspective is also to be unearthed in unexpected places; examples include guidelines issued in relation to such wide-ranging activities as football on the one hand, and the pig industry on the other. These semi-official comments are invariably of wider interest than just for the intended audience and several are included in appendices to this book.

Statutory and case law references are provided at all appropriate points to give authority to what the authors have written. HMRC guidance notes are referred to where these add something to what is already clear from the legal authorities. The HMRC view is occasionally challenged where it seems to the authors that the view is not correct, or where there may be different legitimate interpretations of the law on a particular item.

1. Capital allowances

1.1 Introduction

Capital allowances are relevant for virtually every business in the UK, as well as for investors in commercial property. They have been described as the tax equivalent of depreciation which, though an imperfect analogy, is not a bad starting point.

The law governing capital allowances changes frequently, and recent years have seen the demise – after many decades – of industrial and agricultural buildings allowances. New allowances were introduced from April 2007 for the costs of business premises renovations and flat conversions, but both of these schemes have now been closed.

The most commonly claimed allowances, by far, are for expenditure on plant and machinery, and here too the scheme is in a constant state of flux. Innovations are brought in every year but 2008 saw some particularly radical changes, including the introduction of the concepts of "integral features" and of the "annual investment allowance". 2012 introduced important further changes, this time relating specifically to fixtures in property.

Before allowances can be given for "plant or machinery" it is obviously necessary to know what that term encompasses, yet this is often far from clear. Statutory rules introduced in the 1990s went some way towards creating a firmer definition, but those rules, now starting at section 21 of CAA 2001, still leave many questions unanswered. In essence, the distinction is drawn between the premises or setting within which a qualifying activity is conducted, and the apparatus used in the course of that activity. In practice, the setting and the apparatus can overlap and there are many grey areas. Dozens of cases have been taken to court where it has not been possible for a business to reach agreement with the tax authorities about where the line should be drawn.

One complication is that the correct capital allowances treatment of a particular asset is coloured by its context. A ship, for example, will normally qualify quite clearly as an item of plant or machinery, yet the best known capital allowances case concerning a ship determined that it did not so qualify in the particular circumstances of the case (as it was functioning only as the premises for the business in question).

For this reason, any simple list of assets will rarely provide a satisfactory statement of the correct tax treatment. What is required is a more nuanced and sophisticated analysis, where the likely outcome is explored in the context of the statutory rules and of case law precedents. In practice, it is also helpful to understand (though not to accept unquestioningly) the HMRC perspective. This book aims to bring together those three elements (statutes, case law, HMRC guidance) and to wrap them within an expert commentary based on the authors' experience of working with capital allowances for real businesses over many years.

1.2 Illogical distinctions

Case law shows that it is notoriously difficult to pin down the meaning of "plant". As Stephenson LJ commented in his judgment in *Cole Bros*:

> "The more definitions multiply, the less enviable grows the task of H.M. Inspectors of Taxes. If they 'traverse the whole gamut of reported cases' crossing the border into Scotland and the seas to Australia in their search for guidance, they find plant in the most unlikely objects, from a horse to a swimming pool, from a dry dock to a mural decoration. Faced with such applications of the word, all supported by cogent reasoning, they may be pardoned for finding anything, or almost anything, to be or not to be plant and may be justified in making any number, or almost any number, of inconsistent concessions and illogical distinctions. It all depends on the circumstances, especially the work of the particular taxpayer, and (I feel bound to add) on how it strikes the particular judges of the question, whether in tax administration or on the judicial bench."

It is unfortunate that such a fundamental concept, affecting all businesses and often involving substantial amounts of expenditure, should have been left so open to the whims of individual interpretation. The comments quoted above pre-date the legislation now beginning at s. 21, but in reality that legislation has been of limited help in defining the slippery notion of "plant". At least the 2008 legislation, whereby certain assets are categorised as "integral features", has brought a greater degree of certainty to some common types of expenditure, including electrical work and cold water systems. These developments are very welcome, though even here the scope of the legislation is at times unclear.

Case: *Cole Brothers Ltd v Phillips* [1982] BTC 208

1.3   How the law works

1.3.1   Overview

It is essential to understand how the statutory provisions relating to plant and machinery work, as it is easy to misapply the rules at sections 21 to 23 (reproduced at **Appendix 1**). There follows an overview of the legislative structure for this issue.

1.3.2   Qualifying expenditure

Section 11(1) provides that plant and machinery allowances can only be given if a person incurs qualifying expenditure.

Section 11(4) gives a "general rule" whereby expenditure is qualifying expenditure if "it is capital expenditure on the provision of plant or machinery" and if other conditions are met.

1.3.3   Buildings

Section 21(1) then states that "expenditure on the provision of plant or machinery does not include expenditure on the provision of a building" and s. 21(2) explains that "the provision of a building includes its construction or acquisition".

A broad definition of "building" is given for these purposes, including any items in list A that are "in, or connected with, the building". List A includes the essential framework of a building incorporating (by way of examples only) walls, floors, ceilings, windows, mains services, and drainage systems.

Without further provision, all (or virtually all) fixtures in property would be excluded from allowances on the grounds that they are incorporated in the building.

Section 21 is, however, subject to s. 23 (see **1.3.5** below).

1.3.4   Structures

Just as s. 21 excludes buildings from qualifying as plant or machinery, so s. 22 provides a similar outcome for "structures, assets and works". The exclusion in fact applies to works involving the alteration of land, to fixed structures except buildings, and to a range of listed assets (list B). The "provision" of a structure is defined to include "its construction or acquisition" (s. 22(2)).

List B includes (among many other items) roads, canals and bridges. It also covers, by default, all other fixed structures apart from certain specified exceptions.

Once more, however, the section is subject to s. 23.

1.3.5   Exceptions

Section 23 contains some very important provisions, but the precise effect of the section can be confusing. Indeed, when the legislation now at sections 21 to 23 (reproduced at **Appendix 1**) was enacted, the Institute of Taxation complained that the new rules introduced a complex hybrid system for distinguishing building from plant (IoT 6/94: representations on FA 1994, s. 117, 118).

To avoid confusion, it is advisable to look at s. 23 as constituting two halves that work independently from one another. First, s. 23 lists certain particular provisions that are unaffected by the restrictions for buildings and structures (given by s. 21 and s. 22 respectively, as described immediately above). These provisions relate to thermal insulation, personal security, integral features, and software.

For each of these categories, the legislation has particular rules saying that the expenditure in question specifically qualifies for plant and machinery allowances. For example, allowances for integral features or for thermal insulation are given "as if ... the expenditure were capital expenditure on the provision of plant or machinery". Section 23 thus ensures that sections 21 and 22 cannot override those deeming provisions that allow certain types of expenditure to qualify as plant or machinery.

The remaining part of s. 23 works differently, though. This provides a long list of assets ("list C"), being "expenditure unaffected by sections 21 and 22". The key point to note is that inclusion in list C does not guarantee that expenditure on the item in question will qualify as plant or machinery; the effect of this part of s. 23 is merely to remove the automatic bar on claiming allowances on the items in question. The background to what is now list C was a perception that the Courts were starting to err too much in favour of the taxpayer in various appeals regarding plant and machinery. Consider, for example, these words in the Revenue response to the IoT back in 1994:

> "As you know, court cases have, over the years, increasingly reclassified expenditure on buildings and structures as being expenditure on plant. This erosion in the plant/structure boundary has affected Exchequer receipts and has in itself created continuing uncertainty.
>
> The intention behind the legislation is therefore to strengthen the current boundary, and to ensure that no further erosion takes place. It would of course be difficult for the new rules to replicate past treatment in every case. Nevertheless, the broad aim is to provide exclusions for assets currently regarded as plant as a result of Court decisions, so as to leave the present position unchanged."

The point was made in stronger terms by Stephen Dorrell, speaking for the government when the clauses were debated in Parliament. He was clear that the purpose of the new legislation was "to prevent further changes in the law" and again "to prevent further development of case law". He stated specifically that "we are not seeking to revisit the law established by the Courts" and again that "it is not our intention to change the capital treatment of any class of asset". Once more, he stated that "nothing in the clause is intended to change existing practice of how cases are treated". Occasionally, in areas of doubt, the Courts will try to fathom the intentions of Parliament. In such cases, it may be useful to refer to these assurances that the government was not seeking to change "existing practice".

"Thus far but no further" was the approach. This was a strange concept, for it meant that if an asset happened to have been the subject of a successful appeal the tax treatment of that particular asset was frozen into the legislation. The statutory rules were being made subservient to the case law, rather than the other way round. This accounts for the bizarre range of assets captured in list C that have little internal logic (though even that unusual approach does not account for other oddities such as the doubling up of refrigeration equipment at items 5 and 9).

To reiterate the key point, inclusion in list C does not guarantee that an item qualifies as plant or machinery. If an asset is initially caught by s. 21 or s. 22 (in broad terms, being respectively a building or a structure) the effect of inclusion in list C is simply to remove the statutory restriction that would automatically prevent a claim. The actual tax treatment of the asset can then be considered on its own merits, using the case law precedents established before or since the statutory rules were introduced in 1994.

This point has caused confusion both outside and within HMRC. See under **Pictures** below for an example of where HMRC seem to be misapplying the rules in this respect.

1.4 Applying the law in practice

Establishing the correct capital allowances treatment of a particular asset is not straightforward. In brief, though, the following steps may be followed:

- Check that the expenditure in question is capital expenditure. If it is not, capital allowances will not be due but tax relief may be available through other mechanisms.
- Do the assets being considered fall into any of the restricted categories at s. 21 (buildings) or s. 22 (structures)?
- If the assets are potentially caught by those restrictions, is the chance to claim capital allowances saved by any of the provisions listed at s. 23?
- If the assets in question fall within the categories listed at s. 23(2), then allowances will be due but in some cases the costs incurred will be "special rate" expenditure, which may attract tax relief at a slower rate.
- If an item is caught by s. 21 or s. 22, and is not rescued by s. 23(2), allowances will be prohibited unless the expenditure is on an asset shown in list C.

- If an item is not caught by s. 21 or s. 22, or if it is initially so caught but it is shown at list C, case law principles must be applied to determine whether or not allowances are due.

- In applying the case law principles, it is also worth checking if HMRC guidance is available to help to determine the correct tax treatment. It should always be remembered, however, that the HMRC manuals and other guidance material have no statutory force and that such commentary may be incorrect in some cases.

To illustrate this with a practical example, take the question of a hut put up by a builder to provide canteen and toilet facilities for workers at particular sites. The reasoning to follow will be:

- Assuming that the hut is to be kept in use for at least two years, it should be clear that the cost is capital expenditure.

- The cost of the hut is potentially caught by either s. 21 (as a building) or by s. 22 (as a structure).

- There is nothing relevant at s. 23(2), but item 21 at list C refers to "moveable buildings intended to be moved in the course of the qualifying activity".

- That does not of itself mean that the hut can qualify for allowances, but it can at least be considered using case law principles.

- Case law coverage of moveable buildings is not always helpful, but HMRC guidance does in this case come to the rescue, as allowances are specifically permitted for such buildings. (See **Buildings (moveable)** for a much fuller discussion.)

If, instead, the huts in question were used for some other trade – perhaps for selling items at trade fairs around the country – the HMRC guidance is less favourable. It would then be necessary to apply general principles to determine the correct outcome. In this case, it may be appropriate to question the HMRC view, so as to see if it can stand up to scrutiny.

2.   Case law

2.1   Introduction

Any claim for capital allowances under Part 2 of the *Capital Allowances Act* 2001 must begin with by addressing the question of whether the expenditure in question qualifies as plant or machinery. Although there are some statutory principles, as well as case law stretching back to the nineteenth century, the definition of this key concept remains uncertain in many day-to-day circumstances.

Given that the capital allowances legislation contains no positive definition of "plant or machinery" it has fallen to the courts to develop an interpretation over the years. The meaning of "machinery" has caused relatively few problems and is considered under **Machinery** in the A to Z section below.

Defining "plant" has been a far greater challenge, and it is here that a familiarity with the relevant case law is required in any cases of doubt.

2.2   Capital expenditure

It is a fundamental principle (s. 1(1)) that expenditure must be capital in nature if it is to qualify for capital allowances.

It is likely today that an item that fails to qualify for allowances on these grounds will qualify for a revenue deduction in computing business profits (though the "wholly and exclusively" concept is not identical for capital allowances and for revenue expenditure). At various times in the past, however, it has suited the taxpayer to argue (under the rules as they then applied) that the expenditure was capital rather than revenue in nature.

Several cases have therefore been heard in which one consideration was whether the expenditure was capital.

The case of *Maden & Ireland* concerned knives and lasts with a low unit cost and a relatively short shelf life. The House of Lords had a difference of opinion, but found in favour of the company by a majority. As Lord Jenkins put it (for the majority view):

"The machines in conjunction with which the knives and lasts are used are admittedly capital assets. For the present purpose I see no ground for distinguishing the former from the latter in this respect apart from the small cost and relatively short life of the knives and lasts as compared with the machines. As to the cost, if the knives and lasts had an unlimited life the fact that they cost only a matter of £1 each would not, so far as I can see, afford any ground for denying them the character of capital assets. As to length of life, if each knife or last was worn out by one day's work it would lack the element of permanence which is undoubtedly essential to the conception of a capital asset. The knives and lasts worn out by each day's work would on this supposition have no better claim to rank as capital than would be possessed by the coal consumed daily in firing the boilers in a factory where the machines were worked by steam. On the other hand, I repeat that if each knife or last endured for ever I can see no ground for holding that it would not be a capital asset.

The case, therefore, appears to me to turn in the end on the question of permanence, which is largely a question of degree. I think the element of permanence looms larger in the conception of a capital asset than it does in the conception of plant. Nevertheless, I see no reason for holding that the average life of three years possessed by sole knives and making and finishing lasts is too short to justify their acceptance as capital assets. The average life of only 12 months possessed by upper knives seems to me to be near the line, but no attempt has been made to separate these knives and the other appliances, and I do not know whether it would have been practicable to do so. In point of function there is no distinction, so far as I can see, between the upper knives and the rest. I would therefore give the upper knives the benefit of the doubt and for the present purpose treat them as possessing the requisite degree of longevity."

In *Rose & Co*, by contrast, the court accepted the view of the commissioners that expenditure on pattern books did not constitute plant, as the books were not capital in nature:

"The life of each set of pattern books is a little more than two years. The sole faction of the pattern books is to supply prospective customers during that period with patterns of papers currently in stock. The books have from the very start no value at all as a separate asset. At the end of each period the function of the books is spent. Then the books are scrapped and a new cycle begins. On these facts the cost of the books is, I think, simply an outlay incurred in selling the Company's papers. It is comparable to expenditure upon sale catalogues, or indeed any other advertising material.

There was no expert evidence before the Commissioners as to accountancy principles and practice, but it seems to me that upon the ordinary principles and practice of accountancy, as I understand them, such expenditure would be regarded as properly attributable to revenue. It would not, I think, be normal practice to bring in this intrinsically valueless article as a capital asset at the cost of manufacture and write it off during the period of its life.

I should mention that, by an arrangement with the Revenue which appears in para. 4(c) of the Case Stated, the expenditure on the pattern books was in practice spread over the two years of their life. Nothing, I think, turns on this point in the present case one way or the other. Clearly being spread over two years is no indication that the expenditure ought properly to be treated as capital."

Wear and tear allowances were not permitted for greyhounds with an average racing life of less than two years, in *Albion Greyhounds*.

The distinction between revenue and capital expenditure is considered in depth in **Chapter 3** below.

Cases: *Abbott v Albion Greyhounds (Salford) Ltd* (1945) 26 TC 39; *Hinton v Maden & Ireland Ltd* (1959) 38 TC 391; *Rose & Co. (Wallpaper & Paints) Ltd v Campbell* (1968) 44 TC 500

2.3   The wide definition of "plant"

2.3.1   *All apparatus, goods and chattels*

The starting point should always be a recognition that the term "plant" has been very widely defined by the courts over the years.

Lindley LJ attempted a definition in a case, *Yarmouth v France,* heard back in 1887 on a matter that had nothing to do with taxation:

> "There is no definition of plant in the Act: but, in its ordinary sense, it includes whatever apparatus is used by a businessman for carrying on his business – not his stock-in-trade which he buys or makes for sale; but all goods and chattels, fixed or moveable, live or dead, which he keeps for permanent employment in his business."

This quotation has been approved over and over again, in all courts, in discussions of the meaning of plant for capital allowances purposes. It can be seen as the cornerstone definition and – subject only to statutory provisions that restrict or expand its scope – it is thus of pre-eminent importance in determining what does or does not qualify as plant.

The key concepts to be drawn out of the quotation are the use of the term "apparatus" and the breadth of the definition, encompassing "all goods and chattels, fixed or moveable, live or dead". In other words, Lindley gave to the word "plant" the widest possible meaning. The term "apparatus" has sometimes been given a narrow interpretation, but "whatever apparatus" clearly indicates that it actually embraces a wide category of assets. That wide interpretation is made explicit in the last part of the quotation, encompassing "all goods and chattels".

Lindley LJ in that case also specifically refuted the notion that the concept of plant had to be confined to inanimate chattels.

Comprehensive meaning

The wide definition of "plant" was re-affirmed in the *Scottish & Newcastle Breweries* case. In the House of Lords, Lord Lowry approved the words of a lower court as follows:

> "The question of what is properly to be regarded as 'plant' can only be answered in the context of the particular industry concerned and, possibly, in light also of the particular circumstances of the individual taxpayers' own trade ... . I think that much difficulty is caused by seeking to place limitative interpretations on the simple word 'plant': I do not think that the classic definition propounded in *Yarmouth v*

France suggests that it is a word which is other than of comprehensive meaning."

Cases: *Yarmouth v France* [1887] 4 TRL 1; *CIR v Scottish & Newcastle Breweries Ltd* [1982] BTC 187

HMRC guidance

In the context of annual investment allowances, HMRC guidance states that:

> " 'Plant or machinery' actually covers almost every sort of asset a person may buy for the purposes of his/her business."

However, it is suggested that this should be taken with a large pinch of salt, first because it is simply not true and second because the guidance goes on to say, confusingly, that:

> "Really the only business assets not covered are land, buildings and cars (which are excluded by one of the 'general exclusions')."

Taken at face value, this would mean that the definition of plant or machinery would encompass a bridge (which it does not) but would not encompass a car (which it does). Such bland statements from HMRC are therefore dangerous and should not be relied on when planning significant capital expenditure.

The guidance does go on to list various "typical examples of plant or machinery" and these are covered under their own headings in this book.

Guidance: CA 23084

2.3.2   Extended meaning for capital allowances purposes

In holding that a barrister's law library was plant, the Court of Appeal in *Munby v Furlong* overturned the principles of a decision on essentially the same issue 50 years previously (*Daphne v Shaw*). Lord Denning first drew a distinction between capital and revenue expenditure on the library, and the case was then concerned only with the former.

In the 50 years between the two decisions, other courts had felt uncomfortable with the earlier decision but were constrained to follow it. In *Arthur Sanderson*, for example, Cross J had commented that:

> "If a barrister has to buy a new edition of a textbook in order to help him to write his opinions, I cannot see as a matter of principle why the book should not be regarded as a tool of his trade just as much as the typewriter on which his opinions are typed."

Lord Denning in *Munby v Furlong* agreed with this view, noting that case law precedents, including those established in the House of Lords:

> "... show quite conclusively that in this taxing statute the courts do not apply the meaning to the word 'plant' as the ordinary Englishman understands it. It has acquired by the course of decisions a special meaning in tax cases. It has acquired a special meaning, it seems to me, in the interests of fairness, that 'plant' extends virtually to a man's tools of trade — that is the phrase which Cross J used. It extends to the things which he uses day by day in the exercise of his profession."

Lord Denning was therefore clear that the term "plant" should not be restricted to "things used physically like a dentist's chair or an architect's table".

Cases: *McVeigh v Arthur Sanderson & Sons Limited* (1969) 45 TC 273; *Munby v Furlong* (1977) 50 TC 491

2.3.3 Wear and tear not a pre-requisite

A small point, but one worth noting in passing. In *Jarrold v Good*, which concerned the treatment of movable partitions, the court rejected the idea that the term "plant" should be restricted to something that is normally the subject of wear and tear. As Ormerod LJ put it:

> "I am not satisfied that it is proper to say that the word 'plant' in the context of the Income Tax Acts must be construed as something capable of being the subject of wear and tear, although that, I agree, may very well be the case. We do not have to decide it."

Case: *Jarrold v John Good & Sons Ltd* (1963) 40 TC 681

2.4 Premises or plant

2.4.1 Premises and setting not necessarily synonymous

The courts have not always been careful to draw a clear distinction between the "setting" of a business and the "premises" from which the business is carried on. When reviewing case law, it is therefore necessary to consider whether "setting" is being used merely as a synonym for the premises or building from which the trade is conducted, or whether it is being used in a more specialised sense, typically in relation to décor in the hospitality industry.

In the *Scottish & Newcastle Breweries* case, Counsel for the Revenue argued that "the setting of a trade was synonymous with the premises or place *in* which the trade is carried on, in contrast to the apparatus, or plant, *with* which it is carried on". However, Lord Cameron in the Court of Appeal brought out an important distinction, referring to "the 'setting' (as opposed to the structure or place within which the businessman conducts his business)". In the House of Lords, Lord Lowry clearly approved the distinction:

> "My Lords, the Crown's primary fallacy, in my opinion was to identify 'setting' inevitably with 'premises' or 'place' by misapplying to this case the observations of the judges in *Jarrold* when facing the question whether the articles are part of the premises or setting in which the business is carried on or part of the plant with which it is carried on. This was in a case where the word 'setting' had no theatrical or artistic significance, as it would have in the phrase 'appropriate setting' meaning 'the right atmosphere'."

So whilst the terms "premises" and "setting" may have the same meaning in some contexts, they will not invariably do so, and the distinction must be respected where it will make a difference. The concept of setting in the context of trades that provide a certain atmosphere as part of the "product" they are selling is considered at **2.4.5** below (**Décor**).

The *Scottish & Newcastle Breweries* quotation then continues by erasing the distinction that has just been drawn:

> "Even if one assumes that 'the setting' is the same thing as 'the premises', it is fallacious to say that articles used to adorn the

> setting thereby ceased to be apparatus used by the taxpayer company for carrying on their business."

Although this seems to muddy the waters somewhat, it is in reality helpful in clarifying that both meanings of "setting" are legitimate. In other cases, it is clear the terms "setting" and "premises" are indeed used synonymously, as for example in the *Leeds Permanent* case, which concerned screens offering privacy in a building society:

> "In applying [the *Yarmouth v France*] conception of the apparatus used by a business man for carrying on his business, it was found convenient to draw a distinction between the setting in which a business is carried on and the apparatus with which a business is carried on."

Similarly, the case of *J Lyons & Co* considered the treatment of lighting (long before the introduction of the rules for integral features, of course) and the judge commented:

> "In the present case, the question at issue may, I think, be put thus: Are the lamps and fitments properly to be regarded as part of the setting in which the business is carried on or as part of the apparatus used for carrying on the business? The presence of lamps in this building is not dictated by the nature of a particular trade their carried on, or by the fact that it is for trade purposes that the building is used."

In this case, too, it seems clear that the term "setting" was used in a generic sense to refer to the premises in which the trade was being carried on.

The case needs some caution, as the distinction between setting and apparatus has been questioned (in *Jarrold v Good*). Furthermore, Fox LJ in *Wimpy* has suggested that the lights in *Lyons* were neither plant nor part of the premises.

Cases: *Yarmouth v France* [1887] 4 TRL 1; *J. Lyons & Co. Ltd. v. Attorney-General* [1944] Ch. 281; *Jarrold v John Good & Sons Ltd* (1963) 40 TC 681; *CIR v Scottish & Newcastle Breweries Ltd* [1982] BTC 187; *Leeds Permanent Building Society v Proctor* [1982] BTC 347; *Wimpy International Ltd. v Warland* [1989] BTC 58

2.4.2   *Plant or premises*

The references in the *Yarmouth v France* quotation to "apparatus" and to "goods and chattels" can be used to differentiate between plant on the one hand and the premises (or "setting" – but see **2.4.1** above) on the other. This theme was to emerge more fully and specifically in later case law. For example, nearly a century later, the distinction was developed in the *Cole Bros* case where the judge explicitly drew out the etymological link between the taxation use of the term "plant" and its more familiar botanical use:

> "I think it worthwhile spending a moment's time in reflecting briefly on what the botanical analogy is. In the field of botany 'plant' is used in three quite separate contexts. It can mean a vegetable organism synthesizing its nourishment from inorganic materials by the use of chlorophyll. In this sense an oak tree is a plant, whilst the Matterhorn is not. It can mean a vegetable organism with a soft stem. In this sense a bluebell is a plant, but an oak tree is not. Neither of these senses affords the analogy. But the word can mean a vegetable organism deliberately placed in an artificially prepared setting.
>
> A gardener can say 'I am going to dig my flower beds in readiness for my plants' or, 'I am going to buy some plants at my garden centre'. It is this sense which gives it its analogical meanings, e.g. in medicine ('an organ transplant'), in crime ('it was planted on me'), or in industry, which is the sense we are now discussing, as the means by which a trade is carried on in an appropriately prepared setting. In each case, the contrast is between the thing implanted, i.e. the plant, and the prepared setting into which it is placed."

A good starting point is therefore to ask: is this the prepared setting into which other assets may be placed (in which case it is not plant) or is this asset itself being placed within a prepared setting (in which case it is)?

The point was brought out in a second world war compensation claim case, that of *J. Lyons & Co*, where it was held that "the electric lamps and fittings were not part of the apparatus used for carrying on the business, but were part of the setting in which the business was carried on, and, therefore, were not 'plant' ". In reaching that conclusion, the judge noted that the items in question presented "no special feature either in construction, purpose or position".

In the case of *St John's School*, too, a school laboratory and a gymnasium were held not to be plant as "the building was only the structure within which the function of educating the boys was carried on"; neither the laboratory nor the gymnasium had any function to perform other than to shelter the pupils. Similarly, the allowances were refused for the ship in the *Yard Arm Club* case as it functioned only as the premises and not as apparatus used for carrying on the trade.

And in the more recent case of *McMillin*, some holiday cottages were (rather clearly) not plant. In *Rogate*, too, the Tribunal was in little doubt that the "car valeting bays" under consideration were simply the place where people worked – a building, in fact – and not plant.

But the divide between setting and apparatus is not black and white. In *Jarrold v Good*, the judge specifically commented that "the setting in which a business is carried on, and the apparatus used for carrying on a business, are not always necessarily mutually exclusive". On that basis, a claim for the cost of moveable partitions was permitted.

In *Scottish & Newcastle*, again, some metal seagull sculptures, which were fixed in place and not easily removed, were "clearly part of the setting" but were nevertheless "properly described as apparatus which in view of the nature of the Company's trade, functions as plant".

The division between plant and premises has been explored in relation to a number of sport venues. A football stand (*Burnley Football & Athletic*) and an all-weather horse-racing surface (*Lingfield Park*) were both held to be premises rather than plant, but an artificial football pitch was accepted as plant (*Anchor International*).

One of the best, and most recent, cases to explore the boundary between apparatus and setting is that of *Andrew*, considered in detail under **Gazebos** below.

Cases: *Yarmouth v France* [1887] 4 TRL 1; *J. Lyons & Co. Ltd. v. Attorney-General* [1944] Ch. 281; *Jarrold v John Good & Sons Ltd* (1963) 40 TC 681; *St. John's School (Mountford and Another) v Ward* (1974) 49 TC 524; *Benson v The Yard Arm Club Ltd* (1979) 53 TC 67; *Brown v Burnley Football and Athletic Co Ltd* (1980) 53 TC 357; *CIR v Scottish & Newcastle Breweries Ltd* [1982] BTC 187; *Wimpy International Ltd. v Warland* [1989] BTC 58; *Shove (HMIT) v Lingfield Park* [2003] BTC 422; *Anchor International Ltd v CIR* [2005] BTC 97; *Andrew v HMRC* [2010] UKFTT 546 (TC); *McMillin v HMRC* [2011] UKFTT 65 (TC); *Rogate Services Ltd v HMRC* [2014] UKFTT 312 (TC)

2.4.3 *Entity or separate elements*

In some cases, the issue may arise of whether the asset should be considered as a whole or whether it needs to be broken down into its constituent parts.

In the Australian case of *ICI Australia and New Zealand*, concerned with acoustic ceilings, the judge had commented as follows:

> "Their sound-absorbing qualities do, no doubt, make working in the building more comfortable, and consequently, I presume, more efficient, and to that extent they are better ceilings than sound-reflecting ceilings would be. But every part of a building makes some contribution to the comfort and efficiency of those who work in it. To take it notionally to bits and describe as 'plant' any bit that has a function which is useful in connection with the business carried on there, seems to me indefensible. The truth is that the ceilings with which we are concerned do nothing for the appellants' business that they would not do for the business of any other occupier."

Australian law is not directly relevant for our purposes, but these comments were approved in the Court of Appeal and again in the House of Lords in the *Cole Bros* case.

There is really no substitute for a thorough reading of the House of Lords decision in *Cole Bros* in any case where the arguments may turn on whether the asset should be considered as a whole or broken down into its constituent parts. The unusual aspect of that case is that a majority of the five law Lords, and indeed possibly all of them, would have reached a different conclusion from the general commissioners. Nevertheless, they felt unable to overturn their decision, respecting their role as the fact-finding tribunal, and acknowledging that at least some of their decisions were close enough to the dividing line between plant and premises to allow a decision to go either way.

The specific issue in the case – the treatment of electrical costs – has been largely superseded by the statutory provisions introduced in 2008 that treat electrical costs as integral features.

Case: *Cole Brothers Ltd v Phillips* [1982] BTC 208

2.4.4   Structures

In *case law* terms, the fact that an asset is a structure, even a large one, is not fatal to a claim that it constitutes plant. This is illustrated by the cases of *Beach Station Caravans* (swimming pool), *Schofield v Hall* (grain silo) and *Barclay Curle* (dry dock), where in each case the substantial asset was held to be plant.

However, the government perceived that the courts were being too lenient, so a line was drawn in the sand with the legislation now at CAA 2001, s. 22. As such, an asset that is a fixed structure is now subject to a statutory bar that prevents a claim for it to be treated as plant, subject only to the very specific exceptions given at list C at s. 23.

Cases: *CIR v Barclay, Curle and Co Ltd* (1969) 45 TC 221; *Cooke v Beach Station Caravans Ltd* (1974) 49 TC 514; *Schofield v R & H Hall Ltd* (1975) 49 TC 538

2.4.5   Décor

The term "setting" is used in its more specialised sense in trades (such as hotels and restaurants) where the provision of a particular atmosphere is deemed to have a particular importance.

In *Wimpy*, Hoffman J provided a useful summary of the earlier case of *Scottish & Newcastle Breweries*, explaining it as follows:

> "The items in dispute in that case were wall decor, plaques, tapestries, murals (which were in fact detachable), pictures and metal sculptures used to decorate hotels. All of these

were held to be chattels or trade fixtures and not integral parts of the premises. The Revenue refused them capital allowances as plant on the ground that they formed part of the 'setting', which in one sense, and probably the most obvious sense, they certainly did. But the House of Lords held that they nevertheless passed the business use test because they were used to please and attract customers, and therefore were for the promotion of the trade."

In that *Scottish & Newcastle* case, the principle of providing a certain "ambience" was explored as follows by Lord Wilberforce:

"It seems to me ... that the taxpayer company's trade includes, and is intended to be furthered by, the provision of what may be called 'atmosphere' or 'ambience', which (rightly or wrongly) they think may attract customers. Such intangibles may in a very real and concrete sense be part of what the trader sets out, and spends money, to achieve. A good example might be a private clinic or hospital, where quiet and seclusion are provided, and charged for accordingly. One can well apply the 'setting' test to these situations. The amenities and decoration in such a case as the present are not, by contrast with the *Lyons* case, the setting in which the trader carries on his business, but the setting which he offers to his customers for them to resort to and enjoy. That it is setting in the latter and not the former sense for which the money was spent is proved beyond doubt by the commissioners' findings."

Two contrasting decisions relating to false ceilings illustrate the importance of the décor factor. In *Fortes Autogrill*, where little attention was paid to the concept of "ambience", allowances were denied for the cost of a false ceiling in a restaurant. There was a more ambiguous outcome in *Wimpy*. The judges felt that it was open to the commissioners to conclude that the false ceilings were not plant but there was an implication that they might not have reached the same conclusion themselves. A further ceiling was found by the commissioners to be plant, and that decision was allowed to stand. It was noted that "its primary function was the creation of atmosphere by reducing the height of the ceiling and giving visual interest".

Cases: *Hampton v Fortes Autogrill Ltd* (1979) 53 TC 690; *CIR v Scottish & Newcastle Breweries Ltd* [1982] BTC 187; *Wimpy International Ltd. v Warland* [1989] BTC 58

2.5   Function

Another test to have emerged from the courts is that of function, but this test has rarely proved helpful in practice. Going back more than half a century, knives and lasts were held to be plant in the *Maden & Ireland* case as they "performed an indispensable function in the process of manufacture".

In reality, though, every business asset has a function of some sort and the test generally leads back to the question of whether it functions as apparatus or as premises/setting. Particular weight was given to the concept of function in the case of *Fitch's Garage* ("the right test is the functional test") but the House of Lords in *Cole Brothers* (Lord Hailsham) suggested that *Fitch's Garage* had been incorrectly decided. The decision was also noted in *Scottish & Newcastle* as a borderline one that might have gone either way, so little reliance can now be placed on that case.

In *St John's School*, Templeman J did not attach much importance to the notion of function:

> "It is necessary to find, not the name of the building or its function, but whether the building is in truth a building within which the business is carried on or ... whether it is apparatus used by the businessman for carrying on the business."

HMRC specifically agree that the functional test leads back to the distinction between apparatus and setting:

> "Note that the functional test is not whether an asset has a function. All business assets have a function. The functional test is whether the asset functions as apparatus used in carrying on the activities of the business. For example, an asset that functions as the business premises is not plant. It is not apparatus used in carrying on the activities of the business."

It is, though, worth making the point that a building that is designed in a particularly suitable way does not thereby become an item of plant. In *London Electricity*, for example, the fact that features of the structure (a substation) were carefully designed, to accommodate the equipment within, did not convert what was otherwise plainly the premises in which the activity was conducted into the plant or apparatus with which that activity was conducted.

A similar point was noted by Fox in the *Wimpy* case, as follows:

> "It is proper to consider the function of the item in dispute. But the question is what does it function as? If it functions as part of the premises it is not plant. The fact that the building in which a business is carried on is by its construction particularly well-suited to the business, or indeed was specially built for that business, does not make it plant. Its suitability is simply the reason why the business is carried on there. But it remains the place in which the business is carried on and is not something with which the business is carried on."

Conversely, an asset that would normally be plant will not qualify as such if they way it is used shows that its function is merely to act as the setting within which the qualifying activity is carried out. So a floating restaurant was held not to be plant in the *Yard Arm Club* case, even though a boat would normally qualify clearly as plant:

> "If land, premises or structures operate as the means by which a trading operation is carried out, then they rank as plant. If chattels are used as premises and are not part of the means by which the relevant trade is carried out, then those chattels do not rank as plant."

Nobody in that case seems to have considered the possibility that the boat as a whole might have qualified as a machine. HMRC currently accept that any vessel propelled by engines is a machine, and it would certainly have been interesting to hear an exchange of views on whether the floating restaurant was within that definition.

Very often, the line between plant and premises can only be drawn with a very clear understanding of how the asset functions within the context of the business, and taking account of special features that make (or fail to make) the asset into more than just the property or setting within which the business is carried out. See, for example, the relevant headings of this book for the treatment of greenhouses, kennels, poultry houses.

Cases: *Yarmouth v France* [1887] 4 TRL 1; *Hinton v Maden & Ireland Ltd* (1959) 38 TC 391; *St. John's School (Mountford and Another) v Ward* (1974) 49 TC 524; *Dixon v Fitch's Garage Ltd* (1975) 50 TC 509; *Benson v The Yard Arm Club Ltd* (1979) 53 TC 67; *CIR v Scottish & Newcastle Breweries Ltd* [1982] BTC 187; *Cole Brothers Ltd v Phillips* [1982] BTC 208; *Wimpy International Ltd v Warland* [1989] BTC 58; *Bradley v London Electricity plc* (No. 2) [1996] BTC 451
Guidance: CA 21100

2.6   Difficulty of definition

Each case has to be considered on its own merits, and there is no single flowchart-style approach that will determine whether or not a particular item qualifies as plant in any given context.

The difficult of defining plant was noted by Stephenson LJ in the *Cole Bros* case (see **1.2** above). Two practical matters follow from this.

First, a business may be justified in making reasonably bold plant and machinery claims. This principle, though, should only apply where there is genuinely a proper basis on which a court might decide that a particular item should be treated as plant. Tax advisers taking this approach will obviously need to manage client expectations, however, and will also wish to consider the extent to which a fuller disclosure should be made at the outset for any items that fall nearer the dividing line.

The second point is that the first (Tribunal) stage of any tax appeal will be critical. In *Wimpy* (considered in more depth at **2.7** immediately below), the courts were very reluctant to overturn the initial findings of the commissioners. In this respect, Lord Justice Lloyd noted that "all the items in dispute were items which could have fallen on either side of the line".

Cases: *Cole Brothers Ltd v Phillips* [1982] BTC 208; *Wimpy International Ltd. v Warland* [1989] BTC 58

2.7 Wimpy

This chapter has considered the key case law principles that apply (subject, of course, to any statutory override) to determine whether or not an asset will qualify as plant.

The *Wimpy* case, however, merits consideration in its own right. The decision drew a distinction between something that had become part of the premises (which would not be plant) and something that merely embellished them (which might be). This was subject to "the rare case" where the premises themselves were plant. The case was heard initially by the special commissioners, then by Hoffman J in the Chancery Division, and finally by Fox, Lloyd and Glidewell LJJ in the Court of Appeal.

The commissioners upheld the claim in relation to a number of items, but rejected the claim – in the context of the business – in relation to shop fronts, floor and wall tiles, a suspended ceiling, a mezzanine floor, raised floors, balustrading, stairs, accessory work, light fittings, a trapdoor and ladder, "artex" and other wall finishes, flooring other than tiles, fire doors and fireproofing of walls and other surfaces.

Hoffman allowed the companies' appeal only in relation to the light fittings. More generally, he said that the question was whether it would be more appropriate to describe the items as having become part of the premises rather than as having retained a separate identity. The company took the rather different view that the test was whether the asset in question performed the sole function of housing the business or whether it also had some other distinct business purpose. If it did, the company argued, it should be treated as plant even if it would otherwise be described as part of the premises.

The Court of Appeal unanimously upheld the decision reached by Hoffman in the lower court. Fox LJ brought out the following principles:

- Something which becomes part of the premises, instead of merely embellishing them, is not plant, except in the rare case where the premises are themselves plant;
- A distinction can be drawn between the premises in which the business is carried on and the plant with which the

business is carried on. That can be illustrated by the example of the creation of atmosphere in a hotel by beautiful buildings and gardens on the one hand and fine china, glass and other tableware on the other. The latter are plant; the former are simply the premises in which the business is conducted, and are not plant.

- The fact that the building in which a business is carried on is, by its construction, particularly well-suited to the business, or indeed was specially built for that business, does not make it plant. Its suitability is simply the reason why the business is carried on there. But it remains the place in which the business is carried on and is not something with which the business is carried on.

- It is not only the bare shell of the business premises that is outside the definition of plant. So wallpaper, and paintings on the wall surface – which are there to make the premises attractive to potential customers – are not thereby plant.

- Similarly, the function of floor tiles is to provide a floor and, as such, they are part of the premises. Even if they are chosen because they are attractive, they remain simply part of the floor of the premises, just as a beautiful building which houses a hotel is simply the premises on which the hotel business is conducted.

- The question is whether it would be more appropriate to describe the item as part of the premises rather than as having retained a separate identity. Items such as fixed floor tiles and shop fronts are more naturally to be regarded as part of the "housing" of the business than as mere embellishments having a separate identity.

- Whether something is "plant" for these purposes is a matter of law. There is no precise definition of the word. In most cases the question depends on fact and degree.

- Where items of embellishment are capable, on the facts of the case, of being classed as apparatus used in the trade it does not matter whether those items are fixed or movable. But to determine whether an item is a "mere embellishment" for the purpose of that distinction it might be relevant to consider the extent to which it is fixed to the premises.

Lloyd LJ acknowledged the difficulty of defining "plant" and was clear that the decisions of the fact-finding tribunal (then the commissioners, today the tax tribunal) should normally be left to stand:

> "The answer is, I think, that in these cases the courts should be especially reluctant to upset the decisions of commissioners, unless it can be shown not only that they have erred in law but also that their error is palpable. It is not enough to show that they may have applied the wrong test ... or that they have not stated the test in the most precise language, or that they have omitted to refer to some factor which they ought to have taken into account. Where the judges have themselves failed to find a universal test, the commissioners are not to have their language examined too closely, or dissected line by line."

This is a very relevant consideration in this case, where the decisions of the commissioners were accepted in relation to many different items. The fact that the courts accepted those outcomes does not necessarily mean that they would have reached the same conclusions themselves.

Counsel for the companies criticised the decision of the special commissioners in relation to shop fronts, where the commissioners found as a question of fact that "their principal function is to form a necessary part of the premises since restaurants, in our climate, are normally conducted within walled premises: and doors are needed for ingress and egress". The companies argued that the question was not whether keeping out the weather was the *principal* function but whether it was their *sole* function. But Lloyd LJ (and his fellow judges) rejected that approach:

> "I cannot accept that it is correct to subject the commissioners' decision to this sort of linguistic analysis."

Lloyd LJ gave many examples where the commissioners had balanced the different function of various assets, for example referring to "the borderline between apparatus and *mere* setting" and to whether a suspended ceiling "served *only* to contain or conceal light fittings" (emphasis added each time). In other words, Lloyd LJ affirmed the basic principle that something may be plant if it acted both as premises and apparatus, but did not feel the commissioners could be criticised for failing to make that distinction explicit in relation to every item, given that they had made clear in other contexts that they were applying the correct tests.

Lloyd therefore concluded that "the commissioners did not misunderstand or misapply the functional test" but rather did exactly what they were meant to do. In a fascinating acknowledgment of the difficulty of pinning down the meaning of plant, Lloyd said that "all the items in dispute were items which could have fallen on either side of the line". So the decision could have gone either way, but that meant that the courts would be slow to reach an opposing conclusion. The third judge, Glidewell LJ, agreed that the commissioners had "made decisions of fact and degree with which this court cannot interfere".

Finally, Lloyd approved the following summary given by Hoffman J in the High Court:

> "Adopting the words of Lord Lowry, the question seems to me to be whether it would be more appropriate to describe the item as having become part of the premises than as having retained a separate identity. This is a question of fact and degree, to which some of the relevant considerations will be: whether the item appears visually to retain a separate identity, the degree of permanence with which it has been attached, the incompleteness of the structure without it and the extent to which it was intended to be permanent or whether it was likely to be replaced within a relatively short period."

This is an important quotation, but one that needs to be used with care. It is clear that this is not presented as a definitive list of factors to be considered, never mind a list of criteria that must all be met. Rather, these are given as "some of the relevant considerations".

Case: *Wimpy International Ltd. v Warland* [1989] BTC 58

3. Revenue or capital expenditure

3.1 Introduction

It is a fundamental principle that capital allowances are only given (as the name suggests) for capital expenditure. The point is stated at the start of the very first section of CAA 2001.

The *Capital Allowances Act* does contain some guidance (s. 4) on what is meant by capital expenditure, but this is expressed only in negative terms. As such, the term does *not* include any of the following:

- any amount that may be deducted in calculating the profits or gains of a trade, profession, vocation or property business;
- any amount that may be allowed as a deduction under certain specified provisions (e.g. as mileage allowance relief) from the taxable earnings from an employment or office;
- certain amounts paid under deduction of income tax (annual payments, patent royalties, and certain royalties etc. where the usual place of abode of the owner is abroad).

Beyond these statutory provisions, the concept of capital expenditure relies on accounting principles and on judicial interpretations. In most cases, it is obvious whether expenditure is capital in nature or not, but there are some circumstances where it is not so straightforward.

This is not a merely theoretical issue, even at a time when the annual investment allowance may give immediate tax relief. If expenditure is classified as repairs, it is likely to be allowable in full. If it has to be capitalised, by contrast, it is quite likely that it will only qualify in part for capital allowances, or indeed that no allowances will be due at all. There are plenty of types of expenditure that have to be capitalised but that do not attract allowances (e.g. goodwill, or the costs of the walls and floors of an office block).

A good illustration of the difficulties is the case of a property refurbishment. A hotel may, for example, build an extension to add some new rooms and – at the same time – take the opportunity to spruce up some areas of the original property. Depending on the facts, it may be that the refurbishment costs are allowable as revenue expenditure. The cost of the new rooms will clearly be capital, however, and only a part of that capital cost will attract capital allowances.

Law: CAA 2001, s. 4, 10

3.2   HMRC guidance

HMRC acknowledge the difficulty of distinguishing between revenue and capital expenditure. One example is in the *Business Income Manual* where paragraph BIM 35005 includes the following:

> "What is and what is not capital expenditure has taxed the minds of judges, tax advisors, Revenue officials, business people and others for more than two centuries. No one has produced a single simple test that will determine the issue in all circumstances. A variety of judicial pronouncements has resulted in recipes that are applicable to particular circumstances but which lead to inconclusive or even incorrect results in others. As the body of case law has expanded the margins of uncertainty have retreated. But those margins remain to this day. Resolving a case on the borderline is far from easy. The various judicial recipes may point to conflicting conclusions. You will have to come to a balanced judgement. To do so you will need to establish the relevant facts that applied at the time the expenditure was incurred.
>
> The day-to-day running costs of a business (staff wages, purchase of trading stock, rent of business premises, and so on) are referred to as revenue expenditure. Revenue expenditure is sometimes described as circulating capital. This description reflects the fact that the capital in question leaves the owner's possession (changes masters) to produce profit or loss. The capital may be considered as being 'turned over'. In the process of turning over, profit or loss ensues.

Capital expenditure (goodwill, the purchase of business premises, plant and machinery used in the business process and so on) in practice is the opposite of revenue expenditure.

The profit making structure within which the business is conducted is sometimes called the fixed capital of the business. A trader does not part with the fixed capital (there is no changing of masters); it is retained and not turned over in the same way as circulating capital. The fixed capital provides the opportunity for the business to make profits or losses."

HMRC also publish a "toolkit" entitled *Capital v Revenue Expenditure*, which organises the topic under the following headings:

- Acquisition, improvement and alteration of assets
- Legal and professional fees
- Finance costs
- IT costs
- Corporate intangible assets
- General

Elsewhere, HMRC have linked capital expenditure to the "acquisition, improvement or disposal" of an asset:

"For expenditure to be capital it must be spent for the acquisition (*Rolfe v Wimpey Waste Management Ltd* [1989] 62TC399, see BIM 35605), improvement (*Tucker v Granada Motorway Services Ltd* [1979] 53TC122, see BIM 35320) or disposal (*Mallet v The Staveley Coal & Iron Co Ltd* [1928] 13TC972, see BIM 35625) of a capital asset. It is not sufficient that it was paid in connection with (or on the occasion of) the acquisition, improvement or disposal of the asset. For example, the goodwill of customers may be a valuable capital asset. But that is not enough to make expenditure such as the pay of staff (who, by serving customers well, may have helped create the goodwill) a capital outgoing."

Guidance: BIM 35000ff., 35901; CA 11530, 21200; www.hmrc.gov.uk/agents/toolkits/capital-v-revenue.pdf

3.3 Enduring benefit

The most useful (and often quoted) judicial guidance in this area is probably that of Viscount Cave in the *Helsby Cables* case, when he stated that:

> "When an expenditure is made, not only once and for all, but with a view to bringing into existence an asset or an advantage for the enduring benefit of a trade, I think that there is very good reason (in the absence of special circumstances leading to an opposite conclusion) for treating such an expenditure as properly attributable not to revenue but to capital".

The "once and for all" element should not be applied literally as some businesses will obviously incur capital expenditure on a frequent basis. Conversely, expenditure may be incurred once only but still be revenue in nature.

However, the concept of the "enduring benefit" gets to the heart of the matter – capital expenditure is normally incurred with a view to putting the acquired asset to good use for an extended period of time. That would apply, for example, to a business that pays to acquire goodwill or a building or a car (assuming that such assets are not bought with a view to selling on at a profit).

The courts have been clear that a formulaic approach to the matter cannot be used. In current terms, we might say that a flow chart approach to the question of whether expenditure is capital or revenue is unlikely to resolve the more difficult questions. In *Granada Motorway Services*, for example, Lord Wilberforce commented that:

> "It is common in cases which raise the question whether a payment is to be treated as a revenue or as a capital payment for indicia to point different ways. In the end the courts can do little better than form an opinion which way the balance lies. There are a number of tests which have been stated in reported cases which it is useful to apply, but we have been warned more than once not to seek automatically to apply to one case words or formulae which have been found useful in

another ... . Nevertheless reported cases are the best tools that we have, even if they may sometimes be blunt instruments."

Cases: *Atherton v British Insulated and Helsby Cables Ltd* (1925) 10 TC 155; *Tucker v Granada Motorway Services Ltd* (1979) 53 TC 92

3.4 Property expenditure

In the context of this book relating to plant and machinery, the difficulty of distinguishing between revenue and capital expenditure is likely to arise most frequently for expenditure on property. Normal principles apply, so expenditure in improving or enlarging the property will be capital in nature, whereas the costs of restoring or repairing a property will in principle be allowed as revenue.

Entirety

Two early cases concerned factory chimneys, and the courts focused on the question of whether there was a replacement of the "entirety" (capital expenditure) or of just a part of the property (revenue expenditure). In *Bullcroft*, a new and improved chimney was built on a site nearby. The commissioners held that the cost should be capitalised and Justice Rowlatt in the High Court agreed:

> "If you replace in entirety, it is having a new one and it is not repairing an old one. I think that it is very largely a question of degree, but it seems to me the Commissioners have taken the only possible view here."

In *Samuel Jones*, by contrast, the cost of a replacement chimney was held to be revenue expenditure. Although it was again built on a slightly different site (and the old chimney was demolished), there was held to be no improvement in this case. The commissioners, feeling bound by the *Bullcroft* decision, disallowed the costs of the new chimney but the decision was overturned in the Court of Session. In the words of the Lord President:

> "The facts seem to me to demonstrate beyond a doubt that the chimney with which we are concerned is physically, commercially and functionally an inseparable part of an 'entirety', which is the factory. It is quite impossible to describe this chimney as being in the words of Rowlatt, J., the 'entirety' with which we are concerned. It is doubtless an indispensable part of the factory, doubtless an integral part;

but none the less a subsidiary part, and one of many subsidiary parts, of a single industrial profit-earning undertaking."

Both of the judges who gave substantive rulings in *Samuel Jones* also noted that the costs of replacing the chimney were small (about 2%) compared with the overall value of the factory.

The judges were also clear that the costs of taking down the old chimney had to be treated in the same way as the costs of building the new one. As such, these costs were also allowed.

Help can also be gleaned from two further contrasting cases, this time concerning the pipes of gas suppliers. HMRC have summarised the decisions in those two cases as follows:

"The cases of *Auckland Gas Co Ltd v CIR* (2000) 73 TC 266 and *Transco Plc v R A Dyall* (2002) Sp C 310 both involved the insertion of polyethylene pipes into existing cast iron and steel pipes ... . In the case of *Auckland Gas*, the Privy Council found that the work on replacing a pipe network was capital expenditure and not allowable as a deduction. In the Transco case, the work was a repair to a part of the network and allowable. The Special Commissioners in *Transco* set out the differences between the two cases.

1. In *Transco*, the replacement pipes did the same job as the old pipes, there was no increase in capacity and there was no increase in pressure.

2. In *Auckland Gas* the new pipes were able to take higher pressure/higher capacity.

3. In *Transco* the old pipes had been successfully carrying natural gas for years unlike in *Auckland Gas*, where the old pipes were not suited for natural gas.

In *Transco*, the pipeline was simply restored to its previous efficiency. As a result the cost of the work was revenue expenditure and *Transco* could claim a deduction for the cost of the work when it was recognised in accordance with GAAP."

In the *Transco* decision, the commissioners were "satisfied that what was done was repair by renewal of subsidiary parts of the entirety of the pipeline system". Furthermore:

> "It was not renewal or improvement of substantially the whole of the subject matter. There was no 'wholesale' renewal, or renewal sector by sector, but only renewal of individual pieces and so the character of the whole did not change".

As such, the commissioners concluded that "it remained a pipeline through which gas was transported; neither the pressure nor the capacity was materially increased".

HMRC summarise this case by noting that:

> "The expenditure was allowable because all that was being done were repairs to the existing asset. There was no new asset when the work was done, nor was there any real difference to the asset, it still transported gas in the same way that it had before it had been repaired."

The HMRC guidance also contains the following useful example:

> "Sophia owns a number of residential properties that she lets. The properties are not furnished lettings.
>
> The boiler in one property needs replacing. As the new boiler has to be located in a different position, Sophia decides to modernise the kitchen as a whole.
>
> All the existing base units, wall units and sink etc, are stripped out and replaced, as is the fitted cooker and hob. New units of an equivalent quality are installed but in a different layout to allow for the re-location of the boiler, finally the kitchen is re-plastered and re-tiled.
>
> The entirety is the house, not the fitted kitchen. The new kitchen is slightly different but it does the same job as before. Sophia has simply replaced the old kitchen with a modern equivalent. This is a repair and allowable expenditure.
>
> Shortly afterwards, the fridge freezer breaks down and has to be replaced.

> This is not part of the building but is an asset in its own right. Sophia has not repaired an asset; she had incurred capital expenditure on a new asset. As the fridge freezer is used in a dwelling house it is not qualifying expenditure for capital allowances purposes."

This example is of interest partly because it concerns a residential property where capital allowances will not be due. The distinction between revenue and capital expenditure is therefore particularly stark. The example brings out an important distinction between fixtures – where HMRC accept that "the entirety is the house, not the fitted kitchen – and non-fixtures, which are assets in their own right, rather than being part of the larger entity. In other words, the replacement cost of fixtures is more likely to qualify as repairs and renewals (though this is subject to the special rules for integral features: see note 3 at **Appendix 4**), whereas the replacement of a standalone item is in principle capital expenditure.

Cases: *Bullcroft Main Collieries Ltd v O'Grady* (1932) 17 TC 93; *Samuel Jones & Co (Devonvale) Ltd v CIR* (1951) 32 TC 513; *Auckland Gas Co Ltd v CIR* (2000) 73 TC 266; *Transco Plc v R A Dyall* (2002) Sp C 310
Guidance: BIM 35470

3.5   Newly acquired assets

Particular issues can arise in relation to assets that have just been acquired.

If further expenditure on a newly acquired asset has to be incurred before the asset can be used in the trade (or very soon after acquisition) then that expenditure may have to be treated as part of the cost of acquiring the asset. This principle arose from the *Law Shipping* case, concerning a vessel that was acquired in a very poor state of repair. By contrast, expenditure will normally be allowable as a revenue cost if it has been possible to use the asset to generate profit for a period before the repairs are undertaken. This was the outcome in the *Odeon* case, where cinemas were acquired in a poor state of repair just after the war, but where the costs of putting matters right were allowed as a revenue deduction.

In *Odeon*, Lord Buckley provided a useful summary of the issues as follows:

"The cost of acquiring or creating a physical capital asset for use in a trade or business is clearly capital expenditure. The cost of improving such an asset by adding to it or modifying it may well be capital expenditure. On the other hand, the cost of works of recurrent repair or maintenance of such an asset attributable to the wear and tear occurring in the course of use of the asset in his trade or business by the person carrying out the works is revenue expenditure, and so constitutes a proper debit item in the profit and loss account of the business.

Whether, where there has been a change of ownership, the cost of works of repair or maintenance attributable to wear and tear which occurred before the change of ownership should be regarded as revenue expenditure or capital expenditure is a question the answer to which must, in my opinion, depend upon the particular facts of each case. The Solicitor-General has argued that any repair must improve the article repaired, and, avoiding undue cynicism, I think that that proposition must be accepted. He says further that, if the state of the article when repaired is better than its state was when it was acquired by the person carrying out the repairs, the cost of repairs should *pro tanto* be regarded as capital expenditure. A tradesman, for example, who acquires a dilapidated shop in which to carry on his business and, either before he commences business or as soon thereafter as he can afford to do so, puts the shop into a state of repair and decoration suitable for his business, has incurred the cost not only of acquiring the shop but also of repairing and decorating it in a suitable manner in order to provide himself with a capital asset of a character which he regards as appropriate to his business. The whole of this expenditure, it is said, is capital expenditure because it constitutes the cost of acquiring such a capital asset as the trader requires for the purpose of his business. The argument is an attractive one, but should not, in my opinion, be accepted without careful consideration."

The court found compelling differences of fact between the two cases and had no hesitation in allowing the deduction in the *Odeon* case. Key factors that led the Court of Appeal to distinguish the cases were summarised by Lord Justice Orr as follows:

"In my judgment there are a number of important differences between that case and this.

One is that in that case the purchaser knew at the time of acquisition of the ship that after one further voyage a Lloyd's survey would be required and would involve very substantial expenditure if the ship were to continue to be used in the trade, whereas here what was in the purchaser's contemplation was that the theatres could be used profitably (as in the event they were) without making good the deferred repairs, and that substantial expenditure in making them good could not be lawfully incurred for an indefinite period of time.

A second difference is that in the Law Shipping case the Court drew, and in my judgment correctly drew, the inference that if the Lloyd's survey had not been overdue the seller would have exacted and the buyer would have paid a larger price, whereas here it has been found as a fact that the dilapidated state of the theatres did not materially affect the price.

A third difference is that there was not in the Law Shipping case any accountancy evidence, whereas in the present case there was such evidence which was accepted by the Commissioners.

A fourth difference is that in the Law Shipping case the repairs or replacements necessary to satisfy the Lloyd's survey were carried out after the first voyage of the ship, whereas in the present case the repairs and replacements in question were carried out over a period beginning two years and ending ten years after the acquisition, and there is no evidence to indicate that (apart from inflation, which was taken into account in the percentage calculation or estimate) they cost any more than would have been incurred if the theatres had been acquired in good repair and subsequent dilapidations had been made good in the ordinary course of prudent maintenance."

Cases: *Law Shipping Co Ltd v CIR* (1923) 12 TC 621; *Odeon Associated Theatres Ltd v Jones* (1970) 48 TC 257

A-Z of Plant & Machinery

A-Z of Plant & Machinery

A1   Abortive expenditure

A business may incur expenditure on a proposed project which – in the event – does not go through. Professional costs are one common example; another might be a business that pays for a van in good faith, only to discover that it is stolen and that it therefore has to be returned to the former owner or to an insurance company.

Case law is clear that expenditure that is capital in nature does not change its character because it proves to be abortive. HMRC guidance refers to the *ECC Quarries* case, which was concerned with costs incurred in relation to an unsuccessful planning application. The matter was also discussed in the *Sargent v Eayrs* case, which included the following:

> "What the Respondent did in this case appears to me, applying the principles so laid down, to have been something in which he incurred not revenue but capital expenditure. In the result the business was not extended, because he found prices in Australia prohibitive, and therefore the expenditure was abortive. But *Lothian Chemical Co. Ltd. v Rogers* (1926) 11 TC 508 shows, as one would expect, that that is an irrelevant consideration. The expenditure does not change its nature according to whether it be successful or unsuccessful."

The fact that expenditure is capital in nature does not, however, mean that capital allowances are automatically due. Indeed, the normal outcome for abortive expenditure will be that no allowances may be claimed, at least under the regime for plant and machinery. This is because of the fundamental condition given at s. 11 for claiming allowances, namely that "the person incurring the expenditure owns the plant or machinery as a result of incurring it". By definition, such abortive expenditure will not meet that condition.

Law: CAA 2001, s. 11(4)(b)

Cases: *Lothian Chemical Co. Ltd. v Rogers* (1926) 11 TC 508; *Sargent v Eayrs* (1973) 48 TC 573; *ECC Quarries Ltd v Watkis* (1975) 51 TC 153

Guidance: BIM 35325

A2   Active façades

Active façades are forms of technology operating on the exterior of a building to have a beneficial impact on the way heat is transmitted through the windows. Solar energy may be transferred into the building, or shading may be provided to reduce temperatures at warmer times of year. The façade may involve so-called "smart glass" and/or shading systems or a variety of other technologies.

HMRC have made the following observations in relation to active façades:

> "In the run up to the 2007-08 public consultation on the FA08 Business Tax reform package, including the new 'integral features' classification, key stakeholders suggested that two environmentally beneficial features of buildings, namely external solar shading and active façades, should be included within the new integral features classification. S.33A includes expenditure on the first but not on the second asset.
>
> This is because it is already accepted that the external skin of the active façade system is not eligible (as it is basically a window and so excluded by section 33A (6) CAA01), but that the inner skin is eligible, because it is, in effect, creating a duct within which the cooling/heating air circulates. In short, the relevant parts of these systems already qualify as 'integral features', by virtue of being considered part of the air cooling or heating systems of the building, so there is no need to specify this expenditure separately in the list."

Law: CAA 2001, s. 23 (list C, item 15)
Guidance: CA 22330

A3   Advertising hoardings

Advertising hoardings are included in list C and may therefore qualify as plant even though affixed to a building. Whether they do in fact qualify will depend on the exact nature and use of the hoardings.

CA 21230, based on the Revenue's earlier *Football League* letter (see **Appendix 2**), indicates that advertising hoardings and perimeter boards "would normally qualify as plant or machinery" unless they are simply part of a perimeter fence or other structure.

If the hoarding is in reality simply part of the building, however, it may not be possible to claim that it is an item of plant and machinery. In the *Fitch's Garage* case, a canopy over the area in which petrol was served was held not to be plant. That canopy included a fascia used to advertise the service station itself. The canopy was held to be part of the premises in which the fuel was served, rather than playing any active part in the commercial process. However, the decision was subsequently questioned, as discussed under **Canopies** below.

Law: CAA 2001, s. 23 (list C, item 15)
Case: *Dixon v Fitch's Garage Ltd* (1975) 50 TC 509
Guidance: CA 21230, 22030, 22110

A4   Aerials

An aerial used to transmit programmes will clearly qualify as an item of plant for the activity in question.

For a receiving aerial, typically on the roof of a building, it will be necessary first to show that any expenditure is incurred for the purposes of a qualifying activity.

Assuming that it is, there should be no problem claiming plant and machinery allowances on the aerial. Arguably, an aerial is "incorporated in the building" (though the author would not readily accept that description). However, list C refers to "computer, telecommunication and surveillance systems (including their wiring or other links)" which would seem to cover a receiving aerial for television or radio. If so, the cost may be considered on ordinary principles and it would seem reasonable to conclude that such an aerial would be an item of plant.

Law: CAA 2001, s. 22 (list B, item 7(3)), s. 23 (list C, item 8)
Guidance: CA 32217

A5   Air conditioning systems

Air conditioning systems qualify as integral features, and therefore attract allowances without any doubt, but only at the lower "special rate".

According to HMRC guidance, the special rate allowances are available for:

"all parts of air conditioning systems including, for example:

- ventilation shafts
- ACNV (automatically controlled natural ventilation) shutters
- Metal mesh & curtain arrangements for controlling airflow".

No allowances will be due, however, for "any asset whose principal purpose is to insulate or enclose the interior of a building or to provide an interior wall, floor or ceiling which (in each case) is intended to remain permanently in place". So a wall which is one of the four sides of a ventilation pipe will not thereby qualify for plant and machinery allowances.

Law: CAA 2001, s. 33A(5)
Guidance: CA 21200; R&C Brief 03/10 (see **Appendix 4**)

Enhanced capital allowances

In some cases, air conditioning equipment will attract 100 per cent first-year allowances under the scheme for **Enhanced capital allowances** (ECAs).

The qualifying category of "heating, ventilation and air conditioning (HVAC) equipment" includes two separate categories:

- close control air conditioning equipment; and
- building environment zone controls (formerly known as heating, ventilation and air conditioning zone controls).

In each case, enhanced allowances are due only if the specific product is named on the energy technology product list, having met the eligibility criteria.

The first category is described on the official site as follows:

"Close control air conditioning equipment is used to control temperature (and optionally humidity) in rooms and enclosures containing heat generating equipment, such as servers, computers or telecommunications devices, and in some types of manufacturing process (e.g. clean rooms). The equipment typically operates continuously and has a much higher unit floor area cooling load requirement than conventional air conditioning."

The ECA scheme, here as elsewhere, aims to encourage consumers to buy higher efficiency products.

Building environment zone controls can, according to the official guidance, "help a company save energy by matching actual demand to the operational requirement in each zone". This is a more generic description than the predecessor HVAC controls, for which the official site used to state as follows:

> "HVAC zone controls are used to control the environmental conditions (i.e. temperature, ventilation rate and/or air condition) in individual zones (i.e. rooms or areas) within a building. They can be programmed to maintain these environmental conditions within pre-set limits in a manner that reflects occupation schedules or occupation status, whilst also taking account of environmental conditions, and specific operating requirements. Some products are also able to switch lighting and electrical appliances in a zone on and off in line with its occupation schedule or occupation status."

Law: SI 2018/268, art. 3(2)(f)

Guidance: https://www.gov.uk/energy-technology-list

A6   Air-to-air energy recovery devices

Equipment falling into this category will qualify for plant and machinery allowances in all normal circumstances. In some cases, it will attract 100 per cent first-year allowances under the scheme for **Enhanced capital allowances** (ECAs).

According to the earlier ECAs guidance:

> "This process involves recovering energy from air expelled into the atmosphere, and using it as supply air. This means not as much energy is needed to heat the supply air, so less is used and emissions are reduced.
>
> Various devices can be used, including plate heat exchangers, thermal wheels, run-around coils, heat-pipe generators and regenerators."

The energy technology criteria list includes the following:

> "Air-to-air energy recovery devices are heat exchanger products that are specifically designed to recover (or salvage) waste heat from the exhaust air stream from a building ventilation system, and use it to heat the incoming air stream to the same building ventilation system."

The guidance goes on to give the following technology description:

> "Air-to-air energy recovery devices use heat exchanger technology to recover heat from the exhaust air of building ventilation systems that would otherwise be lost to atmosphere. The heat exchangers are incorporated into the supply air and extract air ventilation ducts. Some products may also be used to reduce the energy used by air conditioning systems by removing heat from the incoming air."

At the time of writing, two categories of air-to-air energy recovery equipment are included in the ECA scheme:

- plate heat exchangers (or recuperators); and
- rotating heat exchangers (including thermal and desiccant heat wheels);

The category of run-around coils is no longer included.

Investments in these devices will only attract ECAs if the specific product is named on the energy technology product list, having satisfied the eligibility criteria. The list is in a constant state of flux, with new products being added and old ones removed on a monthly basis.

Law: SI 2018/268, art. 3(2)(a)

Guidance: https://www.gov.uk/energy-technology-list

A7   Airstrips

Airstrips and runways are included in list B at s. 22. As such, they are excluded from the definition of plant and machinery and allowances are not due.

HMRC guidance confirms that plant and machinery allowances will not be given "on the provision, construction or acquisition" of such assets.

Law: CAA 2001, s. 22 (list B, item 2)
Guidance: CA 22020

A8   Alteration of land

In principle, allowances are not available for the cost of "any works involving the alteration of land" (s. 22(1)(b)). However, that general restriction does not apply to "the alteration of land for the purpose only of installing plant or machinery" (list C, item 22). As such, HMRC's instruction at CA 22020 that tax officers should not give allowances "on any works involving the alteration of land" needs some refinement.

There can be substantial sums involved but the correct treatment is not always clear cut.

In guidance issued for the pig industry, HMRC made the following observation:

> "Expenditure on the provision of P&M (for example, transportation & on site installation costs) and alteration of land for the purpose only of installing P&M, can qualify for PMAs at the rate applicable to the P&M being installed. However, expenditure on works involving the alteration of land more generally do not qualify. For example, the cost of levelling land in order to provide a stable base for a heavy machine would qualify, but the cost of levelling land in order to lay a hard standing or a foundation for a building would not qualify."

That is fine as far as it goes, but it does not address the grey areas that can arise. One classic example raised with one of the authors recently was that of roads put in place across large areas of desolate land in connection with the installation of power-generating wind turbines. If (for the sake of considering this particular aspect) it is accepted that such turbines qualify as plant or machinery, does the cost of building roads similarly qualify?

It may be necessary to ask whether the roads are put in place *only* for installing plant or machinery, or whether they are also put in place so that the plant or machinery can subsequently be serviced and used. This may seem an odd distinction to be made in practice, but a similar argument won the case for HMRC in *Wetherspoon*, where it was necessary to decide whether certain building alterations were incidental to the installation of plant or machinery (a different statutory test: see **Alterations to buildings**).

The Tribunal referred to Lord Reid's comment in the *Barclay, Curle* decision, in which he stated that "installation of machinery or plant for the purposes of the trade" should be understood as meaning installation so that the machinery or plant can function properly by reference to the purpose for which it was installed. The Tribunal then noted the evidence that "as a result of installing the cooking equipment and the sinks it was a requisite under [health and safety legislation] to install a non-slip wipe-clean floor surface for spillages from the equipment" before making the following distinction:

> "Although we acknowledge that we are making a fine distinction, we interpret this evidence as meaning that the floor surfaces were needed for the operation of the equipment, not for the installation of the equipment in a state in which they could be used for the purposes of the trade."

So the distinction is made between expenditure needed for the *operation* of the equipment or for its *installation*. Returning to the example of the roads that have to be put in place for the wind turbines to be built, it is then legitimate to ask if the expenditure is purely for the installation of the turbines or whether it is also required for their operation. If an existing road has to be widened purely to take the vehicles that deliver the turbines to site, then there will be a good case for claiming relief. If it is a completely new site, and a wide road has to be built, it may be possible to show that a part of the overall cost is incidental to the installation, even if part will be used also for servicing the site.

An attempt was made, in *McMillin*, to claim allowances for an "earth bund" created during the construction of some "eco" cottages. The bund had been created out of building work spoil and a somewhat tenuous argument was put forward that it was in some way linked to the heating system. On the face of it, allowances were excluded by virtue of s. 22(1)(b) ("works involving the alteration of land"). That exclusion is potentially subject to s. 23, but none of the relieving items was held to apply; in particular, the Tribunal did not accept that the earth bund could be described as "the alteration of land for the purpose only of installing plant or machinery".

Law: CAA 2001, s. 22(1)(b), 23 (list C, item 22)

Cases: *CIR v Barclay, Curle & Co Ltd* (1969) 45 TC 221; *J D Wetherspoon plc v HMRC* (2007) Sp C 657; *McMillin v HMRC* [2011] UKFTT 65 (TC)

Guidance: R&C Brief 03/10 (see **Appendix 4**)

A9   Alterations to buildings

A person is treated as incurring expenditure on plant or machinery if:

a. he is carrying on a qualifying activity;

b. he incurs capital expenditure on alterations to an existing building; and

c. those alterations are incidental to the installation of plant or machinery for the purposes of the qualifying activity.

The alterations are then treated as if they were part of the plant or machinery. It follows that if the plant is an integral feature, the incidental costs will also need to be allocated to the special rate pool rather than to the main pool.

Existing building

There is no statutory definition of "existing building". It is clear that the legislation does not apply to a new construction. However, there is nothing to prevent a business from making a claim if it buys a new building but then has some alterations made before moving in.

Arguably, relief could be due under these rules not just for alterations within the footprint of an existing building, but also for an extension. It would be necessary to show that it is all part of the same building and that the works could properly be described as "alterations".

Scope of rules

According to HMRC:

"The legislation is intended to cover the direct costs of installation, that is those works which are brought about by

53

the installation of the plant and which are associated with it in such a way that their cost can properly be considered to be part of the cost of providing the plant. The use of the word 'incidental' makes it clear that the primary purpose of the work must be the installation of plant or machinery."

The HMRC guidance goes on to refer to Lord Reid's words in the *Barclay, Curle* case, very slightly misquoting him. The original version of the words quoted by HMRC is that:

"the exigencies of the trade require that, when new machinery or plant is installed in existing buildings, more shall be done than mere installation in order that the new machinery or plant may serve its proper purpose".

HMRC guidance then states that there must be a direct link between the incurring of the expenditure and the installation of the relevant plant:

"The main purpose of the alterations must be the installation of plant or machinery. Work done for some other purpose such as the better operation of the asset does not qualify. When you are trying to decide whether expenditure on alterations qualifies under Section 25 as expenditure on alterations incidental to the installation of plant or machinery you should think about what would happen if the plant were removed. Would the 'installation' work remain as part of the building or would it be eradicated or abandoned?"

Elsewhere, HMRC mention a lift shaft as an example of expenditure that would qualify under this heading, the cost being incidental to the expenditure on the lift itself, which is an item of plant or machinery.

Wetherspoon

The *Wetherspoon* decisions suggest that HMRC have taken an unduly restrictive approach to interpreting this legislation, though the company was by no means successful across the board in the way it wished to claim under these provisions. The appeal was heard first by the special commissioners, then by the newly formed First-tier Tribunal and finally by the Upper Tribunal. The last of these may for now be seen as the definitive authority on how s. 25

should be interpreted. The decision is quite long but anyone who is involved with a case where the amount of tax at stake is substantial would do well to read through the relevant parts. The key principles are discussed below.

The *Wetherspoon* case was concerned with the predecessor legislation, and so references are made throughout the case to s. 66 of CAA 1990. For clarity, however, these have been changed in the text that follows to s. 25, being the directly equivalent wording in CAA 2001. (In the author's view, there are no significant differences between the wordings of the two Acts. In particular, they both refer to "alterations to an existing building incidental to the installation" of plant or machinery.)

Common ground

Although there was a gulf between the possible interpretations of the legislation, some principles were agreed without controversy.

First, it was agreed that basic installation costs were allowable as part of the cost of the plant and machinery itself. In the case of a cooker, for example, the installation costs would include those of being able to switch it on and being able to open its doors. As such, these costs would be allowable under general principles, in a new building as well as in an existing one. It followed that s. 25 is concerned with "what further expenditure might qualify for relief when plant or machinery was installed in an existing building such that building alterations were made".

Second, it was agreed that the restrictions now in sections 21 and 22 (for buildings and structures respectively) would not apply to expenditure rightly claimed under s. 25. If, for example, expenditure qualifying under s. 25 involved alterations to a wall incidental to the installation of a cooker, such expenditure would be deemed to be expenditure on the cooker and not on the wall. It would follow that the s. 21 restrictions for walls would not apply.

Third, it was noted that with the exception of some fairly brief references in the *Barclay, Curle* case, there were no judicial precedents offering guidance on the correct interpretation of these provisions.

Finally, there was agreement that certain categories of expenditure would definitely qualify under this heading. HMRC examples quoted included "the moving of a staircase in an existing building where the installation of plant might prevent people accessing other floors that they had previously been able to access". HMRC also accepted that relief would be due under these provisions for building alterations consequent upon the installation of the plant "if a large item of plant was installed in an existing building, and it blocked the windows so that old windows had to be bricked up and new window apertures created".

Most generous interpretation

The company argued for a very wide interpretation, reminding the Tribunal that Lord Reid in *Barclay, Curle* had commented that the word "incidental" was wider than just "necessary". As Lord Reid had ruled:

> "It may be that the exigencies of the trade require that, when new machinery or plant is installed in existing buildings, more shall be done than mere installation in order that the new machinery or plant may serve its proper purpose. Where that is the case this section enables the cost of the additional alterations to be included."

Counsel for Wetherspoon interpreted this very broadly, as is made clear in the following extract from the Tribunal decision:

> "Accordingly, because:-
>
> - the installation of a cooker required walls to be plastered and covered in wipe-clean tiles throughout the kitchen to meet Health and Safety requirements;
> - the installation of toilet bowls, where there had hitherto been no toilet block, in practice necessitated the construction of partitions, blockwork dividing-walls, doors, and the provision of floors with wipe-clean tiled surfaces to enable anyone to use the sanitary ware; and
> - the provision of beer cooling machinery in the cool room necessitated a drain to enable the floor to be

> cleaned and spilt beer to be removed, and a slightly
> inclined floor to direct water to the drain,
>
> it was contended that all the expenditure on building
> alterations relevant to those items was expenditure
> 'incidental to the installation' of the relevant items of plant."

The problem with this approach was that – at least in relation to
some of the costs – it created an asymmetry between the treatment
of expenditure on new and existing buildings:

> "It was implicit in these contentions that allowances would be
> available for expenditure in relation to existing buildings
> under [s. 25] for many items that might equally be needed in
> constructing kitchens, toilets and cold rooms in new
> buildings, regardless of the fact that none, or hardly any, of
> them would qualify for allowances when the same plant was
> installed in a new, purpose-built, building."

Later in the judgment, the Tribunal noted that Lord Reid in *Barclay
Curle* had warned against creating such asymmetry. The Tribunal
itself also felt that such a result could not be justified:

> "There appears to be no ground for assuming some
> Parliamentary purpose that an additional subsidy should be
> given for renovations, and the re-use of existing buildings, to
> account for the asymmetry that the Appellant's contentions
> would generally involve."

Least generous interpretation

The Tribunal noted the "stark contrast" between the wide
interpretation sought by the company and the narrow view taken by
HMRC. In HMRC's view, relief was due only "for alteration works
incidental to the pure physical installation of the plant in an existing
building, and not to alterations geared to facilitating the better use
of the installed items".

HMRC argued that the expenditure had to be incidental to the
installation of the plant, which should be interpreted less widely
than being incidental to the *provision* of the plant. To avoid the issue
of asymmetry, the Tribunal was asked:

"to confine the application of [s. 25] to situations where installations in existing buildings might occasion the need for alterations in a way that would generally be irrelevant with installations in new buildings".

To illustrate this, HMRC gave an example of where they had allowed expenditure under s. 25 in this case:

"The restaurant required a food-hoist for food to be sent up from the basement kitchen to the restaurant area, and the hoist and accompanying machinery were obviously plant or machinery. Relief was then claimed, and given, under [s. 25], for shuttering that had to be constructed around the line of travel of the hoist. In a new building, the walls would have been built around the lift shaft, and expenditure on those walls would have been building expenditure, not qualifying for allowances ... . Where the existing building had to be altered however, as an immediate and direct result of the installation of the plant and machinery, [s. 25] applied to that expenditure."

In HMRC's view, this was "the typical, relatively limited, situation" to which the legislation was directed.

Purposive interpretation

The Tribunal began its decision by giving the following "purposive" view of the legislation:

"The focus of the section is on the point that if plant is installed in an existing building rather than in a purpose-built new building, it is entirely possible that something will not fit, and that this will lead to alterations having to be made to the existing building. In the case of a purpose-built new building, there will generally be no equivalent need for such expenditure. Thus [s. 25] levels the playing field between new and existing buildings by affording taxpayers relief for expenditure on existing buildings which would not be needed in relation to the installation of the same plant in new buildings, or in the open."

The Upper Tribunal then approved the distinction drawn by the special commissioners between:

- expenditure that was "truly incidental" to the installation of plant; and

- expenditure that was consequential to its installation.

Developing this theme, the Tribunal noted that "while particular alterations may, viewed in isolation, contribute to the better use of particular plant, viewed in the round, they may also serve wider purposes which are not 'incidental' to the installation of that or any other plant".

Tail wagging the dog

To illustrate this, the Tribunal referred to the claim made by the company for the costs of constructing toilet blocks. Although rather long, the following quotation is very helpful in gaining clarity on this point:

> "The Appellant's contention starts with the sanitary ware. We are almost asked to visualise toilet bowls in an empty void, whereupon we are then asked to conclude that nobody would use the toilets, unless cubicles were created. Having created the partitions, and then naturally attached cubicle doors, floor and wall tiling is then said to be incidental, as are the partitions to screen off the cisterns. The resultant position is that it is suggested that the entire building work on the toilet blocks is said to be expenditure on building alterations, incidental to the installation of the plant, namely the actual toilet bowls and cisterns.
>
> We consider that description to be extremely unrealistic. The realistic summary is that the overall renovation involved the construction of luxurious toilet blocks, into which various items of plant were installed. Whatever the precise order of construction and installation, we consider that the Appellant's contention that the building works are all incidental to the installation of the toilet bowls and cisterns involves the tail wagging the dog."

As it happens, the special commissioners had – according to the Upper Tribunal – been unduly generous in relation to the toilet block expenditure. Although not all items had been the subject of an HMRC appeal, the Upper Tribunal commented that:

"no allowances should have been granted for any expenditure in relation to the construction of luxurious toilet blocks for men and women in the previous void area of the basement".

Nevertheless, the special commissioners had in other areas correctly applied these principles. In relation to kitchen work, for example, the special commissioners had correctly concluded that:

"It would be stretching [s. 25] beyond its evident purpose to allow expenditure on the construction of kitchen walls to qualify, on the basis that the exigencies of the Appellant's trade, including statutory or regulatory requirements, require that kitchen walls themselves must be constructed so that the cooker may serve its proper purpose. The construction of the kitchen walls was not incidental to the installation of the cookers (or other kitchen equipment). It was part of the creation of a kitchen, in which the cookers and other kitchen equipment could function properly."

The Upper Tribunal approved both the reasoning and the conclusion, noting that it exemplified "the need to start with a broad assessment of what is incidental to what". As such, the Upper Tribunal declared itself "curious" as to why the commissioners had initially granted allowances for cubicle partitions when they had taken the opposite and correct approach in relation to the kitchen alterations.

Relative cost

The Upper Tribunal rejected the notion that incidental costs should always be less than the associated plant to which the alterations were incidental:

"We see no reason why qualifying expenditure on incidental alterations to an existing building should have to be less, or not disproportionately more than, the expenditure on the provision of the plant items to which the alterations are incidental. We imagine that such expenditure would usually be less, but can see no reason why it should not, in an appropriate case, be significantly more."

Reinforcement of kitchen floor

The kitchen floor had to be strengthened to support the weight of commercial cooking equipment. These costs were allowed, even though they effectively created a floor for the kitchen, as "it was a special floor, whose characteristics were determined by the fact that the kitchen equipment needed to be installed in the kitchen".

This might seem to contradict the "asymmetry" argument explained above but the Upper Tribunal felt that a distinction could properly be made:

> "It does not incidentally conflict with our general proposition that [s. 25] will usually confer allowances for alterations to existing buildings, where similar expenditure would not have to be incurred with a purpose-built new building. In that case, the appropriate floor would be designed into the building as an integral part of the overall building work, and this is why the need to make specific alterations on an installation in an existing building deals with a somewhat different situation."

Later, the Upper Tribunal commented that this was in fact "one of the very best examples of a building alteration that is incidental to the installation of plant, and that was properly allowable". This was based on the finding of fact that the reinforcement was needed because of the weight of the equipment, and not because of the weight of people moving around in the kitchen.

Splashbacks and general tiling

In some instances, specific areas around a sink or basin were tiled to protect the brickwork. HMRC accepted that the cost of these could be treated as allowable alterations. The First-tier Tribunal had ruled that "the cost of a splashback is allowable even if the splashback is to cater for the use of splash-producing equipment other than sinks or lavatory basins".

The Upper Tribunal confirmed that ruling, but also felt that HMRC had been wrong to allow an apportionment where there was a more general area of tiling:

> "If a whole room or a kitchen is being tiled for numerous purposes, then even the area around a sink or basin is being tiled because the whole kitchen or work-areas in the kitchen

are being tiled. There is therefore a distinction between the specific splash-back tiling, created simply because of the installation of the sink, and the continuation of the entire tiling around the work areas of the kitchen for numerous reasons. In our view, neither such general tiling, nor any 'fractional element' of it, would qualify under [s. 25]."

Inclined floor

A claim was made for the cost of creating an inclined floor in the cold store to deal with anticipated spillages and washing down. HMRC had argued in front of the First-tier Tribunal that only 5.6 per cent of the cost related to the provision of the incline. However, that Tribunal took the view that the entire cost of the inclined floor was allowable, being incidental to the installation of the drain or pumping equipment:

"the fact (if it be such) that the cost altering the existing building to provide the inclined floor was relatively higher than the cost of the machinery or plant to whose installation the alteration was incidental is on the facts immaterial".

The Upper Tribunal confirmed that allowances were correctly given under s. 25 for these costs, and for the associated trade-specific drainage equipment.

Lighting

Much of the analysis in the earlier appeals related to whether lighting costs were allowable, which would not now be an issue (as they would certainly qualify as integral features). Although the facts were fairly thin, the First-tier Tribunal accepted that the incidental costs of installing the lighting were eligible as alterations to the building. Similarly, the affixation of a pelmet was incidental to the installation of the lighting fixture.

The Upper Tribunal ignored this issue as HMRC had not appealed.

Wipe-clean floors

The First-tier Tribunal regarded it as "unreal" to treat the cost of a wipe-clean floor as incidental to the installation of WCs and urinals. This view was not disturbed by the Upper Tribunal.

Plastering

The First-tier Tribunal ruled "that the plastering provided a wall finish, rather than that it was an inherent part of the process of making the wall surfaces wipe clean". No allowances were therefore due.

That conclusion was not reversed by the Upper Tribunal which clearly rejected the notion that "allowances be claimed for kitchen tiling, the plastering under the tiling, and for kitchen doors all because of spills, fumes and smell from cookers".

Cement and flooring

The company argued that latex cement performed the function of creating a level surface to receive vinyl flooring. This was rejected by the First-tier Tribunal, and that rejection was not disturbed at the Upper Tribunal. Non-slip and wipe-clean floors were desired and necessary for the proper performance of the trade, but their provision was not carried out specifically to enable any machinery or plant to be installed. The floor surfaces were needed for the operation of the equipment, not for its installation.

PVC floor sheeting

This was agreed by all parties to be incidental to the installation of the disabled toilets. The First-tier Tribunal confirmed that the cost was incurred specifically to enable plant or machinery to be installed in the toilets. The point was not considered by the Upper Tribunal.

Law: CAA 2001, s. 25

Cases: *CIR v Barclay, Curle and Co Ltd* (1969) 45 TC 221; *J D Wetherspoon plc v HMRC* (2007) Sp C 657; *J D Wetherspoon plc v HMRC* [2009] UKFTT 374 (TC); *J D Wetherspoon plc v HMRC* [2012] UKUT 42 (TCC)

Guidance: CA 21190, 22010

A10   Amusement parks

An amusement park as such will always be the premises within which a business operates, rather than a large item of plant and machinery. It seems inconceivable that the principle that allowed, for example, a dry dock to be treated as plant could ever be applied to a whole amusement park.

There is a statutory reference to "the provision of structures and other assets for providing the setting for any ride at an amusement park or exhibition". It follows that such structures or other assets are not subject to a statutory bar from being treated as plant, but can be considered on ordinary principles. HMRC's *Capital Allowances Manual* at CA 23084 includes amusement park rides in a list of "typical examples of plant or machinery".

Any machinery will qualify in its own right, without any need to show that it is also plant. It seems likely that many particular attractions may qualify as plant. Swimming pools qualify as plant and the same principles should ensure similar treatment for many attractions found in amusement parks.

Law: CAA 2001, s. 23 (list C, item 32)
Case: *Cooke v Beach Station Caravans Ltd* (1974) 49 TC 514
Guidance: CA 22030

A11 Anaerobic digestion installations

Background

These are, broadly speaking, plants that take organic waste material ("feedstocks") and convert them to produce renewable energy, fertiliser and clean water.

The feedstocks typically consist of organic waste from agricultural sources or from food processing industries, sometimes supplemented by organic household waste and waste from commercial sources such as hotels, hospitals, supermarkets, schools and prisons. Waste paper and mown grass may also be used.

As the waste decomposes, biogas is produced, which is a mixture of carbon dioxide and methane. The biogas is typically used in a combined heat and power plant, but in other cases the methane may be used to power turbines that generate electricity for feeding into the national grid.

As a by-product of the process, a residual substance ("digestate") is produced. This is rich in nutrients and is typically used as a natural fertiliser or as a soil conditioner.

Construction of an anaerobic digestion plant, which will then provide a local source of electricity, typically takes a minimum of about a year, with a longer timescale required for larger projects.

Plant

The nature of the plant to be used will depend partly on the complexity of the project.

In the simplest cases, the whole process will take place within a single environment. This may be a manufactured holding tank, or use is sometimes made of anaerobic earthen lagoons.

In other cases, different vessels are used for different stages of the overall process. This will involve the construction of two or more connected tanks, with sophisticated heating and pumping systems. The materials may be processed in these tanks over a period of anything from a few hours to many weeks.

A key aspect is the removal of contaminants – such as glass, metal or plastic – from the feedstock. These can block the digester tanks and will reduce efficiency, so more complex plant is required to remove these contaminants.

Pulping or mincing speeds up the digestion speeds, so once more it is common for the plant to include mechanical plant to that end.

Claiming allowances

The question of whether or not capital allowances will be available, and to what extent, will depend on the detailed specification of the plant. A simple earthen lagoon may not qualify at all (though any associated plant or machinery will so qualify). A more complex set-up, on the other hand, will contain substantial amounts of plant and machinery.

Following broad principles, any machinery will qualify, but housing that is merely to protect plant and equipment from the elements will not.

A key feature of all such plants will be the main anaerobic digester tank or tanks. Although these are almost certainly structures, a claim may be justified on the basis that these are processing equipment (item 4 of list C at s. 23) or (possibly) storage tanks (item

28b). Industrial hoppers (for the feedstock) would again be structures but would probably also qualify as part of the processing equipment.

HMRC accept that allowances may be given for **Slurry storage facilities** but not for any buildings or structures that form part of such facilities. See also item 29 at list C. See also **Silos and silage clamps**.

Electricity generators will qualify in their own right as plant or machinery. As these are noisy, special insulated housing may be needed. Depending on the detailed facts, such housing may or may not constitute "sound insulation provided mainly to meet the particular requirements of the qualifying activity" (per item 7). It will be necessary, however, to watch the caveat at s. 23(4), relating to assets whose principal purpose is to insulate or enclose the interior of a building.

Any **Combined heat and power** installation is likely to qualify in full for allowances, and may qualify for enhanced allowances, as discussed at that section.

Any pumps, transformers and related equipment will clearly qualify as plant or machinery. The housing for such equipment would in principle not qualify, though once more it may be worth considering whether such housing might qualify under the heading of trade-specific sound insulation.

Many facilities will have a control room. In principle, this will not qualify but it will no doubt contain substantial amounts of plant or machinery for which a claim will be possible.

Complicating factors

Enhanced capital allowances are likely to be available for combined heat and power installations.

Any equipment with a useful life of 25 years or more may be subject to the rules for **Long-life assets**, and may therefore treated as special rate expenditure.

In appropriate cases, the question of feed-in tariffs may need to be considered, as discussed under **Energy-saving technology**.

A12   Animal feed systems

HMRC guidance confirms that "feed systems (whether or not automated)" qualify as plant and machinery. Such expenditure will be allocated to the main pool.

The guidance, written specifically for the pig industry, also confirms that allowances are due for "specialist equipment for the production, storage, handling & distribution of pig feed".

Guidance: R&C Brief 03/10 (see **Appendix 4**)

A13   Animals

Animals that do not form part of the trading stock of a business (and that are not the subject of a herd basis election: see below) may well qualify as plant, and attract capital allowances accordingly.

HMRC guidance to tax officers is as follows:

> "Accept a claim for PMAs on an animal if the animal functions as apparatus with which the trade is carried on and it has an expected life of 2 years or more. For example, it is likely that a horse used in a riding school or show jumping business, a guard dog or a circus animal is plant.

> Do not accept a claim that a farm animal such as a horse, cow or sheep is plant, unless it is a working animal such as a sheep dog. Farm animals are normally trading stock and their cost is revenue expenditure that bars a capital allowance claim."

The Revenue also wrote on the topic in *Farm Tax and Finance* back in January 1984, as follows:

> "In order to qualify for capital allowances a trader needs to show that he has incurred capital expenditure on the provision of plant .... Where there has been expenditure on a work horse and the practice has not been to write the cost off in computing profits such expenditure may be treated as capital expenditure on plant for these purposes and a capital allowance claimed."

There is plenty of case law backing the idea that animals can be plant. *Yarmouth v France*, in which a cart-horse was held to be plant, is the classic case regarding the definition of plant and machinery, quoted in dozens of later decisions since it was decided back in 1887. The judgment included the following key comments:

> "Plant includes whatever apparatus is used by a business man for carrying on his business – not his stock-in-trade which he buys or makes for sale; but all goods and chattels, fixed or moveable, live or dead, which he keeps for permanent employment in his business."

Elsewhere in the same case, the judge commented:

> "It is suggested that nothing that is animate can be plant; that is, that living creatures can in no sense be considered plant. Why not? In many businesses horses and carts, wagons, or drays, seem to me to form the most material part of the plant: they are the materials or instruments which the employer must use for the purpose of carrying on his business, and without which he could not carry it on at all."

In *Cole Bros*, the judge commented in an aside that "an elephant might be plant".

Greyhounds were held *not* to be plant in *Albion Greyhounds*. The reasoning is not clear but it seems likely that the animals did not qualify as plant simply because they did not live long enough to do so; their average racing life was under two years and they therefore failed the *Yarmouth v France* principle that plant must be kept for "permanent employment" (which is generally interpreted to mean at least two years).

By contrast, the **Human body** does not qualify as plant.

Cases: *Yarmouth v France* [1887] 4 TRL 1; *Abbott v Albion Greyhounds (Salford) Ltd* (1945) 26 TC 39; *Norman v Golder* (1945) 26 TC 293; *Cole Brothers Ltd v Phillips* [1982] BTC 208
Guidance: CA 21220

Herd basis

Farmers may elect to treat certain production animals on the "herd basis" under ITTOIA 2005, s. 111ff. or under CTA 2009, s. 109ff. If an election is made, the expenditure on such animals (or on shares in such animals) is not qualifying expenditure for plant and machinery purposes.

Law: CAA 2001, s. 38

A14   Annual investment allowances

These allowances (AIAs) are not a category of expenditure and are therefore not covered in this volume in depth. Some key principles, however, are as follows:

- AIAs give immediate tax relief for most types of expenditure on plant and machinery, up to a defined limit;
- the limit changes from time to time and is subject to transitional provisions that can be extremely complex;
- AIAs are available for expenditure on integral features and special rate expenditure;
- various general exclusions apply, however, including for expenditure on cars;
- AIAs can only be given for the period in which the expenditure is incurred, and not for historic expenditure claimed in a later period (though such historic expenditure may be claimed by way of writing-down allowances);
- allowances are available for individuals, for partnerships of individuals and for companies, but not for trusts;
- a single amount of AIA must, in broad terms, be shared between group companies or between various associated businesses.

See *Capital Allowances* 2018-19 for full, practical commentary on these allowances, including detailed coverage of the extremely complex transitional provisions that apply when there are changes to the amount that may be claimed. *Capital Allowances* is written by the same authors as this volume and is also published by Claritax Books.

Law: CAA 2001, s. 38A, 38B
Guidance: CA 23080

A15   Aqueducts

Aqueducts are included in list B at s. 22. As such, they are excluded from the definition of plant and machinery and no allowances are due.

HMRC guidance confirms that plant and machinery allowances will not be given "on the provision, construction or acquisition" of such assets.

Law: CAA 2001, s. 22 (list B, item 1)
Guidance: CA 22020

A16   Architraves

The term "architrave" is typically used to denote the framework around a door or window. In the *Wetherspoon* case, it was argued that these items should qualify as plant or machinery, on the grounds that they were removable and therefore not part of the premises. This argument was clearly rejected by the Upper Tier Tribunal, as follows:

> "Having been shown photographs of each of the items in issue, we consider it fanciful to suppose that any of them could be regarded as having retained their separate identities; separate that is from the ceilings, walls and balustrades of which they each form part. Since those ceilings, walls and balustrades are all clearly part of the premises, so are the cornices, architraves and balustrade end-fittings. We cannot, in short, imagine how any legal analysis of the nature of plant, as opposed to premises, could lead to a conclusion that those items were plant."

Case: *J D Wetherspoon v HMRC* [2012] UKUT 42 (TCC)

A17   Artex

The claim for the cost of "artex" and other wall finishes was rejected by the commissioners in *Wimpy* and this view was upheld in the High Court and then by all three judges in the Court of Appeal. Fox LJ commented as follows:

> "This is a proprietary decorative finish for interior wall surfaces. The commissioners, rejecting the contention that

artex expenditure was on plant, said that it was no more than a suitable surface applied to the walls and to enable the premises to be used and kept clean. It was a necessary part of the setting and not apparatus used in trade. The commissioners must, it seems to me, have taken the view that the artex is part of the premises. I see no reason to disagree with that."

Fox LJ went on to add:

"There was expenditure on plaster, paint, varnish and other wall finishes. All of it was incurred to put the premises, including the staff area, into decorative order for use. The commissioners rejected the claim that it was expenditure on plant. I agree with Hoffmann J, that the items were in the same position as the artex claim and were rightly held not to be plant."

Case: *Wimpy International Ltd. v Warland* [1989] BTC 58

A18   Automatic monitoring and targeting (AMT) equipment

Such equipment will qualify for plant and machinery allowances in all normal circumstances. In some cases, it will attract 100 per cent first-year allowances under the scheme for **Enhanced capital allowances** (ECAs).

According to the official ECAs guidance:

"AMT equipment can be portable or fixed (systems). Both types monitor how much energy a site is using, identifying any areas where it's being wasted. This helps companies introduce energy-saving measures in the areas where they will provide the most benefit.

The equipment also helps ensure these measures have the desired long-term effect."

Two categories of product are covered, as below. In each case, the descriptive wording is taken from the official ECA site and/or from the energy technology criteria list.

Automatic monitoring and targeting sub-metering systems

"Automatic Monitoring & Targeting sub-metering systems are products that are specifically designed to measure energy consumption, record and distribute metered energy data, and analyse and report on energy consumption."

Portable energy monitoring equipment

"Portable energy monitoring equipment covers products that are specifically designed to temporarily measure energy use in different locations, and to record, analyse and report on energy consumption."

Investments in these systems will only attract ECAs if the complete installation meets the specified eligibility criteria; individual components or products used in the system are not named on the energy technology list.

Law: SI 2018/268, art. 3(2)(b)

Guidance: https://www.gov.uk/energy-technology-list

B1   Balustrades

In the *Wetherspoon* case, it was held by the Upper Tier Tribunal that balustrades (and their associated end fittings) were "clearly part of the premises" and not plant.

Case: *J D Wetherspoon v HMRC* [2012] UKUT 42 (TCC)

B2   Barriers

Many properties have a low barrier around the outside, especially to offer protection where cars would otherwise be able to drive right up to the building itself.

The treatment of these barriers is not clear cut. They are not buildings, but the question of whether or not they are structures is more difficult. Case law suggests that **Structures** must be of a certain degree of size and permanence, and it is arguable that these barriers lack that quality – compared, for example, to roads, dams, docks and other items included at list B at s. 22.

The HMRC view is that fences are always fixed structures, and they may seek to argue that barriers should be treated in the same way.

On the other hand, the author is aware of a case in which HMRC have conceded (albeit on a "without prejudice" basis as part of an overall settlement covering a variety of items) that gallop rails on a race course might be allowed.

If it can be argued that there is no statutory bar on treating the barrier as plant, the next stage is to look at case law principles, asking whether the barrier functions as part of the premises or setting within which the trade is carried on, or whether it functions as part of the apparatus used to carry on the trade. HMRC would probably argue for the former, but the matter is not entirely clear cut.

Law: CAA 2001, s. 22

B3   Baths

Baths are included in list C at CAA 2001, s. 23. They will normally fall clearly within the definition of plant and machinery, attracting allowances at the standard rate. HMRC guidance specifically states that baths should be accepted as plant.

Law: CAA 2001, s. 23 (list C, item 5)
Guidance: CA 21200

B4   Batteries and battery chargers

Battery chargers are clearly plant if used in normal circumstances.

Batteries themselves will qualify as long as they have a shelf life of at least two years. (If they do not, the cost should probably not be capitalised but will normally be allowable as a revenue deduction.) In the *B & E Security Systems* case, the cost of a power supply and back-up batteries was allowed as part of the qualifying expenditure. Back-up units for emergency lighting would also qualify.

Battery technology is at the forefront of the green energy revolution, and is set to grow in importance as the world harnesses more renewable energy, and as we all switch to electric cars. The world's "biggest battery" (in reality a vast network of batteries generating 100 megawatts and covering an area the size of a football pitch) was installed by Tesla in South Australia towards the end of 2017.

In a written answer in Parliament, recorded in Hansard on 1 December 2017, the Exchequer Secretary Andrew Jones confirmed that standard rate allowances are available for battery storage technologies.

Case: *B & E Security Systems Ltd v HMRC* [2010] UKFTT 146 (TC)

Guidance: www.theyworkforyou.com/wrans/?id=2017-11-23.115 378.h

B5   Bicycle holders

Bicycle holders were included in the list of items "which would normally qualify as plant or machinery" in the Revenue's *Football League* letter of January 1991 (see **Appendix 2**). That predated the legislation now at s. 21 and 22 and so it would be necessary to show that the bicycle holder was not incorporated in the building or of a kind normally incorporated in a building.

Law: CAA 2001, s. 21, 22

Guidance: CA 21230

B6   Bicycles

Bicycles used for transport purposes, as well as exercise bikes in a sports facility, should clearly qualify as plant or machinery in normal circumstances.

B7   Blinds

Blinds will normally qualify as plant, in much the same way as **Curtains** will, as long as they are being used for the purposes of a qualifying activity. This is obviously subject to the restriction for plant used in a **Dwelling house**.

In *Cole Bros*, Oliver LJ made the following observation in the Court of Appeal:

> "I would have thought that the blinds fitted to shop windows to protect the goods displayed there from excessive sunlight were as much 'plant' as the heating system which prevents them from freezing."

In *Cadogan Gardens*, blinds in a hotel were accepted as plant.

As regards blinds used as part of refrigerated display units, see **Refrigerators and refrigeration equipment**.

Cases: *Lupton v Cadogan Gardens Developments Limited* (1971) 47 TC 1; *Cole Bros Ltd v Phillips* (1981) 55 TC 188 (Court of Appeal)

B8   Boilers

A boiler used as part of a central heating system or for the provision of hot water will in principle clearly qualify as plant or machinery.

The HMRC view is that a boiler is an integral feature, attracting allowances at the lower "special rate". This is on the basis that the boiler forms part of "a space or water heating system, a powered system of ventilation, air cooling or air purification ...".

The author's view is that the question of whether a boiler is an integral feature or standard plant and machinery is not entirely clear cut, for the reasons discussed under **Lifts** below. Nevertheless, the HMRC view will almost certainly prevail, at least until there is a test case.

Enhanced capital allowances

Boiler equipment is one of the categories in the "energy technology list" that may qualify for **Enhanced capital allowances**, where the necessary conditions are met.

The following categories of equipment are *or have historically been* specified for the purposes of claiming ECAs. In each case, investments in these devices will only attract ECAs if the specific product is named on the energy technology product list, having satisfied the eligibility criteria. The descriptions in inverted commas are in each case copied or condensed from the official ECAs guidance:

Biomass boilers

This category was known as "biomass boilers and roomheaters" until 2016. The following explanation is included in the energy technology criteria list:

> "Biomass boilers are products that are specifically designed to burn solid biomass fuels in order to heat water."

The heat produced by these boilers is transferred, by means of radiation and convection, to the surrounding area within a building. They may also heat water for space heating and domestic uses by means of a heat exchanger incorporated into the product.

Burners with controls

The details of this sub-category were revised in 2018.

"Burners with controls are used to provide heat for hot water, steam and thermal oil boilers, heaters and processes. They are widely used in industry and commerce."

This sub-category "covers products that are specifically designed to create and burn air and fuel mixtures in a safe, efficient and controlled manner, and to direct the heat released through combustion into a pressurised vessel (or other combustion chamber)".

Condensing economisers

"These recover sensible and latent heat from boiler flue gases and ensure fuel is used in the most efficient and economic way. Any heat that is recovered can then be used to provide low-grade thermal energy to heat the rest of the site."

Condensing economisers are thus a type of heat exchanger. This heat is normally used to preheat the boiler's feedwater and to supply low grade heating requirements.

Flue gas economisers

"These are heat exchangers designed to recover sensible heat from boiler flue gases."

Once more, the heat is normally used to preheat the boiler's feedwater. The technology is said to work best in systems with a low return water temperature, where the overall efficiency of the system can be increased by up to 6%.

Gas-fired condensing water heaters

"Gas-fired condensing water heaters are products that are specifically designed to continuously provide hot water either by the direct heating of water as it passes through the product, or the heating of water contained in an integral storage vessel."

"Gas-fired condensing water heaters are used to provide hot water for domestic purposes or process heating, and offer an energy efficient method of generating hot water. They can be installed close to the point of use, or in a central plant room.

Gas-fired condensing water heaters are described as 'storage' type products if they generate hot water by heating water stored within the product itself."

Heat recovery from condensate and boiler blowdown

"Steam boilers need to be blown down to control the level of total dissolved solids. The water discharged from this process contains useful heat that can be recovered and used to pre-heat the boiler's feed water.

Recovering heat in this way increases the overall efficiency of the system."

Heating management controllers for wet heating systems

These were formerly known as "Optimising controllers for wet heating systems".

"These controllers reduce the amount of energy a boiler uses by ensuring that the firing and heating are distributed in a way that closely matches demand. They are available as stand-alone units that can be added to existing systems, or as modules that can be integrated into a new boiler design."

Hot water boilers

The guidance in the energy technology criteria list states that "hot water boilers are products that are specifically designed to heat water by means of a heat exchanger that transfers heat from combustion into the water as it passes through the product."

Retrofit burner control systems

"Burner controls maintain the quality of combustion over the boiler's complete firing range, optimising efficiency and minimising emissions.

Precise and repeatable control is essential, but traditional mechanical methods are not considered accurate enough to provide this. However, the necessary precision can be achieved by retrofitting microprocessor-based controls."

Steam boilers

The details of this sub-category were revised in 2018.

"Steam boilers are products that are specifically designed to convert water into pressurised steam by means of a burner that converts fuel into heat and a heat exchanger that transfers the heat into the water as it passes through the product."

Former sub-categories

The criteria for boilers are subject to frequent change and the following sub-categories have been removed in recent years:

- automatic boiler blowdown control equipment (removed 2013);
- combustion trim controls (removed 2012);
- condensate pumping equipment (removed 2013);
- localised rapid steam generators (removed 2018);
- sequence controls (removed 2012).

Law: CAA 2001, s. 23, 33A(5)(c); SI 2018/268, art. 3(2)(c)
Guidance: https://www.gov.uk/energy-technology-list; R&C Brief 03/10

B9   Bollards

Many businesses will incur expenditure on bollards (indoors or out), whether to offer a form of protection against crime or accident, or perhaps as part of a system of channelling people who are standing in queues.

Indoor bollards will typically (but not invariably) be moveable. These would seem to qualify as plant and machinery without any problem. They are equipment used for the purposes of the business activity and are not fixed structures.

The treatment of fixed bollards, usually outside a building, may be more problematic.

Retractable bollards – and telescopic posts – would probably constitute **Machinery** (according to the wide HMRC definition discussed under that heading), and would therefore seem to qualify without too much difficulty.

The question of whether fixed, heavy duty, "ram raid" bollards (typically made of cast iron and/or steel) would qualify is less straightforward. These may obviously serve a business purpose – deterrence, counter-terrorism, demarcation, or whatever it may be – but these items may be thought to constitute a **Structure** (the definition of which is considered under that heading). If such items are not mechanical, and if it has to be conceded that they are indeed fixed structures, there would appear to be nothing in list C at s. 23 that could allow them to qualify as plant. However, it may reasonably be argued that a bollard is too small, and insufficiently complex, to constitute a structure.

Law: CAA 2001, s. 22

B10   Books

Books that are bought for genuine business purposes will qualify as plant unless a revenue deduction can be claimed for the cost.

Early case law ruled that books were *not* plant but this decision was overruled in the *Munby v Furlong* case, in which two judges gave a clear ruling on the point. Sir John Pennycuick worded it as follows:

> "[Plant] seems to me quite plainly to cover books purchased by a barrister for the purpose of his profession. Those books do indeed represent apparatus used by him for carrying on his profession, and that to my mind is the end of the case."

And Lord Denning gave a longer explanation:

> "I do not think 'plant' should be confined to things which are used physically. It seems to me that on principle it extends to

the intellectual storehouse which a barrister or a solicitor or any other professional man has in the course of carrying on his profession. The difficulty has arisen because the Legislature, when it extended this provision to professions, did not make clear the scope of the word 'plant' in that context. It seems to me, in the context of a profession, the provision of 'plant' should be so interpreted that a lawyer's books – his set of law reports and his textbooks – are 'plant'."

HMRC guidance is that "the initial cost of establishing a technical library may qualify for capital allowances" and that a revenue deduction may be given for the following:

- new editions of, and supplements to, books already owned;
- replacements of books rendered obsolete by extensive changes in the law;
- technical periodicals, and periodical parts of law reports and similar items;
- binding of supplements, periodicals, etc.

In practice, HMRC are unlikely to bother about capitalising the cost of occasional books where the amounts involved are not substantial.

Case: *Munby v Furlong* (1977) 50 TC 491
Guidance: BIM 46970; EIM 36710

B11   Boreholes

Boreholes come in widely varying sizes and their tax treatment will depend on the nature of the borehole and its function within the business.

If a borehole is sunk as part of a process of supplying water for a business (e.g. a farm), and if a pump is installed as part of the system, it may be possible to argue that the cost of the borehole is part of the cost of the overall installation.

In the *RTZ* case, not concerned with capital allowances and presumably dealing with a borehole on an altogether larger scale, Vinelott J commented:

"I cannot see that any distinction can fairly be drawn between the boreholes, well heads and flow lines on the one hand and the rig, the manifold and the loading lines and buoy on the other hand. All are part of a comprehensive installation designed to obtain access to and to win and transport oil from the oil field to onshore facilities."

It is understood that HMRC have confirmed the cost of drilling a borehole to an underground salt cavern does qualify for capital allowances where this is for the purposes of gas storage. This was reported in an article dated 23 April 2009 on the *Mondaq* site.

Case: *RTZ Oil and Gas Ltd. v Elliss* [1987] BTC 359
Guidance: www.mondaq.com

B12   Bridges

Bridges are specifically mentioned in list B at s. 22. As such, they are excluded from the definition of plant and machinery and no allowances are due.

HMRC guidance confirms that plant and machinery allowances will not be given "on the provision, construction or acquisition" of such assets.

Law: CAA 2001, s. 22 (list B, item 1)
Guidance: CA 22020

B13   Briefcases

As a briefcase is likely to last for more than two years, the cost should strictly be capitalised. In the *Employment Income Manual*, HMRC accept that a briefcase is likely to be plant (though allowances for employees themselves will normally be denied on the grounds that the case is not necessarily provided for use in the performance of the employee's duties: see **Employee expenses**).

B14   Building management systems

Building management systems may be used to control many aspects of the electrical systems within a property – heat, light, etc. Such systems will normally qualify unambiguously as plant and machinery.

It is understood that HMRC have insisted that such systems should be allocated to integral features rather than being treated as general fixtures. This would be on the basis that the management controls form part of "an electrical system (including a lighting system)".

Arguably, the cost should in some cases be apportioned between integral features and general fixtures. This would seem to be justified if, for example, the controls also related to fire and burglar alarm systems.

Law: CAA 2001, s. 23, 33A

B15   Building works in connection

It is common to see an entry for "Building Works in Connection" as part of the overall cost of a large construction project. This term, often abbreviated to "BWIC" covers such items as drilling holes, concrete bases, support trays and all those works which allow wires and pipes to be threaded through a building.

The treatment should follow that of the underlying expenditure. If, for example, the works are in connection with the installation of cold water pipes, the costs will be treated as expenditure on integral features.

B16   Buildings for aircraft testing

Any building will in principle fail to qualify for plant and machinery allowances. Some buildings, or parts of buildings, may however qualify by virtue of particular exemptions.

Item 20 at list C refers to "buildings provided for testing aircraft engines run within the buildings". The reasoning behind this exemption from the statutory restriction is not clear, but it means that such buildings can be considered on case law principles. Presumably there is some sort of understanding between HMRC and the aircraft industry.

Law: CAA 2001, s. 23 (list C, item 20)

B17   Buildings generally

The general principle is that "expenditure on the provision of plant or machinery does not include expenditure on the provision of a building". The term "building" is then defined to include any asset incorporated in a building, and also an asset which "although not incorporated in the building (whether because the asset is moveable or for any other reason), is in the building and is of a kind normally incorporated in a building".

However, the reality is much more complex than this, as many fixtures in buildings do indeed qualify as plant or machinery. Indeed, a majority of the categories listed in this A-Z section relate to fixtures in property, showing that they will often qualify for allowances. The treatment of fixtures is one of the more complex aspects of the capital allowances system and is considered in depth (over 100 pages) in *Capital Allowances* 2018-19, also available from Claritax Books.

For a discussion of the term "incorporated in the building" (and of "normally incorporated in the building") reference may usefully be made, albeit in a different tax context, to the *Taylor Wimpey* case heard in the Upper Tribunal in 2017. The case makes the point that " 'incorporates' is not the same as 'installed as fixtures' ".

Law: CAA 2001, s. 21-25
Case: *Taylor Wimpey plc v HMRC* [2017] UKUT 34 (TCC)

B18 Buildings (moveable)

The statutory restriction on buildings does not apply to "moveable buildings intended to be moved in the course of the qualifying activity". If a building falls within this category, the question of whether or not it is plant must therefore be considered on first principles, using case law precedents.

The key case is that of *St John's School*, in which a claim was made for the cost of a laboratory and a gymnasium. The description of the buildings included the following:

> "(a) each is constructed of a number of prefabricated, timber-framed, asbestos-lined panels bolted together, supplied separately and erected on the site; the appropriate windows and doors form part of the panels;
>
> (b) the outside surfaces of the panels are cedar strip cladding;
>
> (c) each has a gable roof covered with roof felt on laths, and a ridge and guttering;

   (d)   both have mains electricity service; and

   (e)   neither structure is affixed to the ground or the concrete base on which it stands."

In rejecting the claim for plant and machinery allowances, the judge carried out a thorough analysis and brought out some important principles:

- the fact that a building could be taken down by inexperienced workmen and put up in a different way, or that the interior could be changed from two small rooms to one large one, did not alter the basic question of what is the structure, and if the structure was a building or premises it remained a building or premises;

- in considering whether a structure was plant or premises one had to look at the finished product and not at the bits and pieces as they arrived from the factory;

- it might happen that within the whole, if it be premises or a building, one might find that there are one or more items of plant;

- the fact that a building, or part of a building, held plant in position (e.g. the roof holding in place the climbing ropes) did not, by some magic wand, convert the building itself into plant;

- if a building had special features it generally speaking remained a building and was not plant, although it may be that the special features attached objects which were themselves plant;

- it was necessary to find, not the name of the building or its function, but whether the building was in truth a building within which the business was carried on or whether it was apparatus used by the businessman for carrying on the business;

- the treatment of a whole building could be distinguished in a number of ways from the treatment of moveable partitions within a building: in the present case the subject-matter of the inquiry was a structure which, however it may be altered, remained a building;

- the fact that there were special features of a building or that it could be altered to provide a different setting did not suffice to turn a building into plant;

- if one asked whether the laboratory and the gymnasium were the premises in which the business is carried on or were part of the plant with which the business was carried on, the answer had to be the former. Education was not carried out *with* these particular buildings but *in* these particular buildings;

- neither the laboratory nor the gymnasium had any function to perform other than to shelter the persons who were being educated inside – the building was only the structure within which the function of educating the boys was carried on.

The case proceeded to the Court of Appeal where (subject to one element of detail about apportionment of costs) the Court "entirely accepted and adopted" the arguments as summarised above.

In view of the very clear rejection of the taxpayer's arguments in this case, it is possibly surprising that the statutory exemption is given for moveable buildings. This is a clear illustration of how sections 21 and 23 are interwoven and of how the inclusion of an item in list C does not guarantee that it will qualify as plant.

In practice, the only circumstances in which HMRC are clearly willing to apply the list C exception is in relation to builder huts. As the guidance states:

> "Treat temporary huts which are moved from one site to another and used by builders and contractors to provide canteen and toilet facilities or as storage sheds as site plant. They will then qualify for plant or machinery allowances."

There is no statutory reason why huts used by builders and contractors should be treated any differently from huts used by any other trade. As such, it may be possible to make an analogous claim by reference to this HMRC guidance. Where temporary buildings are put up at sporting events, for example, it seems likely that a claim will be possible in appropriate cases. A key issue will be to look not just at the physical nature of the building but at how it is in reality used within the context of the particular trade or other activity.

Law: CAA 2001, s. 23 (list C, item 21)
Case: *St. John's School (Mountford and Another) v Ward* (1974) 49 TC 524
Guidance: CA 22110

B19   Burglar alarm systems

Burglar alarm systems are included in list C at s. 23 and will clearly qualify as plant and machinery in normal circumstances. The associated wiring will likewise qualify, whether in a new building or an existing one.

Burglar alarm systems do not need to be classified as integral features, as confirmed by HMRC:

> "The term [electrical system] does not include other building systems intended for other purposes, which may include wiring and other electrical components. For example, communication, telecommunication and surveillance systems, fire alarm systems or burglar alarm systems. These other systems are all separately identified in S23 (3) List C of CAA01."

The guidance from HMRC goes on to confirm that the cost of a ducting system within a building or structure will follow the tax treatment of the system or systems that the ducting supports. So ducting for general electrical work will be classified as integral features, and will accordingly attract a lower tax rate. Ducting for a burglar alarm system will qualify as plant and machinery in its own right and will attract the higher rate.

Law: CAA 2001, s. 23 (list C, item 11)
Guidance: CA 22330

B20   Bus shelters

Bus shelters are clearly structures and are thus caught initially by s. 22. In *J C Decaux*, no allowances were allowed for the bus shelters. The case was complex and was concerned in part with the question of who had a licence to occupy the land, but the following comment is relevant:

"A bus shelter has to be fixed into a slab laid in the ground in order to hold it securely and hold its component parts together, otherwise it would fall down. Its base or slab is part of the chattel in this instance as in the following instances, as Mr Thornhill submitted. In my opinion a bus shelter loses its chattel nature on being so erected. I hold it becomes part and parcel of the land. It is firmly fixed into the ground. It is not a temporary structure."

A bus shelter is not a building and thus cannot benefit from the potential exemption given at item 21 in list C at s. 23 ("moveable buildings intended to be moved in the course of the qualifying activity").

There is a possible argument, however, that bus shelters are in fact not caught by s. 22. The legal technicalities are complex and unclear but item 7a in list B at s. 22 catches any structure *other than* a structure that falls within the meaning of industrial building for the purposes of the now repealed IBA rules. Those former IBA rules do not state specifically that certain items are to be treated as industrial buildings; rather they talk about buildings in use for the purposes of a qualifying trade (s. 273). Table B at s. 274 then lists (or, strictly, listed – but the point remains valid for plant and machinery purposes: see FA 2008, Sch. 27, para. 33) certain undertakings that are qualifying trades if carried on by way of trade.

On the face of it, a bus shelter could therefore be protected by reference to s. 274 as Table B includes references to both a transport undertaking and a highway undertaking.

If this reading of a particularly difficult part of the legislation is correct, it does not follow that a bus shelter would be correctly treated as plant, but it would mean that there was no statutory bar against such treatment.

Where shelters are used for advertising, HMRC accept that they may qualify as plant, but subject to a caveat:

"Advertisers sometimes lease shelters which they have erected and which they use to display advertisements to bus companies or local authorities. If they do that you should accept that the shelters are plant or machinery but note that where the assets are fixtures the claimant must have an interest in the relevant land."

Law: CAA 2001, s. 22, 23, 273, 274

Case: *J C Decaux (UK) Ltd v Francis* (1996) Sp C 84

Guidance: CA 22110

C1   Cabling

The treatment of electrical installations and equipment in general is considered at **Electrical Installations and Equipment** (at E1) below. However, electrical (and other) cables raise technical considerations of their own.

Internal cabling

Cabling costs within a building would clearly seem to fall within the HMRC definition of an "electrical system" ("a system for taking electrical power (including lighting) from the point of entry to the building or structure, or generation within the building or structure, and distributing it through the building or structure, as required"). As such, they qualify as integral features.

External cabling

For external cabling, leading from the site boundary to the point of entry to the building, the position is more complex. This can be a big issue for certain qualifying activities; for example, a caravan park may incur substantial costs in providing reliable, high wattage electrical supplies to each caravan location on the site.

The definition quoted above of "electrical system" is only the one used by HMRC. As it has no statutory force, it is open to challenge and one line of argument would be that this external cabling too forms part of the electrical system of the building. Given that HMRC's definition is well established, it is unlikely that this argument would prevail without at least a First-tier Tribunal hearing.

If that does not work, then it is necessary to turn again to the detail of sections 21 to 23.

If the cabling costs can be said to be "connected with" the building (which they must presumably be, by definition) and if they constitute "mains services ... for ... electricity" then they are caught initially by s. 21(3) (list A, item 2). The statutory effect of this is that they do not constitute plant or machinery unless there is a let-out elsewhere.

Nor should s. 22(1)(b) be overlooked, which says that expenditure on "any works involving the alteration of land" is not expenditure on plant or machinery.

Section 25 ("Building alterations connected with installation of plant or machinery") does not seem to help, for two reasons. Primarily, the installation of external cabling would not seem to constitute alterations to a building. As a secondary problem, that section would only apply to alterations to an *existing* building, which would rule out any relief in many cases.

Turning to list C at s. 23, item 25 removes any statutory restrictions for "the provision of pipelines or underground ducts or tunnels with a primary purpose of carrying utility conduits".

The relationship between the general restriction for "mains services for electricity" and the relieving wording re "underground ducts or tunnels" needs to be considered carefully. The legislation should be interpreted on the basis that both elements carry some force and, on the face of it (but see below), this would seem to mean that the cabling costs themselves do not qualify (as they constitute mains services) but that the ducts or tunnels may do so. Inclusion in list C does not, of course, guarantee that those elements will qualify, but there is perhaps a general presumption that they will qualify in normal circumstances as they are specifically identified within list C.

However, the conclusion that the ducts qualify but the cables do not is problematic in principle (in that it is difficult to identify any logical reason for ending up at that conclusion). Furthermore, HMRC guidance at CA 21200 includes the following (with our emphasis added near the start):

> "If you receive a capital allowance claim for an underground cable system (including television, telecommunications, *or electricity supply systems*) the costs of installing the cables will include the costs of excavating the land and providing ducting that houses the cables. The cabling and the ducting may be recognised as separate components of the asset in the

claimant's accounts (so that they are depreciated at different rates). Where the ducting is installed as a direct incident of the installation of the cabling, the costs of the ducting and the associated excavation are, for capital allowance purposes, part of the costs incurred on the provision of the cabling regardless of the treatment in the accounts. In these circumstances, if the cabling is not itself a long-life asset, the long-life asset rules are not separately applicable to the ducting."

This can, on the face of it, be read as implying (though not quite stating explicitly) that cabling costs qualify for allowances (as an asset cannot be a long-life asset unless it is plant in the first place: see the definition at s. 91(1)).

However, this appears to be in contradiction of the restriction in s. 21. We also have guidance from HMRC back in the 1970s (a reply from the then Inland Revenue to a query raised by the Consultative Committee of Accountancy Bodies) in which the Revenue stated that "expenditure on the provision of main services to buildings such as electrical wiring ... is regarded as part of the cost of the building, and therefore, as not qualifying for capital allowances". That predates the legislation now at sections 21 to 23, but these sections were never intended to broaden the scope of what qualifies.

It may perhaps be argued that the wording at CA 21200 is not as broad as it may seem, and that it only applies to cabling provided for specified items of plant or machinery. But the wording does clearly refer to television and telecommunications on the one hand, and to electricity supply systems on the other.

If cabling is installed specifically for particular electrical equipment then it would qualify, but if we take the line that the whole electrical system qualifies (as integral features) and that the whole of the mains cabling is incidental to that system, then it is difficult to understand what purpose is served by the general restriction for mains cabling, which will always be to serve an electrical system of some sort.

To add one further clue, HMRC guidance suggests that **Fibre optic cabling** qualifies, as this is included at CA 23084 in a list of "typical examples of plant or machinery".

In short, there does not appear to be a definitive answer on this, even though it must come up all the time in practice. We should perhaps not be too surprised, though, as *Wetherspoons* and other cases have shown that the treatment of many common items of expenditure can often remain unclear. It may be possible to rely on the wording of CA 21200 (and to a more limited extent CA 23084) to justify a claim for external cabling costs, but there is certainly no cast iron guarantee that the claim would be accepted; it might in fact be relatively difficult to defend if it went to Tribunal and if we were relying on statutory wording rather than on HMRC guidance. For the ducts and tunnels, there is no statutory restriction, so it comes down to whether or not these qualify as plant on first principles. Although it is not clear cut, their inclusion at item 25 would seem to provide a reasonable justification for a claim.

Law: CAA 2001, s. 21, 23, 25
Guidance: CA 21200

C2   Cameras

A portable camera used for the purposes of a qualifying activity will be treated as plant on ordinary principles.

The position regarding fixed cameras is more complex, though the end result will normally still be that such cameras will qualify as plant or machinery.

A camera is unlikely to be a structure but may be incorporated in the building. Arguably, some security cameras are "of a kind normally incorporated in a building". In either case, they would initially be caught as part of the building, with no allowances due (s. 21(3)).

In most cases, however, the camera will be rescued from the restrictions of s. 21 by falling within one of the exemptions contained in list C at s. 23. Possible categories would include:

- item 1 (machinery);
- item 8 (computer, telecommunication and surveillance systems); and (possibly)
- item 11 (burglar alarm systems).

Once there is no statutory rule preventing a camera from qualifying as plant, it is probable that it will so qualify. Cameras were listed in the *Football League* letter (see **Appendix 2**) as one type of asset that "would normally qualify as plant or machinery".

It is also possible that a camera will qualify under the special rules applying for **Personal security**. However, these provisions apply only in specific and restricted circumstances.

Law: CAA 2001, s. 21, 23, 33
Guidance: CA 21230

C3   Canopies

The treatment of a canopy, in the sense of a protective covering that serves effectively as a roof, is not black and white. In *Fitch's Garage*, a canopy over the petrol filling station was held not to be plant or machinery as the only function it played was to offer protection from the weather. Nevertheless, the precedent value of that case is weak as Lord Lowrie observed in *Scottish & Newcastle Breweries* that the earlier case had been "capable of decision either way". A stronger comment was made by the Lord Chancellor in *Cole Bros*, who doubted that the *Fitch's Garage* case could now stand.

A canopy would, though, probably now be barred from allowances as a fixed structure. As such, it would be necessary to find a let-out option within s. 23 to allow it to qualify as plant or machinery. The choice of appropriate categories from list C will depend on the circumstances, but it is conceivable that a canopy might constitute machinery (item 1), display equipment (item 4), or advertising hoardings, or signs, displays and similar assets (item 15).

In some circumstances, a canopy might constitute external **Solar shading** and qualify (as special rate expenditure) accordingly. It will be a question of fact to determine whether the canopy is in place to shade the building or for some other purpose, such as to provide shelter from the elements more generally.

Taxation magazine of 6 January 2000 (on p. 295) included an "editorial note" indicating that a major supermarket had successfully persuaded the commissioners that a canopy should be treated as plant, but without fuller details it is not possible to attach much weight to the decision.

Law: CAA 2001, s. 22, 23

Cases: *Dixon v Fitch's Garage Ltd* (1975) 50 TC 509; *CIR v Scottish & Newcastle Breweries Ltd* [1982] BTC 187; *Cole Brothers Ltd v Phillips* [1982] BTC 208

C4   Capital gains tax

There can be confusion about the interaction between capital allowances and capital gains tax, especially in relation to property sales. The topic is covered in depth in *Capital Allowances*, also published by Claritax Books. In brief, however, the position is as follows.

The general principle is that claiming capital allowances does not increase a capital gain when property is sold at a profit. This is made clear at s. 41 of TCGA 1992, which provides that:

> "Section 39 shall not require the exclusion from the sums allowable as a deduction in the computation of the gain of any expenditure as being expenditure in respect of which a capital allowance or renewals allowance is made."

So if a company buys a property for £500,000 and sells it for £600,000, there is a capital gain of £100,000 (ignoring legal and other incidental costs). This is the case whether or not any capital allowances are claimed for fixtures in the property (and whether or not the value of those allowances is retained when the property is sold).

This general principle is amended in two circumstances:

- where property is sold at a loss; or
- where the asset is a wasting asset.

Where property is sold at a loss, the CGT loss is restricted, broadly by reference to capital allowances that have been given and retained on the property. In HMRC's words, the purpose of the restriction "is to prevent relief being given twice for the same expenditure, once under the capital allowances code and once under the capital gains code".

Law: TCGA 1992, s. 41
Guidance: CG 15401

C5 Car hoops

Car hoops – typically an inverted U-shaped piece of metal embedded in concrete – are often used as a protective barrier, especially by car dealerships. The hoops present several advantages over a traditional wall or fencing, in that they allow the cars to be seen from outside while offering an enhanced level of security.

On ordinary case law principles, it would seem entirely reasonable to view these as apparatus used to carry on the qualifying activity, rather than as simply a part of the premises or setting within which the business is carried on.

For allowances to be due, however, it will also be necessary to consider whether the hoops constitute **Structures**, as discussed under that heading. The legislation at s. 22 is silent on the definition of "structure", beyond saying that the term encompasses "a fixed structure of any kind". However, most dictionary definitions of "structure" refer to complexity, or to size or to something made up of a multiplicity of parts, and all such definitions would tend to suggest that a simple car hoop – effectively a single piece of metal that has been moulded into shape – would not be caught as a structure. If that is the case, there would seem to be proper grounds for claiming allowances for these car hoops.

See **Fencing** for a discussion of knee rail restraint fencing when used to prevent vehicle theft.

Law: CAA 2001, s. 22

C6 Car parks

"A park for vehicles or containers" is included in list B at s. 22 (alongside such related items as roads, railways, etc.). As such, a car park is excluded from the definition of plant and machinery and no allowances are due.

HMRC guidance confirms that plant and machinery allowances will not be given "on the provision, construction or acquisition" of such assets.

In *Anduff*, the following comment was made in the Court of Appeal:

> "It is impossible to say that the bays where the cars are parked whilst the vacuum cleaning is done have any function other than as premises. The fact that the site is purpose-designed as a whole cannot turn a site which functions as premises into plant".

HMRC have commented as follows:

> "One thing that you should remember when you are considering your case is that the fact that an asset is a means of generating profit does not necessarily mean that it is plant. The business premises are a means of generating profit but they are not plant. For example, the classrooms, car parks, playgrounds, playing fields of a school are part of the means of generating profit and are all part of the premises".

Although this is not a capital allowances issue as such, it is worth noting that HMRC have written as follows about the deductibility of costs relating to an existing car park (see **Appendix 3**):

> "HMRC accept that expenditure on, for example, redefining parking areas by repainting parking bays to provide wider, designated bays for disabled parking, is a revenue expense, which is allowable in full for tax purposes.

> Where the work is more substantial, for example, to include car park resurfacing, then as long as there is no improvement element, the expenditure is allowable as normal revenue expenditure on repairs."

Law: CAA 2001, s. 22 (list B, item 2)
Case: *Attwood v Anduff Car Wash Ltd* [1997] BTC 454
Guidance: CA 21260, 22020

C7   Car wash apparatus

Any car wash system will contain significant elements of plant and machinery, which will generally qualify for allowances at the standard rate.

Vehicle wash waste reclaim units are one of the technology classes specified in the water technology criteria list. It follows that such units potentially qualify for **Enhanced capital allowances** when all necessary conditions are met.

Where those criteria are not satisfied, ordinary principles must be applied. It would seem reasonable to assert that such waste reclaim units are plant and machinery on which allowances should be claimed in the general pool.

In *Anduff*, a claim was made to treat the entire car wash site as a single item of plant or machinery. The claim succeeded (but see below) in front of the commissioners, who held that the whole thing should be regarded "not as a building but as a structure akin to a machine which takes into its large maw motor cars at up to four at a time, washes them thoroughly, dries them and ejects them".

That view was overturned in the High Court, and was rejected even more clearly in the Court of Appeal. The fact that the site was purpose-designed as a whole could not turn a site that functioned as premises into plant. In the words of one of the judges:

> "I therefore conclude without hesitation that even if the wash hall were a single unit of plant, it is quite impossible to say that the entire site is a single unit of plant".

The judge in fact then turned his attention to the wash hall itself, and even here he completely disagreed with the way the commissioners had viewed the matter:

> "[Their] analysis of the wash hall seems to me very inadequate. It entirely leaves out of account the fact that the wash hall is a building also containing a lobby and WC, pump room, an inspection area and a store. The building as a whole is certainly not a machine or machine-like, although it houses machinery, and the colourful description of the building as akin to a machine with a maw appears to have led to obfuscation of, rather than casting light on, the question whether the building operated as premises or plant."

Law: CAA 2001, s. 45H; SI 2003/2076, art. 3(2)(l)

Case: *Attwood v Anduff Car Wash Ltd* [1997] BTC 454

Guidance: wtl.defra.gov.uk/product_search_landing.asp; R&C Brief 03/10 (see **Appendix 4**)

C8   Caravan sites

HMRC reached an agreement with the National Caravan Council back in the 1950s. HMRC guidance is that the agreement may still be used but that tax officers "should only apply the agreement if the taxpayer asks for it to be applied".

The effect of the agreement is explained by HMRC as follows:

"Under the agreement expenditure incurred on:

- water supplies (that is mains or other apparatus used to convey water to or around sites – and hot water systems),
- electricity supplies (that is heavy cables, distributive wiring and general electrical apparatus, and diesel generating apparatus),
- sanitary fittings, baths and wash basins,

qualifies for plant or machinery allowances.

Under the agreement no allowances are due for expenditure on:

- roads,
- proposed sites for individual caravans,
- buildings erected as sanitary blocks,
- sewage and drainage pipes installed as public health requirements.

... The taxpayer must accept the disallowances as well as the allowances for the agreement to be applied."

Since the introduction in 2008 of the rules for integral features, the agreement seems to have little continuing relevance. All of the items listed as qualifying would now do so on general principles anyway, in some cases as integral features. If a taxpayer were to ask HMRC to apply the agreement today, it is assumed that HMRC would insist that the cost of mains water and electricity supplies must be added to the special rate pool, attracting allowances at the lower rate only.

Law: CAA 2001, s. 23 (list C, item 19), s. 23(5)
Guidance: CA 22100

C9   Caravans

It is not easy to make sense of the capital allowances treatment of caravans. List C at s. 23 contains an entry (item 19) for "caravans provided mainly for holiday lettings". The implication is that a caravan is either a building or a structure, and that item 19 therefore prevents an exclusion from plant and machinery allowances. However, the question of whether a caravan is indeed a building or structure must be open to debate.

HMRC give the following guidance in relation to caravans:

"A caravan is plant if it does not occupy a fixed site and is regularly moved as part of normal trade usage, even if it is only moved from its summer site to winter quarters.

Accept that a caravan, which is provided mainly for holiday lettings on a holiday caravan site, is plant whether it is moved or not. Caravans occupying residential sites do not qualify for capital allowances. As far as a holiday caravan site is concerned, treat anything that is treated as a caravan for the purposes of:

(1)   the Caravan Sites and Control of Development Act 1960 (c. 62) (CSCDA), or

(2)   the Caravans Act (Northern Ireland) 1963 (c. 17 (N.I.)),

as a caravan. Those acts give caravan a wider meaning than its normal one. In them, caravan covers double units delivered in two sections and then joined together and wooden lodges provided these are moveable. But it does not cover structures that are not moveable, even if these are otherwise identical."

This extended definition of "caravan" now has statutory authority in s. 23(5).

HMRC guidance then instructs tax officers that they must:

"give plant or machinery allowances on a caravan provided by a farmer to house a farm employee even if it occupies a fixed site and is used solely for residential purposes. This treatment applies only to farmers. It does not apply to any other cases".

There is no obvious reason, and there are certainly no statutory grounds, why this special approach should apply only to farmers.

The *Telfer* case concerned an employee of the Caravan Club. HMRC's reasoning in the case left much to be desired, and the taxpayer won on two out of the three points being debated. Nevertheless, it was held on the facts that the caravans in question were not something by means of which the employment duties were carried out but were rather "structures which played no part in the carrying on of those duties". As such, they "were merely the place within which they were carried on" and no allowances were available.

As regards allowances for employees more generally, see **Employee expenses**.

Law: CAA 2001, s. 23 (list C, item 19), s. 23(5)
Case: *Telfer v HMRC* [2016] UKFTT 614 (TC)
Guidance: CA 22100

C10   Carpets

HMRC normally accept that carpets and linoleum are plant (CA 21200). The guidance includes the slightly odd reference to "furniture including carpets". Many might take the view that carpets are not naturally within the definition of "furniture" but carpets have always been treated as plant in practice. In *Anchor International*, a huge synthetic carpet used for playing five-a-side football was held to be plant.

HMRC do not accept, by contrast, that tiles that are stuck down should be treated as plant.

In the *Football League* letter (see **Appendix 2**), the list of items likely to qualify for capital allowances included "floor coverings that are not part of the building or structure; for example, carpets (but not tiles which are stuck down)". Given that the statutory justification for treating carpets as plant is already somewhat tenuous, it is difficult to determine with any confidence whether or not glued down carpet tiles should qualify.

See also **Floors and floor coverings** and **Turfing**.

Case: *Anchor International Ltd v IR Commrs* [2005] BTC 97
Guidance: CA 21200, 21230

C11   Cars

Cars clearly qualify for allowances, both as plant and as machinery, as long as the expenditure is capital in nature. (The question of whether the cost of cars was properly treated as capital or revenue in nature was considered in the *Waterloo Car Hire* case. The Tribunal concluded in that case that the cars were "fixed assets subject to capital allowance legislation and not items that could properly be included in 'cost of sales' ".)

Writing-down allowances

Most allowances for cars will be given by way of writing-down allowances. Expenditure on cars will now normally be allocated either to the main plant and machinery pool or to the "special rate" pool (which attracts writing-down allowances at a slower rate). The allocation is determined according to the level of CO_2 emissions: cars with emissions not exceeding 110g/km go to the main pool and cars with higher emission levels go to the special rate pool. Anti-avoidance measures seek to ensure that a business cannot generate artificial balancing allowances to circumvent these rules.

The figure of 110g/km applies for expenditure incurred since 1 or 6 April 2018. For the five years before that date, the equivalent figure was 130g/km, and it was 160g/km before 1 or 6 April 2013.

Cars with private use (by a business proprietor, but not by an employee driving a company car) are kept in a single asset pool. The rate of allowances is still determined by the emission levels, but a private use adjustment is then made to reflect the level of private use.

Case: *Waterloo Car Hire (a partnership) v HMRC* [2016] UKFTT 752 (TC)

Annual investment allowances

These are not given for cars.

First-year allowances

First-year allowances are generally not given for cars. However, full (100 per cent) allowances are given for expenditure incurred by 31 March 2021 on new (unused) cars with very low emissions.

A car qualifies as having very low emissions if it has a qualifying emissions certificate showing an official CO_2 emissions figure not exceeding a given level.

For expenditure incurred from 1 April 2018, the threshold is set at 50g/km.

For expenditure incurred from 1 April 2015, the threshold was 75g/km.

For expenditure incurred from 1 April 2013, the threshold was 95g/km.

For expenditure incurred up to 31 March 2013, this level was set at 110g/km.

It was announced at the time of the 2016 Budget that the case for continuing the first-year allowance for low emission cars will be reviewed at the time of the 2019 Budget, with a view to implementing any further changes from April 2021.

Leased cars can no longer attract these first-year allowances.

Overview of allowances

In summary, therefore, allowances are currently due as follows for the year of purchase, for expenditure incurred from 1 or 6 April 2018:

- emissions up to and including 50g/km: 100%
- emissions between 51 and 110g/km: 18%
- emissions exceeding 110g/km: 8%

Electrically-propelled cars must be driven entirely by electrical power, so the first-year allowances are not given for hybrid vehicles (unless their emissions do not exceed 50g/km).

Motor cycles, which were formerly classified as cars for capital allowances purposes, are no longer so treated. They will therefore now routinely go into the main pool, but subject to any private use by business proprietors.

Vans, lorries, tractors and other vehicles will all qualify as plant or machinery when used in a normal way for the purposes of a qualifying activity.

No capital allowances are given if a deduction is claimed at a fixed rate (45p per mile for the first 10,000 miles) by virtue of s. 94D of ITTOIA 2005.

Privately owned vehicles

No plant and machinery allowances may be given for privately owned cars that are used by employees for the business purposes of their employers. Employees may instead claim mileage allowances payments from their employer or mileage allowance relief from HMRC.

Unincorporated businesses and, now, unincorporated property businesses, may choose to claim mileage relief rather than capital allowances for cars.

Law: CAA 2001, s. 36, 38B, 38ZA, 45D, 46(2), 59, 104AA, 104F, 206, 268B; ITTOIA 2005, s. 94E; SI 2016/984, art. 4(b)
Guidance: CA 23500ff

Definition: overview

The definition of "car" for capital allowances purposes is a "mechanically propelled road vehicle" *other than*:

- a motor cycle;
- a vehicle of a construction primarily suited for the conveyance of goods or burden of any description; or
- a vehicle of a type not commonly used as a private vehicle and unsuitable for such use.

In practice (although the statutory wording is different) this is the same as the definition used for employee benefit (company car) purposes, but with one exception. The one exception is that an invalid carriage may be treated as a car for capital allowances purposes, but is not a car for employment tax purposes.

By default, therefore, a mechanically propelled vehicle that is designed to drive on the roads will be treated as a car, even if it would not be so treated under any normal definition. One example of this may be seen in relation to motor homes, which are treated as cars for these tax purposes.

Law: CAA 2001, s. 268A

Definition: conveyance of goods or burden

The second bullet above excludes from the definition of "car" a vehicle that is "of a construction primarily suited for the conveyance of goods or burden of any description". The legislation is therefore concerned with the way the vehicle has been made, rather than with the use to which it is put.

People are not "goods or burden" (*Bourne v Norwich Crematorium*) so a minibus or other vehicle that is constructed to carry people is not within this exemption, though the last bullet (considered below) may apply to take such a vehicle out of the definition of "car".

HMRC take the view that "the fact that the manufacturer or dealer describes the vehicle as a 'commercial vehicle' is not conclusive". Nevertheless, such a description is likely to be a relevant factor as the manufacturer knows more about the construction than anyone else.

HMRC interpret the word "primarily" in a literal way, arguing that "[if] neither purpose predominates with regard to the construction of the vehicle, the vehicle is not primarily suited for either purpose and this means that it does not escape from being a car".

HMRC also take the view that a vehicle with side windows behind the driver and front passenger doors will normally be treated as a car rather than as a goods vehicle. Similarly, the HMRC view is that the vehicle will usually be a car rather than a goods vehicle if it is fitted (or is capable of being fitted) with additional seating behind the driver's row of seats.

In most cases, a commonsense approach will determine the correct status of the vehicle.

This definition is considered in greater depth by HMRC in the *Employment Income Manual* at EIM 23110 and following sections. Detailed commentary is also contained in *Employee Benefits & Expenses*, available from Claritax Books.

Case: *Bourne (HMIT) v Norwich Crematorium Ltd* (1964) 44 TC 164

Definition: not commonly used as a private vehicle and unsuitable for such use

This is a two-part definition, and both sub-conditions must be met if the vehicle is to escape being classified as a car:

- the vehicle must be of a type not commonly used as a private vehicle; and
- it must be unsuitable for such use.

Certain vehicles are clearly of a type not commonly used as a private vehicle. Some emergency vehicles (for example ambulances or fire engines) and large buses are cases where this first condition is met. HMRC also accept that fire engines, agricultural tractors, buses, back-hoe loaders and diggers are all of a type not commonly used as a private vehicle.

HMRC accept, based on case law precedents, that modifying a vehicle may establish a different "type". Specifically, HMRC accept that a new type of vehicle may be created by the addition of fixed, flashing blue lights, of dual controls, or of a rooftop sign or loud speaker.

The question of whether a vehicle is unsuitable for private use will be one of fact. The courts have held that a dual control driving vehicle is unsuitable for private use, and also certain emergency vehicles "altered so that, without being reconverted, they cannot be used lawfully on a road by a member of the public".

Once more, this definition is considered in greater depth by HMRC in the *Employment Income Manual* at EIM 23110 and following sections. Detailed commentary is also contained in *Employee Benefits & Expenses*, available from Claritax Books. In brief, however, the following will normally be treated as cars: estate cars, off-road vehicles, multi-purpose vehicles, Land Rover Defender Station Wagons, motor homes. Double cab pick-up trucks are more borderline and will need to be considered closely on the individual facts.

Taxis

Particular issues arise in relation to taxis, considered separately under that main heading in this A-Z section.

Hearses, etc.

See **Hearses and funeral vehicles** for the treatment of these.

Cases: *Bourne (HMIT) v Norwich Crematorium Ltd* (1964) 44 TC 164; *Gurney (HMIT) v Richards* [1989] BTC 326; *Morris v R & C Commrs* [2006] BTC 861

C12   Cash dispenser machines

In the author's view, cash dispensers will clearly qualify as plant and machinery, attracting allowances at the standard rate. Although they may be incorporated in a building, they are undoubtedly machines and there is therefore no statutory bar on claiming allowances (s. 23, list C, item 1). As machines, furthermore, it is not necessary to consider all the case law issues concerning the meaning of plant as machines qualify in their own right.

Law: CAA 2001, s. 11(4), 23 (list C, item 1)

C13   Ceilings

The cost of a ceiling does not usually qualify for plant and machinery allowances. Ceilings are specifically included in list A in the category of "assets treated as buildings" on which no allowances can be claimed.

As such, a ceiling can only be claimed as plant if there is a statutory exception and if case law principles will allow it. The most likely statutory exceptions are at items 7 and 14 of list C, dealing respectively with trade-specific sound insulation and with decorative assets in the hotel and similar trades. Conceivably, a ceiling might fall within item 10 (fire alarm systems; sprinkler and other equipment for extinguishing or containing fires). However, none of these three exceptions can apply if the principal purpose of the asset in question is "to insulate or enclose the interior of a building or to provide an interior wall, floor or ceiling which (in each case) is intended to remain permanently in place".

Clearing out the double negatives, a particular asset is excluded from list C if it has, as its principal purpose, the provision of a permanent ceiling. It then follows that list A will operate to prevent any claim for plant and machinery allowances, irrespective of any case law precedents. If that principal purpose rule does not apply (for example, because it is not intended to remain permanently in place) then the asset may be saved from the effects of list A; in this case, it will be necessary to consider case law principles to determine whether or not it can qualify as an item of plant.

HMRC take the view that "suspended ceilings and acoustic tiles" are not plant. HMRC guidance also refers to the *Fortes Autogrill* case in which allowances were denied for a false ceiling in a restaurant. It is noteworthy, though, that very little attention was paid in that case to the "ambience" issue that can allow expenditure to qualify in certain trades (see **Decorative assets**).

The position in the *Wimpy* decision was, however, much less clearly in HMRC's favour. The judges felt that it was open to the commissioners to conclude that the false ceilings were not plant but they certainly did not indicate that they would necessarily have reached the same conclusion themselves. In relation to a further ceiling, the commissioners concluded that it did fall on the "plant" side of the line and that allowances were due. It was noted that "its primary function was the creation of atmosphere by reducing the height of the ceiling and giving visual interest". HMRC did not even appeal against that decision. In principle, therefore, it seems entirely reasonable to claim plant and machinery allowances on a false ceiling in a hotel or similar establishment. It is noteworthy that no reference is made to this case in the HMRC guidance at CA 22080.

Integral features

A ceiling may qualify for special rate allowances under the heading of integral features, if it forms part of a heating system. HMRC have given their view on this as follows:

> "The [integral features] rules also specifically clarify that the new definition does not extend to any asset whose principal purpose is to insulate or enclose the interior of a building, or to provide interior walls, floors or ceilings which are intended to remain permanently in place. ... So if, for example, a business installs a new, permanent false ceiling in its premises, in order to conceal new wiring and service pipes, expenditure on that ceiling would not qualify for PMAs.

> On the other hand, if a business installs in its premises a plenum floor or plenum ceiling, the principal purpose of

which is to function as an integral part of the heating or air conditioning system (for example, the plenum floor or plenum ceiling may form the fourth side of a duct or channel through which stale air is extracted and treated air is discharged), that expenditure would qualify for PMAs as part of an 'integral feature' of the building or structure."

Such a ceiling would be treated as part of the heating system and the cost would therefore go to the special rate pool.

If there is a mechanical ceiling, one that may perhaps be opened or shut electronically according to the weather conditions, it would be necessary to argue that the ceiling is not intended to remain permanently in place. If that argument is sustainable (even though, presumably, the ceiling would move only a few yards when opened up) then it would probably qualify as machinery.

Law: CAA 2001, s. 21 (list A, item 1), s. 23 (list C, items 7, 10, 14), s. 33A
Cases: *Hampton v Fortes Autogrill Ltd* (1979) 53 TC 690; *Wimpy International Ltd. v Warland* [1989] BTC 58
Guidance: CA 22080, 22320

C14   Central heating

Central heating systems are plant and machinery but must be classed as integral features, thus attracting writing-down allowances at the slower rate. This treatment covers, more specifically, "a space or water heating system, a powered system of ventilation, air cooling or air purification, and any floor or ceiling comprised in such a system".

No allowances are given, however, for "any asset whose principal purpose is to insulate or enclose the interior of a building or to provide an interior wall, floor or ceiling which (in each case) is intended to remain permanently in place". So a wall used as one of the four sides of a central heating pipe will not thereby qualify for plant and machinery allowances.

Enhanced capital allowances

First-year allowances are available for many types of **Energy-saving technology**, subject to the principles described in that section. See, in particular, the following headings for details:

- Air conditioning systems;
- Air to air energy recovery equipment;
- Boilers;
- Combined heat and power;
- Heating, ventilation and air conditioning equipment;
- Heat pumps;
- Pipework insulation.

Dwelling houses

Particular issues arise in a **Dwelling house**, where in principle no plant and machinery allowances are given for the following qualifying activities:

- an ordinary UK property business;
- an ordinary overseas property business; or
- special leasing of plant or machinery.

For these activities (but not, for example, for a trade), no allowances are due for expenditure on plant or machinery for use in a dwelling house. In relation to central heating systems, HMRC have commented that:

> "[a] central heating system serving the common parts of a building which contains two or more dwelling houses will not comprise part of either dwelling house. A central heating system serving an individual residential flat does not however qualify for PMA."

The guidance goes on to explain the practicalities of making a claim as follows:

> "Expenditure on a central heating system serving the whole of the building containing two or more dwelling houses should be apportioned between the common parts should be apportioned between the common parts, which part qualifies for PMA, and the residential flats or individual dwelling houses which do not."

Law: CAA 2001, s. 23(2), 33A(5)(c), 35
Guidance: CA 20020, 21200

C15   Charging points for electric vehicles

First-year allowances at 100% are given for expenditure incurred in the "relevant period" on electric vehicle charging points. The relevant period began on 23 November 2016 (the date on which the measure was originally announced) and is provisionally due to end on 31 March 2019 (corporation tax) or 5 April 2019 (income tax). The end date is, however, subject to possible extension.

The charging points must be "installed solely for the purpose of charging electric vehicles". For these purposes, an electric vehicle is defined as "a road vehicle that can be propelled by electrical power (whether or not it can also be propelled by another kind of power)". An electric vehicle charging point is defined to mean a facility for charging an electric vehicle.

The plant or machinery in question must be "unused and not second-hand".

First-year allowances under this heading are subject to the usual "general exclusions" – see **F11**.

Law: CAA 2001, s. 45EA

C16   Charities

If a charitable body is not liable to pay income tax or corporation tax, it will not be able to claim capital allowances. That does not mean, however, that allowances can be ignored completely.

A charity selling a property will not be able to sign a fixtures election under s. 198 as it will not have to bring a disposal value into account and therefore does not meet the conditions of s. 198(1). It will also not meet the conditions of s. 187A, so is not subject to the pooling and fixed value requirements. As such, a person buying a property from a charity can in principle claim allowances, without having to worry about those requirements. However, if the charity bought the property from a third party in or after April 2012 then the third party may be a past owner for the purposes of applying the s. 187A legislation.

A charity buying a property should normally sign a fixtures election so as to protect the value of the fixtures for a future owner, thereby helping to maximise the value of the property when it eventually comes to be sold.

Charities cannot claim first-year tax credits (see **F12** below).

Law: CAA 2001, s. 187A, 198; Sch. A1, para. 1

C17   Checkouts

Checkouts are included in list C at CAA 2001, s. 23. As such, they may qualify as plant even though affixed to a building. There is no further guidance but it seems likely that a checkout in a shop or similar premises will qualify on normal principles.

Law: CAA 2001, s. 23 (list C, item 4)

C18   Chicken cages

According to HMRC, "the fixed chicken cages inside a poultry house should not be accepted as plant".

It seems to the author that the point is not as clear cut as this HMRC guidance would suggest. If the cages are "incorporated in the building" then they do seem to be caught by s. 21(3). However, that section goes on to recognise that an item may not be incorporated in a building because it is moveable or for some other reason. It probably depends what is meant by "fixed" but it seems possible that there might be some cages that are fixed in place but still easily removable and that could not properly be said to be incorporated in the building. In such cases, a claim that the cages constitute plant or machinery does not seem out of the question.

HMRC would not accept that the exemption afforded to **Zoo cages** should be extended to fixed chicken cages. It is difficult to argue with that view.

See also **Poultry houses.**

Law: CAA 2001, s. 21(1)
Guidance: CA 22110

C19   Cladding

The topic of cladding around buildings was thrown into the spotlight by the tragic events of the Grenfell Tower fire in 2017. It is likely that huge amounts of expenditure will be incurred in the coming years on replacing (or removing) cladding in blocks of flats and other residential and commercial properties.

From the tax point of view, numerous technical issues arise.

The first question will be to determine whether the cost of the cladding will properly be treated as revenue in nature, or whether it needs to be capitalised. That distinction – which moves beyond the scope of this book, but see briefly **2.2** above – will be made on normal principles, taking account of case law distinctions, accounting principles and HMRC guidance.

If the cost has to be capitalised, the next question is therefore whether allowances can be claimed. Answering this will depend on the full circumstances of each case. It may be appropriate to consider the materials from which the cladding is made, and it will certainly be necessary to understand the purpose it is intended to serve and the nature of the affixation to the property.

Cladding can be made of metal, wood, vinyl, brick or of a range of composite materials. Its primary purpose may be to protect against rain penetration, to insulate the building or to control noise, or there may be any combination of these and other purposes.

It would seem clear that the cost of cladding would initially be denied by s. 21. If a capital allowances claim is to succeed, it will therefore be necessary to consider the basis on which that statutory hurdle can be overcome.

The taxpayer will need to determine whether a claim may be possible under s. 28, which deals with the thermal insulation of existing buildings. See **Thermal insulation** for a discussion of the issues arising, including the question of where expenditure is incurred with dual reasons in mind.

For residential properties, it will be necessary to consider whether the restrictions under s. 35 for **Dwelling-houses** apply.

Internal cladding

Cladding may also be added internally to a property, often for reasons concerned with hygiene. Internal panels may be impregnated with anti-bacterial materials for use in GP surgeries, hospital wards or childcare centres.

It is not easy to see that these would qualify for relief, as they would appear to be caught by s. 21 initially, as being attached to the building. As such, a statutory let-out within s. 23 is needed if a claim is to be justified. It is understood that the cost of these items is in practice often claimed, possibly by categorising the items in question as "sanitary ware" to fall within item 5. This may be pushing the definition beyond what would commonly be understood by the term, though its etymological origin (with its connotations of hygiene enhancement) would arguably not rule out such an interpretation.

Law: CAA 2001, s. 28, 35
Guidance: CA 22220

C20   Cleaning in place equipment

"Cleaning in place equipment" is one of the technology classes specified in the water technology criteria list. As such, the equipment may qualify for first-year allowances as **Environmentally beneficial technology** when all necessary conditions are met, as explained in that section.

According to the official website:

> "Cleaning in place (CIP) saves water by delivering it more efficiently or in a more controlled way. This equipment is primarily used in businesses that regularly clean vessels, pipe-work and fittings. The process is particularly beneficial to companies with high standards of hygiene such as those in food and drinks or chemical industry. A good cleaning-in-place system operates efficiently and will provide substantial savings on water, chemicals, energy and labour time."

Two types of equipment may qualify under this heading. In each case, the specific item must be included on the water technology product list.

The first category is for monitoring and control equipment, which may consist of just software or of a combination of software and hardware.

The second category is for spray devices, defined to mean "a rotating unit (single or twin axis) producing a specific uniform and repeatable spray pattern with a defined coverage area".

Law: CAA 2001, s. 45H; SI 2003/2076, art. 3(2)(h)
Guidance: wtl.defra.gov.uk/product_search_landing.asp

C21   Clocks

Clocks used for the purposes of a qualifying activity will qualify for plant and machinery allowances at the standard rate.

Even if they are incorporated into a building, clocks should be outside the restrictions of s. 21 on the basis that they are machinery. In a capital gains tax context, HMRC accept that "antique clocks and watches, such as 'Tompion' clocks, are regarded as machinery". There is no statutory distinction, relevant for this category of expenditure, between the meaning of machinery for CGT and capital allowances purposes. Nor is there any obvious reason to distinguish between antique and more modern clocks (unless it is argued that modern clocks have fewer and much smaller moving parts).

In *Cole Bros*, the cost of wiring to clocks was accepted by the Revenue as expenditure on plant and machinery. The logic must be that the clocks themselves were accepted as plant or machinery.

Law: CAA 2001, s. 21, 23 (list C, item 1)
Case: *Cole Brothers Ltd v Phillips* [1982] BTC 208
Guidance: CG 76904

C22   Clothing

In most cases, it will not be possible to claim allowances for clothing costs. If costs are incurred by employees directly, relief will be due only if the clothing is "necessarily provided" for use in the performance of the employment duties.

The definition of "necessarily provided" is notoriously tight and was tested in the *Williams* case, where a television newsreader was denied plant and machinery allowances for clothing she wore when presenting. The Tribunal held that the clothing in question presented "no special feature either in construction, purpose or position". Principles from the earlier *Hillyer v Leeke* case were applied. Broadly, the requirement to use the item in question must be imposed by the nature of the employee's duties, and not by the personal circumstances of the employee.

HMRC guidance in relation to this "necessarily" condition is covered more fully under **Employee expenses**.

If allowances are due, an adjustment will be required (on a "just and reasonable basis") if the item in question is used partly for private purposes. The "wholly and exclusively" principle that applies to general employee expenses does not apply for capital allowances.

HMRC do appear to accept that protective clothing may qualify for plant and machinery allowances:

> "In general, fixtures and fittings are plant if they are of a permanent and durable nature, that is if they satisfy the 2-year test ... and they were bought for the purposes of the trade. Treat furniture including carpets, curtains and linoleum and items like cutlery, crockery, glassware, linen, kitchen utensils and protective clothing in the same way."

Law: CAA 2001, s. 36(1), 205ff.

Cases: *Hillyer v Leeke* (1976) 51 TC 90; *Williams v HMRC* [2010] UKFTT 86 (TC)

Guidance: CA 21200; EIM 36560

C23   Cold rooms and cold stores

A clear factual analysis will be required in order to determine whether plant and machinery allowances can be claimed on a cold room or cold store.

It is likely that these items will initially be caught as buildings or parts of buildings. However, the statutory bar on allowances is overruled by item 4 of list C (which includes "storage equipment (including cold rooms)") and item 18 (which refers simply to "cold stores"). Normal principles and case law precedents must therefore be applied.

Plant and machinery allowances will be available, subject to an important distinction made by HMRC as follows:

> "A refrigerated building, which is used as a cold store, may be incapable of an independent existence as a building. That is, it may consist of a refrigeration unit plus a framework and the

framework may be incapable of a separate existence as a building. In that case the whole is effectively a large fridge that qualifies as plant."

But:

"where the building houses an insulated 'box', which provides the insulation, and the building, is capable of an independent existence, it is only the insulated box within the building or structure that qualifies as plant or machinery".

Law: CAA 2001, s. 23 (list C, items 4 and 18)
Guidance: CA 22120

C24   Combined heat and power

Where power is generated, heat may be given off in the process and the heat will typically be wasted. Combined heat and power systems generate heat and power (normally electricity) in a single process, thus cutting down on the waste.

Such equipment will qualify for plant and machinery allowances in all normal circumstances. In some cases, it will attract 100 per cent first-year allowances under the scheme for **Enhanced capital allowances** (ECAs). However, CHP systems are subject to their own special rules if they are to attract these enhanced allowances.

According to the official ECAs guidance:

"Most large conventional power stations generate electricity at 30-50% efficiency (before transmission and distribution losses) and throw away most of the heat generated in the process.

CHP generates electricity and uses the otherwise wasted heat in other industrial applications or community heating. The schemes are typically much smaller than conventional power stations and can be built to whatever size meets the customer's demands.

Using these schemes can help achieve efficiency levels between 60-80%, saving money and reducing carbon emissions."

A certificate must be held before ECAs are claimed under this heading. As this certificate is required, individual products are not included on the energy technology product list. According to other official guidelines (CHPQA ECA Note (v2) – January 2017), "expenditure incurred on a CHP scheme before a certificate has been issued can qualify for the ECA, but the claim cannot be made until certification is given".

Combined heat and power systems also attract a more favourable treatment under the climate change levy rules.

Law: SI 2018/268, art. 4

Guidance: https://www.gov.uk/energy-technology-list; www.chpqa.com; www.gov.uk/government/uploads/system/uploads/attachment_data/file/583663/CHPQA_ECA_Note.pdf; HMRC Reference Notice CCL1/2 (June 2014)

C25   Commercial property standard enquiries

When property is being bought and sold the buyer's solicitors will normally ask the other side to complete these enquiries (CPSEs). The enquiries cover much more than just capital allowances but the final section (section 32) of the form (as updated in February 2014) deals with capital allowances for plant and machinery.

The CPSEs certainly act as an aid to eliciting the correct information, but should not be viewed as a checklist of all the questions it is necessary to ask the vendor at the time of sale. More often than not, it will be necessary to ask additional questions at the outset, or follow-up questions once the replies to the CPSEs have been received.

The wording of the CPSEs is in some respects poor and cannot be relied upon to produce safe answers on which the purchaser can rely. The problems are considered in depth in the accompanying volume to this book, *Capital Allowances* – written by the same authors and also available from Claritax Books.

C26   Compressed air equipment

Such equipment will qualify for plant and machinery allowances in all normal circumstances. In some cases, the equipment will attract

100 per cent first-year allowances under the scheme for **Enhanced capital allowances** (ECAs).

According to the official ECA guidance:

> "Compressed air systems are found on many industrial premises and can often be used as an alternative to a direct electricity supply.
>
> Compressed air is often referred to as the fourth utility after electricity, gas and water. Unlike the other three, it's generated onsite. So users have much more control over costs and the amount they use. Compressed air represents one of the best opportunities for immediate energy savings on any site, and often requires only a modest level of investment."

Three categories of equipment are specified for the purposes of claiming ECAs. In each case, investments in these devices will only attract ECAs if the specific product is named on the energy technology product list at the time of purchase, having satisfied the eligibility criteria. Items are added to, and removed from, the list on a monthly basis.

Desiccant air dryers with energy saving controls

These were added to the official list in 2014. The official ECAs guidance explains that:

> "Desiccant air dryers are products that are specifically designed to extract water vapour from industrial compressed air systems by absorbing moisture using a desiccant material which is then, for example, regenerated by blowing air through the dryer."

Flow controllers

According to the official ECAs guidance:

> "Flow pressure controllers are products that are specifically designed to reduce the pressure fluctuations that normally occur in compressed air distribution systems when machines turn on and off or air demand is variable. They consist of a control unit that monitors the pressure and adjusts the airflow into the compressed air distribution system until it

117

matches compressed air demand, thereby maintaining pressure at a preset level."

Master controllers

According to the official ECAs guidance:

"Master controllers are products that are specifically designed to improve the control of compressed air systems with two or more compressors. They are microprocessor-based systems that provide facilities to co-ordinate the operation of multiple compressors, schedule changes in compressor operation, to operate at lower pressures at off-peak times and to remotely monitor/optimise compressor operations, thereby realising energy savings."

Refrigerated air dryers with energy saving controls

The official ECAs guidance explains that:

"These controls adjust the flow of the refrigerant gas before it enters the compressor. This means the dryer can be controlled according to the heat load."

Law: SI 2018/268, art. 3(2)(d)
Guidance: https://www.gov.uk/energy-technology-list

C27   Computer software

HMRC instructions to tax officers are that they should "treat computer software as plant whether or not it would normally be treated as plant". This is based squarely on the statutory provisions of s. 71.

The guidance goes on to state that officers "should also treat the right to use or otherwise deal with computer software and the software to which the right relates as plant". Again, this is based clearly on the statutory provisions.

HMRC guidance also makes it clear that expenditure incurred on acquiring software outright qualifies for allowances even though there may be no physical asset.

Elsewhere, HMRC have confirmed that abortive capital expenditure on computer software still qualifies for plant and machinery allowances.

The question of whether the expenditure on computer software is revenue or capital in the first place is beyond the scope of this work but is considered in depth in the *Business Income Manual.*

Special rules apply to determine the disposal value if a capital or equivalent sum is received by granting to a third party a right to use or otherwise deal with the whole or part of the software.

Law: CAA 2001, s. 71-73
Guidance: BIM 35800ff, CA 22280

C28   Computers

Computers, and any associated wiring, will clearly qualify as plant and machinery. This will be on first principles and item 8 at list C ensures that "computer, telecommunication and surveillance systems (including their wiring or other links)" will not be denied allowances on the grounds that they have in any sense become part of a building. In *Munby v Furlong*, the commissioners accepted by implication that computers were plant. HMRC in fact take the view that "computers and similar electronic devices" are machinery.

Computers should normally be the subject of a short-life asset election unless the full cost is covered by the annual investment allowance for the year of purchase. Few computers will be kept in the business for eight or more years, and most will depreciate fast, so the use of the election will generally accelerate the tax relief.

HMRC do not normally accept that an employee can claim tax relief for the cost of a computer used for work purposes, but there are exceptions. The point is considered in some detail in the *Employment Income Manual.*

See also Computer software and, in particular, Employee expenses.

Law: CAA 2001, s. 23 (list C, item 8)
Case: *Munby v Furlong* (1977) 50 TC 491
Guidance: CA 21010, 23130; EIM 36730

C29   Consumables

Consumable items that are used up in the ordinary course of the trade – e.g. stationery in an office, plastic bags in a retail shop – will be treated as an ordinary revenue expense; tax relief will in principle be due as long as the cost of the items in question is incurred wholly and exclusively for the purposes of the trade. They lack the durability (broadly, two years) that is needed to be classed as plant.

Guidance: CA 21100

C30   Containers

Many businesses need to hold containers for their produce, which may then be re-used. Examples would include beer kegs or milk crates.

If these items have a shelf life of under two years, the cost will normally be written off as a revenue expense in the accounts. If they do satisfy the two year test, and are used for business purposes, they will be treated as items of plant for which capital allowances may be claimed.

In the past, tax relief may have been given for such items using the so-called renewals basis; in such cases, no capital allowances claim will have been possible. It was announced at the time of the 2016 Budget that the use of the renewals basis was to be discontinued and that:

> "Tax relief for expenditure incurred on replacement of tools will be obtained under the same rules as those which apply to other capital equipment. Businesses can claim tax relief under the normal capital allowance regime ... ."

Those changes were duly implemented.

Guidance: BIM 46903; CA 29220;
www.gov.uk/government/publications/budget-2016-documents/budget-2016

C31   Contributions

A person who makes a contribution to another person's capital expenditure may be entitled to claim plant and machinery allowances where specified conditions are met.

The detailed rules are beyond the scope of this book but, broadly, the contributor can claim allowances if the recipient would otherwise have been able to claim plant and machinery allowances. The contribution must have been made for the purposes of the contributor's trade or other qualifying activity. The two parties must not be connected persons.

HMRC give the following simple example of how these rules can operate:

> "Johnny runs a restaurant. June has a market garden where she grows herbs that Johnny uses in the restaurant. June buys new equipment for the market garden and Johnny makes a contribution towards her costs. Johnny's contribution is deducted from June's expenditure qualifying for PMA ... and Johnny can claim PMA on the contribution.
>
> But if Johnny and June are married Johnny cannot claim capital allowances on his contribution because they are connected persons. However June can then claim capital allowances on all of her expenditure – the contribution is within the exception for contributions by someone other than a public body who cannot get relief for it."

See *Capital Allowances* 2018-19 for commentary on these contribution allowances, including detailed coverage of the position of both contributor and recipient. *Capital Allowances* is written by the same authors as this volume and is also published by Claritax Books.

Law: CAA 2001, s. 537, 538
Guidance: CA 14400

C32   Cookers and ovens

Cookers are included in list C at CAA 2001, s. 23. As such, they may qualify as plant even though built in or otherwise affixed to a building.

In practice, it is difficult to envisage any circumstances in which allowances could be denied for ovens used as such for the purposes of a qualifying activity. Such expenditure will normally go into the main pool, though it will be allocated to the special rate pool if it forms part of a space or water heating system.

Law: CAA 2001, s. 23 (list C, item 5), s. 33A(5)(c)

C33   Cooling equipment

Cooling equipment is included several times in list C at CAA 2001, s. 23, as "machinery", as "refrigerators and similar equipment" and as "refrigeration or cooling equipment". Such equipment will clearly fall within the definition of plant and machinery if used to provide refrigeration for a qualifying activity.

Refrigerators and refrigeration equipment will qualify as general plant or machinery. The expenditure must be allocated to the special rate pool if the asset forms part of "a powered system of ventilation, air cooling or air purification". Some such equipment may qualify for **Enhanced capital allowances**.

Law: CAA 2001, s. 23 (list C, items 1, 5 ,9), s. 33A(5)(c)

C34   Cornices

A cornice is a horizontal decorative moulding, typically above a door or window. In the *Wetherspoon* case, it was argued that cornices should qualify as plant or machinery, on the grounds that they were removable and therefore not part of the premises. This argument was clearly rejected by the Upper Tier Tribunal, as follows:

> "Having been shown photographs of each of the items in issue, we consider it fanciful to suppose that any of them could be regarded as having retained their separate identities; separate that is from the ceilings, walls and balustrades of which they each form part. Since those ceilings, walls and balustrades are all clearly part of the premises, so are the cornices, architraves and balustrade end-fittings. We cannot, in short, imagine how any legal analysis of the nature of plant, as opposed to premises, could lead to a conclusion that those items were plant."

Case: *J D Wetherspoon v HMRC* [2012] UKUT 42 (TCC)

C35   Counters

Counters are included in list C at CAA 2001, s. 23. As such, they may qualify as plant even though affixed to a building. In practice, it seems likely that they will do so as long as they are provided for the particular purposes of the qualifying activity.

Law: CAA 2001, s. 23 (list C, item 4)

C36   Crush barriers

HMRC comment that "crush barriers [e.g. at a football stadium] securely fixed to the ground are not plant or machinery but they may come within the 1975 safety legislation and so qualify under CAA 2001, s. 32".

Section 32 no longer applies, however, as the special legislation regarding safety at sports grounds was repealed with effect from April 2013. See **Sports grounds (safety)** for further details.

Formerly, HMRC guidance in relation to the special relief read as follows:

> "PMAs are available if a person carrying on a qualifying activity takes required safety precautions for a sports ground used for the qualifying activity which is of the kind described in Section 1(1) Safety of Sports Ground Act 1975 but which does not have a designation order."

The legislation applied where the relevant local authority, for the area in which the ground is situated, has certified that certain steps must be taken under specified legislation.

The HMRC view would therefore currently be that no allowances are due for the cost of such barriers. The point is not clear cut, however, so may need to be tested before a definitive view can be given.

Law: *Safety of Sports Grounds Act* 1975, s. 1(1); CAA 2001, s. 32
Guidance: CA 21230, 22240

C37   Curtains

Curtains used for the purposes of a qualifying activity will almost certainly qualify as plant. They were accepted as such in the *Scottish and Newcastle* case, where they also played "an important and intended decorative function in creating the desired atmosphere or setting".

HMRC guidance specifically states that curtains should be treated as plant if they are of a permanent and durable nature and satisfy the two year test. (If they do not satisfy that test, they will almost certainly qualify as revenue expenditure.)

Curtain rails and associated fittings were accepted as plant in *Cadogan Gardens*.

The *John Good* case provided authority for treating stage curtains in a theatre as plant.

The restrictions for plant in a dwelling house should be remembered in appropriate circumstances.

Law: CAA 2001, s. 35

Cases: *Jarrold v John Good & Sons Ltd* (1963) 40 TC 681; *Lupton v Cadogan Gardens Developments Limited* (1971) 47 TC 1; *CIR v Scottish & Newcastle Breweries Ltd* [1982] BTC 187

Guidance: CA 21200

C38   Cushion gas

The term "cushion gas" is used to describe gas "that functions or is intended to function as plant in a particular gas storage facility".

The cost of such gas is treated as **Special rate expenditure**.

Law: CAA 2001, s. 70J(7), 104A
Guidance: www.hmrc.gov.uk/capital-allowances/plant.htm

C39   Customer lists

HMRC will not give plant and machinery allowances for the cost of acquiring a customer list:

> "A customer list is commercial know-how rather than plant or machinery. Where a person buys a customer list what is being acquired is not just a list of customers like a directory but rather the connections with the customers. That is part of the goodwill of the business."

The fact that the list is written down or is on a computer drive of some sort does not affect the matter; the payment is being made for the list, not for the physical means of providing the list.

Know-how allowances are given for certain categories of expenditure. Once more, however, no relief is due for customer lists. As HMRC put it:

> "Things like market research, customer lists and sales techniques are commercial know-how. They do not assist directly in manufacturing or processing operations. Rather, they are concerned with selling goods or materials once they have been manufactured. They are not industrial information or techniques likely to assist in the manufacture of goods or materials or in the working of a mine or in agricultural operations. This means that commercial; know-how is not within the definition of know-how in CAA and so it does not qualify for capital allowances."

Law: CAA 2001, s. 452
Guidance: CA 21210, 70030

C40   Cuttings

Cuttings are included in list B at s. 22 (alongside such related items as embankments, tunnels and bridges). As such, they are excluded from the definition of plant and machinery and no allowances are due.

HMRC guidance confirms that plant and machinery allowances will not be given "on the provision, construction or acquisition" of such assets.

Law: CAA 2001, s. 22 (list B, item 1)
Guidance: CA 22020

D1   Dams, reservoirs, barrages

A "dam, reservoir or barrage" is included in list B at s. 22. The denial of allowances is expanded to cover "any sluices, gates, generators and other equipment associated with the dam, reservoir or barrage". As such, the starting point is that such items are all excluded from the definition of plant and machinery and no allowances are due. HMRC guidance confirms that plant and machinery allowances will not be given "on the provision, construction or acquisition" of such assets. In the *Barclay, Curle* case, concerning a dry dock, a dam was described in passing as "a storehouse for water" rather than as plant.

The actual position is more complex, however. First, the exclusion is disapplied in the case of "any reservoir incorporated into a water treatment works" or "any service reservoir of treated water for supply within any housing estate or other particular locality".

More generally, any machinery qualifies for plant and machinery allowances in its own right and it is difficult to contemplate circumstances in which a generator would not qualify as machinery. Also falling outside the exclusion, in the context of a power generating business, would be "the provision of pipelines or underground ducts or tunnels with a primary purpose of carrying utility conduits".

Law: CAA 2001, s. 22 (list B, item 4), s. 23 (list C, items 1, 25, 27)
Case: *CIR v Barclay, Curle and Co Ltd* (1969) 45 TC 221
Guidance: CA 22020

D2   Decorative assets

To determine the correct tax treatment of decorative assets, it is first necessary to consider whether or not the assets have been incorporated in the property. Different consequences follow accordingly.

If they have been so incorporated, they will initially be caught by s. 21 as forming part of the building. Plant and machinery allowances will then be due only if there is a statutory protection from the effects of s. 21. There are various categories in list C that could offer such protection, including display equipment (item 4) and furniture and fittings (item 5). In either of these cases, allowances will almost certainly be due.

The more specific reference, however, is to "decorative assets provided for the enjoyment of the public in hotel, restaurant or similar trades" (item 14). Based on this exemption, and on the case law precedents, HMRC accept that:

> "if the taxpayer's trade involves the creation of an attractive setting or atmosphere and the sale of that setting or

126

atmosphere to their customers, pictures and removable wall decorations specially chosen to help create that setting or atmosphere will be plant".

This is based on the *Scottish and Newcastle* decision where, for example, Lord Lowry made the following observation:

> "It is fallacious to say that articles used to adorn the setting thereby ceased to be apparatus used by the taxpayers for carrying on their business. It is, in my view, equally fallacious to deny that the creation of atmosphere is, for the purposes of his trade, an important function of the successful hotelier."

But what of decorative assets in other contexts than a hotel or similar establishment? It is certainly the case – for any item of plant – that the function must be viewed in the context of the trade. (A ship, for example, will almost invariably qualify as plant but did not do so in a case where it was simply used as the premises within which the trade was carried on.)

HMRC take the view that decorative assets "are likely to be caught by CAA 2001, s. 21 – s. 22 and not to be plant, except where they fall within item 14 of list C". This assumption is used to justify the notion that allowances for decorative assets are only to be given for hotels and similar establishments.

This seems to the author to be a fallacious starting point. For what of decorative assets that are not incorporated in the property and are not therefore caught by s. 21? In this case, the exemptions in s. 23 are not needed, and it is necessary to turn to case law principles alone. In the *Scottish and Newcastle* case, Lord Lowry commented that "the articles now in dispute were apparatus … and the apparatus was … plant used by the Respondents in their business".

That description leads directly to the original, and very wide, case law definition of plant as "whatever apparatus is used by a businessman for carrying on his business – … all goods and chattels, fixed or movable, live or dead, which he keeps for permanent employment in the business".

Where an asset is not caught as a building or structure by s. 21 or s. 22, the HMRC argument for denying treatment as plant seems fatally flawed. The answer may be that HMRC are reaching the right conclusion but for the wrong reasons, for the distinction between plant and setting existed long before the statutory restrictions now found in sections 21 and 22. One of the leading cases on that distinction was that of *J. Lyons & Co*, which considered the treatment of certain lamps and fitments. As Uthwatt J noted in that case:

> "the presence of lamps in this building is not dictated by the nature of the particular trade there carried on or by the fact that it is for trade purposes that the building is used. Lamps are required to enable the building to be used where natural light is insufficient."

But too much weight can be given to the distinction between apparatus and setting. As Pennycuick J observed in *John Good*, "it seems to me that the setting in which a business is carried on, and the apparatus used for carrying on a business, are not always necessarily mutually exclusive". This view was approved by Donovan L J in the Revenue appeal, who said that "you cannot always answer the question, 'Is this plant?' by asking, 'Is it part of the setting or not?' "

See **Pictures** for further development of this argument.

Law: CAA 2001, s. 21, 23 (list C, items 4, 5, 14)

Cases: *J. Lyons & Co. Ltd. v. Attorney-General* [1944] Ch. 281; *Jarrold v John Good & Sons Ltd* (1963) 40 TC 681; *CIR v Scottish & Newcastle Breweries Ltd* [1982] BTC 187

Guidance: CA 21130, 21200

D3   Demolition costs

There are specific rules to give tax relief for the costs of demolishing plant and machinery. The tax treatment depends mainly on whether or not the demolished assets are to be replaced.

The particular rules apply where the plant (or machinery) is demolished and where the last use of the demolished asset or assets was for the purposes of a qualifying activity.

If the demolished plant is replaced with other plant then the net cost of demolition is treated as expenditure incurred on the provision of the new plant. If there is no such replacement, the net demolition cost is treated as additional expenditure, allocated to the appropriate capital allowances pool. So if the assets in question are integral features, the net demolition costs are allocated to the special rate pool. In most other cases, they are added to the main pool. This takes place in the chargeable period in which the demolition takes place.

The net costs of demolition are the costs that remain after deducting any scrap or sale value for the old plant or machinery.

Special rules apply to ring fence trades (mining and oil industries).

Law: CAA 2001, s. 26, 163
Guidance: CA 22210

D4   Designated assisted areas

Certain enterprise zone expenditure qualifies for first-year allowances under this heading if incurred by companies in the eight-year period beginning with the date on which the area in question was designated. The usual "general exclusions" apply.

The enhanced allowances are not available for all enterprise zones, only for a limited number of designated assisted areas within certain specified zones (see, for example, SI 2016/751 and SI 2018/485).

The expenditure must be incurred on the provision of plant or machinery for use primarily in an area which (at the time the expenditure is incurred) is a "relevant area" (as defined, but broadly a designated assisted area).

The expenditure must be incurred by a company that is within the charge to corporation tax for the purposes of a qualifying activity.

Various other conditions apply and these are considered in greater depth in *Capital Allowances* 2018-19, written by the same authors as this volume and also published by Claritax Books.

D5   Designs and patterns

The question of whether these qualify as plant is not entirely straightforward. In *Arthur Sanderson*, a wallpaper and fabric manufacturer used certain blocks, rollers and screens in order to print the designs. These blocks etc. were held to be plant.

In that same case, however, the designs themselves were held not to be plant. This was clearly based on the reasoning of Rowlatt J in

Daphne v Shaw. Although Rowlatt was a pre-eminent tax judge in his time, his decision in that case was later held (in *Munby v Furlong*) to have been incorrect. As such, there is no satisfactory reason for HMRC to reject a claim to treat designs and patterns as plant, assuming that they are used for the purposes of a qualifying activity and that they have the requisite two-year lifespan.

Former Revenue guidance (in the old capital allowances manual at paragraph 1569) used to state quite clearly that allowances should be given for "the cost of buying designs and patterns incorporated in machinery or tools which qualify for capital allowances as plant". There does not appear to be any reason why that principle should have changed.

Cases: *McVeigh v Arthur Sanderson & Sons Limited* (1969) 45 TC 273; *Munby v Furlong* (1977) 50 TC 491

D6   Dikes, sea walls, weirs, drainage ditches

All of these items are included in list B at s. 22. As such, these items are all excluded from the definition of plant and machinery and no allowances are due.

HMRC guidance confirms that plant and machinery allowances will not be given "on the provision, construction or acquisition" of such assets.

Law: CAA 2001, s. 22 (list B, item 6)
Guidance: CA 22020

D7   Disability Discrimination Act

There are certain statutory obligations on those who provide services to the public regarding ease of access to the premises. In broad terms, providers of such services are obliged to make reasonable adjustments to their premises to remove obstacles that would prevent disabled people from using their services.

The costs of making these changes will sometimes be revenue expenditure, on which tax relief can simply be claimed in the year. Other costs will need to be capitalised and the issue then arises of whether or not the expenditure will qualify for capital allowances.

The relevant part of the former HMRC guidance is reproduced at **Appendix 3**. Where appropriate, the guidance has also been incorporated into the relevant sections of this A to Z commentary.

D8   Dishwashers

Dishwashers are included in list C at CAA 2001, s. 23, both specifically and as falling within the general category of machinery. They clearly fall within the definition of plant and machinery if used in a normal way, for the purposes of a qualifying activity.

Law: CAA 2001, s. 23 (list C, item 5)

D9   Displays and similar equipment

Display equipment is included in list C at CAA 2001, s. 23. Item 4 refers to "display equipment" and item 15 includes a reference to "signs, displays and similar assets". As such, display equipment may qualify as plant even though affixed to a building.

In practice, there should be no problem claiming plant and machinery allowances for such items.

Although capital allowances are not given for shop fronts as such, HMRC instruct their tax officers to "treat showcases associated with a shop front that are distinct from the structure as fixtures and fittings".

Law: CAA 2001, s. 23 (list C, items 4, 15)
Guidance: CA 22110

D10   Docks and dry docks

Docks are included in list B at s. 22, alongside a range of similar assets ("a dock, harbour, wharf, pier, marina or jetty or any other structure in or at which vessels may be kept, or merchandise or passengers may be shipped or unshipped").

As such, docks are in principle excluded from the definition of plant and machinery and no allowances are due. HMRC guidance confirms that plant and machinery allowances will not be given "on the provision, construction or acquisition" of such assets.

There is an exception, however, given at item 23 in list C at s. 23. This is for "the provision of dry docks" (with a further exception for certain jetties or similar assets at item 24). Inclusion in this list does not guarantee that a dry dock will qualify for plant and machinery allowances but the point can be considered on ordinary case law principles.

A dry dock is, in one sense, clearly the premises or setting within which a business may be conducted. However, the *Barclay, Curle* company successfully argued that a dry dock was an item of plant. The court decision was a narrow one (three to two in favour of the company) but as it was in the House of Lords it carries weight over all lower courts. Lord Donovan, giving one of the majority opinions, held that:

> "The dry dock ought, I think, for present purposes to be regarded as a whole, with all its appurtenances of operating machinery, power installations, keel blocks, tubular side shores, and so on."

On that basis, he concluded that the dry dock was an item of plant:

> "This dry dock, looked upon as a unit, accommodates ships, separates them from their element and thus exposes them for repair; holds them in position while repairs are effected, and when this is done returns them to the water. Thus the dry dock is, despite its size, in the nature of a tool of the Respondents' trade, and therefore, in my view, 'plant'."

Expenditure on excavation was also held to be "expenditure on the provision of machinery or plant".

HMRC have commented, in connection with the principles applied in *Barclay, Curle*:

> "The cases where a structure was held to be plant show that a building or structure can be plant if and only if it is apparatus for carrying on the business or employed in the business rather than being the premises or place in which the business is carried on."

The decision may be contrasted with that in the *Anduff Car Wash* case considered under **Car wash apparatus** above.

Law: CAA 2001, s. 22 (list B, item 5), s. 23 (list C, item 25)
Case: *CIR v Barclay, Curle and Co Ltd* (1969) 45 TC 221
Guidance: CA 22020, 22050

D11   Dogs

HMRC accept in principle that a guard dog may be plant for capital allowances purposes. The dog is likely to function as apparatus with which the trade is carried on. The same applies to working dogs used on a farm.

In practice, there may be room for discussion about the tax relief in some circumstances. If the dog is handled by a trained security guard, there should be no restriction on claiming tax relief for the full costs. But if the owner of a pub or shop lives above the business and keeps a dog that can move around at night, it will be a question of fact to determine whether it is really a working guard dog or merely a family pet. In this case, it is possible that everyday costs (food, vet bills, etc.) will be disallowed on "wholly and exclusively" principles, but that a part of the initial cost will still qualify for capital allowances.

If the dogs are bought in, the cost figure will be clear. If they are bred and/or trained by the business, the ongoing costs may be allowable as revenue expenditure. If not, there is an argument that the costs should be capitalised and that allowances can then be claimed on such costs.

Law: CAA 2001, s. 205
Guidance: CA 21220

D12   Door furniture

The *Disability Discrimination Act* guidance, reproduced at **Appendix 3**, confirms that no allowances are normally due for **Doors**. However, it does also indicate that mechanical door *handles* are accepted by HMRC as machinery on which allowances can therefore be claimed.

At CA 21010, too, HMRC state that "door handles with moving parts are machinery". At 21200, the HMRC guidance includes the following:

> "A door handle would normally be an integral part of the door to which it is affixed, with the result that it would not qualify for PMAs. Any subsequent replacement of the door handle would then count as a repair of the door. However you should

not in practice refuse a PMA claim where this is the treatment adopted in the computations. Some mechanical handles can in any event constitute machines in their own right."

If a door handle can qualify as plant (even, by implication, where it is not mechanical), it seems fully justifiable to claim plant and machinery allowances on the cost of any door closer attached to the door. The same principles would apply to panic bolts, push bars, floor springs, locks and even hinges and it is understood that up to 40 per cent of the cost of a door may fall into these categories.

Door mats will normally qualify in their own right, as chattels rather than fixtures.

Law: CAA 2001, s. 21 (list A, item 1), s. 23 (list C, item 1)
Guidance: CA 21010, 21200

D13   Doors

Doors are included in list A at s. 21 and in principle they do not therefore qualify as plant or machinery. Nevertheless, some doors (or parts of doors: see **Door furniture**) may qualify in particular circumstances.

CA 21230, based on the Revenue's earlier *Football League* letter (see **Appendix 2**), indicates that automatic exit doors and gates at a football ground "would normally qualify as plant or machinery". As machinery, such items would be protected (by item 1 in list C at s. 23) from the restrictions in list A.

It is thought that any electric or electronic doors should qualify as items of "machinery". This would be subject to any HMRC argument that the principal purpose of the doors is to enclose the interior of a building (see s. 23(4)). The author's view is that such an argument would fail, as the principal purpose of the door is not to enclose the interior but precisely to break through the enclosing exterior so as to allow ingress and egress.

Any remote opening devices (push pads, etc.) will also qualify.

HMRC have confirmed that, in principle, a reinforced door could qualify as a security asset under the special rules given at s. 33. See **Personal security**.

HMRC accept that the door of a **Squash court** may qualify for allowances.

Fire doors

Fire doors will not generally qualify as plant, simply because they are still doors. It is difficult to argue that fire doors would fall within the wording "sprinkler and other equipment" in list C. The interpretation of "other equipment" would necessarily be coloured by the word "sprinkler" and it seems unnatural to call a door "equipment".

In *Wimpy*, fire doors were held not to be plant. ("The commissioners found that these items played no part in the activities of the trade. Because of fire regulations they merely enabled the premises to be used. The commissioners therefore rejected the contention that the items were plant and I think they were entitled to do so.")

HMRC certainly take the view that fire doors do not qualify. For example, at CA 22230, there is the following para:

> "Treat expenditure that does not already qualify for relief (either an allowance or deduction) that is incurred by a person carrying on a qualifying activity in taking required fire precautions in respect of premises used for the qualifying activity as qualifying expenditure for PMAs. For example, expenditure on a fire door can qualify under Section 29 but only if its installation is required by law."

Section 29 is now repealed, so no claim is possible under that section, but the wording clearly shows the HMRC view that allowances are not available on ordinary principles for fire doors.

There is a possible argument that the doors can qualify if they are linked to electronic controls, on the grounds that they are then machinery. This seems odd but the term "machinery" is given a very wide definition in practice. The point does not appear to have been tested.

As regards the push bar or panic bolt on a fire door, see **Door furniture** above.

See also **Double glazing.**

Law: CAA 2001, s. 21 (list A, item 1), s. 33
Case: *Wimpy International Ltd. v Warland* [1989] BTC 58
Guidance: CA 21230, 22130, 22230, 22270

D14   Double glazing

The costs of adding double glazing to an existing commercial property may be allowable under the rules applying to **Thermal insulation**. See that heading for a general description of the rules applying. These provisions, in appropriate cases, would override the general restriction on claiming allowances for the costs of windows and doors.

HMRC guidance includes the following:

> "Treat capital expenditure on things like roof lining, double-glazing, draught exclusion and cavity wall filling as expenditure on thermal insulation. Sometimes expenditure may be incurred for more than one reason. For example, double-glazing may be installed to insulate against both noise and loss of heat. The expenditure will qualify under Section 28 provided that it is clear that insulation against loss of heat is one of the main reasons why it was incurred."

Law: CAA 2001, s. 27, 28
Guidance: CA 22220

D15   Dwelling-houses

Expenditure is not qualifying expenditure if it is incurred on plant or machinery for use in a dwelling-house to be used in one of the following qualifying activities:

- an ordinary UK property business;
- an ordinary overseas property business; or
- special leasing of plant or machinery.

As such, the restriction does not apply to all qualifying activities, including in particular to trades or to a furnished holiday lettings business.

If plant or machinery is used for mixed purposes, a just and reasonable apportionment must be made to determine how much of the expenditure is disqualified under this rule.

In some cases where no capital allowances are available, a alternative forms of relief may be available. A non-statutory "renewals" basis of giving relief for plant or machinery in a dwelling-house was withdrawn from April 2013. And a new relief for the cost of replacing domestic items was introduced in 2016, replacing the former "wear and tear" allowance: see **Replacement of domestic items**.

Law: CAA 2001, s. 35
Guidance: CA 23060

Meaning of "dwelling house"

HMRC have given the following view on how this term is defined.

> "There is no definition of 'dwelling house' for the purpose of CAA 2001, s. 35 so it takes its ordinary meaning. A dwelling house is a building, or a part of a building. Its distinctive characteristic is its ability to afford to those who use it the facilities required for day-to-day private domestic existence. In most cases there should be little difficulty in deciding whether or not particular premises comprise a dwelling house, but in difficult cases the question is essentially one of fact.
>
> A person's second or holiday home or accommodation used for holiday letting is a dwelling house. The common parts of a building which contains two or more dwelling houses will not comprise a dwelling house, although the individual dwelling houses within the building will do so. A hospital, a prison, nursing home or hotel (run as a trade and offering services) are not dwelling houses.
>
> ...
>
> The common parts (for example, the stairs and lifts) of a building which contains two or more dwelling houses will not, however, comprise a dwelling-house."

Any external plant and machinery, located adjacent to but outside a shared property, is unlikely to form part of any individual dwelling-house, and will therefore normally qualify if the usual conditions are met.

Elsewhere, HMRC give the following specific guidance in relation to central heating systems:

> "A lift or central heating system serving the common parts of a building which contains two or more dwelling houses will not comprise part of either dwelling house. A central heating system serving an individual residential flat does not however qualify for PMA.
>
> Expenditure on a central heating system serving the whole of the building containing two or more dwelling houses should be apportioned between the common parts should be apportioned between the common parts, which part qualifies for PMA, and the residential flats or individual dwelling houses which do not."

Law: CAA 2001, s. 35
Guidance: CA 11520, 20020, 23060

Student accommodation

In 2010, HMRC reviewed their treatment of student accommodation in the light of the earlier *Uratemp* decision (not a tax case as such, but decided under the *Housing Act* 1988):

> "HMRC have concluded that ... each flat in multiple occupation comprises a dwelling-house, given that the individual study bedrooms alone would not afford the occupants "the facilities required for day-to-day private domestic existence". In other words, the communal kitchen and lounge are also part of the dwelling-house. The common parts of the building block (such as the common entrance lobby, stairs or lifts) would not, however, comprise a 'dwelling-house'."

Law: CAA 2001, s. 35
Case: *Uratemp Ventures Ltd v Collins* [2001] UKHL 43
Guidance: HMRC Brief 45/10

D16   Dyehouses

Although a dyehouse was largely held to be plant in an Australian case, the UK position is different.

HMRC guidance on the Australian case includes the reminder that "the external walls and roof were held not to be plant and so the building as a whole was not plant".

As a building or structure, a dyehouse would be excluded from qualifying as plant. Although parts of the overall cost would certainly qualify as plant and machinery (e.g. the electric costs, as integral features), there is nothing in s. 23 that could allow a claim for the entire cost of the dyehouse.

Law: CAA 2001, s. 21, 23

Case: *Wangaratta Woollen Mills v Commissioner of Taxation of the Commonwealth of Australia* [1969] 43 ALJR 324

Guidance: CA 22050

E1   Electrical installations and equipment

This section covers the topic generally. See also **Cabling**.

Electrical equipment used for the purposes of a qualifying activity will almost invariably qualify as plant or machinery. In some cases, it will fall to be treated as integral features, in which case the expenditure must be allocated to the special rate pool, where writing-down allowances are given at a slower rate.

Given the above paragraph, it is perhaps surprising to note that the starting point is still that no allowances are due for mains services, and systems, for electricity (s. 21, list A, item 2). The restriction potentially imposed by that section is, however, neutralised in several ways, which can be summarised by saying that the restriction does not apply:

- in the case of any integral features;
- to "machinery (including devices for providing motive power)"; and
- to a long list of electrical items contained in list C (including, for example, manufacturing equipment, a range

of kitchen equipment, computer systems, and refrigeration or cooling equipment).

Integral features

Since April 2008, certain categories of expenditure have been classed as integral features, including three that fall under this heading of "electrical installations and equipment":

- an electrical system (including a lighting system);
- a space or water heating system, a powered system of ventilation, air cooling or air purification, and any floor or ceiling comprised in such a system; and
- a lift, an escalator or a moving walkway.

Subject to the various rules applying to integral features generally, expenditure on all of these will be classified as special rate expenditure. Allowances will be due, normally at the reduced rate, without any further need to consider case law precedents. In other words, the introduction of the integral feature rules in 2008 was a double-edged sword; more items now qualify for plant and machinery allowances than was previously the case, but some assets (e.g. an air conditioning system) now attract tax relief more slowly than in the past.

The former wording at item 2 of list C, which referred to trade-specific electrical systems, was removed when the rules for integral features were introduced in 2008.

There is no statutory definition of the term "electrical system (including a lighting system)" but HMRC guidance is provided at CA 22330, as follows:

> "An electrical system (including a lighting system) is not defined for the purposes of the legislation, so the term takes its ordinary meaning: a system for taking electrical power (including lighting) from the point of entry to the building or structure, or generation within the building or structure, and distributing it through the building or structure, as required. The system may range from the very simplest to the most complex.

The term does not include other building systems intended for other purposes, which may include wiring and other electrical components. For example, communication, telecommunication and surveillance systems, fire alarm systems or burglar alarm systems. These other systems are all separately identified in S24 (3) List C of CAA01.

The cost of a ducting system within the building or structure follows the tax treatment of the system or systems that the ducting supports. So ducting which relates solely to the building's electrical system would be part of that system and would qualify for WDAs at the rate for the special rate pool, whereas ducting relating solely to a computer system could qualify for WDAs at the rate for the main pool. Where ducting supports two or more systems simultaneously, the relevant expenditure should be apportioned on a fair and reasonable basis, and capital allowances may be claimed on each portion of the total expenditure at the rate appropriate to that portion."

It is thought that the electrical system will include the mains switchboard, fuse switches, sub-mains cabling, distribution boards, etc.

Before the introduction of the integral features rules, HMRC would accept that an electrical system in a building was a single item of plant only in certain very restricted circumstances. Failing that, each item had to be considered on its own merits and might or might not qualify as plant. This broad principle is still contained in the HMRC guidance (at CA 21180) and is based on the HMRC interpretation of the *Cole Bros* case. For taxpayers since 2008, the question arises of whether this principle still applies.

There is a balance to be struck here: the simple approach is to claim allowances on the entire electrical system under the integral features rules. Arguably, however, it would still be open to a particular claimant to adopt the piecemeal approach, and to claim full rate allowances on certain items. (Transformers, for example, were held to be machinery in the *Lancashire Electric Power Company* case.) The obvious risk of taking this approach is that certain items may then not qualify for allowances at all (if the taxpayer is arguing that they do not form part of the electrical system). Given that HMRC seem prepared to take a fairly broad approach, taxpayers will for the most part wish simply to accept that relief is due on the entire electrical system, even though the rate of tax relief is slow.

Machinery

Any item that constitutes machinery qualifies for capital allowances in its own right, without the need to demonstrate that it is also plant. This is subject to the usual conditions, including in particular the requirement to identify a qualifying activity (e.g. a trade).

Other items

Other electrical items specifically identified in the legislation as outside the restrictions imposed by list A include the following:

- manufacturing or processing equipment;
- cookers, washing machines, dishwashers, refrigerators and similar equipment;
- hoists;
- computer, telecommunication and surveillance systems (including their wiring or other links);
- refrigeration or cooling equipment (listed separately from refrigerators as above, though this may have been in error);
- fire alarm systems;
- burglar alarm systems.

The HMRC view seems to be that if there is an overlap between the integral features rules and the items contained in list C, the former must take priority. A lift, for example, is certainly an item of machinery but is now an integral feature. The HMRC view is that it would have to go into the special rate pool, but there is no clear statutory pecking order to determine the matter. This is discussed in more detail under **Lifts** below.

Enhanced capital allowances

Certain energy-efficient assets can attract 100 per cent capital allowances for the chargeable period in which the expenditure is incurred. For further details, see **Energy-saving technology** below.

In this respect, HMRC guidance asserts that:

> "because these systems are now classified as P&M, many businesses may now be able to claim 100 per cent first-year allowances (FYAs), when their expenditure on these systems includes specific items on the 'Green Technology' ECA list (under sections 45A and 45H of CAA)".

Law: CAA 2001, s. 21 (list A, item 2), s. 23 (list C, various), s. 33A

Cases: *Lancashire Electric Power Company v Wilkinson* (1947) 28 TC 427; *Cole Brothers Ltd v Phillips* [1982] BTC 208

Guidance: CA 22330; https://etl.decc.gov.uk/etl/site/etl.html

E2   Electricity substations

An electricity substation is unlikely to qualify as plant in its entirety, as it is a structure caught by s. 22 (list B, item 7).

Even without that statutory bar on claiming the whole station as an item of plant or machinery, case law shows that such a claim would probably fail. In *London Electricity*, the Chancery Division reversed the decision of the special commissioner and held that the sub-station was not plant. No plant-like function was identified for the structure as a whole. The fact that features of the structure were carefully designed, to accommodate the equipment within, did not convert what was otherwise plainly the premises in which the activity was conducted into the plant or apparatus with which that activity was conducted.

Law: CAA 2001, s. 22

Case: *Bradley v London Electricity plc* (No. 2) [1996] BTC 451

E3   Embankments

Embankments are included in list B at s. 22. As such, they are excluded from the definition of plant and machinery and no allowances are due.

HMRC guidance confirms that plant and machinery allowances will not be given "on the provision, construction or acquisition" of such assets.

Law: CAA 2001, s. 22 (list B, item 1)
Guidance: CA 22020

E4   Employee expenses

Statutory rules

To claim plant and machinery allowances a person must be carrying on a "qualifying activity", a term that specifically includes "an employment or office".

Certain restrictions apply to claims by employees (and office-holders), however.

First, such individuals may not claim for the cost of bicycles, cars, vans or any other "mechanically propelled road vehicle". (Employees may instead claim tax-free reimbursement from their employer, failing which they may claim tax relief at specified rates per mile.)

For all other expenditure, employees may claim relief "only if the plant or machinery is necessarily provided for use in the performance of the duties of the employment or office". There is no "wholly and exclusively" test, however, so where necessary an apportionment should be made to take account of any private use of the asset for which allowances are being claimed.

Law: CAA 2001, s. 15(1)(i), 36

HMRC guidance, and case law

The *Employment Income Manual* contains some extensive guidance on capital allowances claims by employees. That guidance includes the following general comments:

> "Capital allowances are not due for expenditure on items which employees provide simply for their own convenience or for other reasons personal to themselves, even if they do in fact use the items in carrying out their work.

To qualify for capital allowances, the duties of an employee must objectively require the use of the machinery or plant. In a disputed case, it is important to establish

- what the employees' duties require; and
- whether it was necessary for the employees to provide the items themselves.

It will not have been necessarily provided by the employee if the employer is willing to provide or pay for it. Note that the machinery or plant does not have to be 'wholly and exclusively' used for the performance of the duties. If there is private use the allowances can be apportioned."

The HMRC guidance makes reference to the case of *White v Higginbottom*, in which allowances were denied for the cost of a slide projector used by a vicar when giving sermons. Nevertheless, the guidance goes on to state the following:

"However you should take care when applying this reasoning to situations where the employee's duties are only vaguely defined. This is particularly so when the equipment purchased represents a more up to date method of carrying out existing tasks which are a necessary part of the duties. In that case, the employee can exercise some element of choice in deciding how to go about those tasks without foregoing [sic] the entitlement to allowances."

HMRC take the view that "if the expense is substantial, it would be reasonable to expect the contract of employment to include a specific reference to the requirement to incur it". If there is no such contractual requirement, tax officers are instructed to "find out whether the employee has approached the employer to provide the item, or to reimburse its cost, and, if so, with what response". If the employer has refused to reimburse the cost, the HMRC view is that this "will clearly weaken the taxpayer's claim, though without being entirely conclusive". HMRC may also "investigate whether other workers with similar duties have also incurred the same sort of expense and if not, how they manage to perform their duties".

HMRC lost on this point (but won overall for other reasons) in the case of *Telfer*, concerning a caravan used by an employee. The caravan was held, on the facts, to function as premises rather than as plant, but in relation to the "necessarily provided for use in the performance of the duties" test the Tribunal was persuaded by the taxpayer argument:

> "We accept that the test imposed by section 36(1)(b) CAA goes beyond a legal requirement by the employer that the asset concerned is provided by the employee and requires an examination of whether or not the duties of the employment objectively require the provision of the asset. In this case, the duties of Mr Telfer's employment did objectively require him to live on site 'in his own outfit'. The duties required Mr Telfer to be on site at all times, and to be ready to move to another site at the Caravan Club's discretion, and on any realistic basis this means that those duties required him to live in his caravan on site. The caravans were used (as shelter and living accommodation) by Mr Telfer in the performance of the duties of his employment(s)."

Case: *Telfer v HMRC* [2016] UKFTT 614 (TC)
Guidance: EIM 36540*ff.*

Minor items

Where capital expenditure is "insubstantial" HMRC have stated that claiming capital allowances can be "impractical and not worthwhile". For such items ("things like tools or small items of office equipment such as cheap pocket calculators or staplers") the HMRC recommendation is that a claim should be made under s. 336 of ITEPA 2003 rather than by way of capital allowances. Claimants will still need to show that the expenditure is necessarily incurred.

Guidance: EIM 36510

Coverage of other specific items

See the following headings of this book for specific guidance on capital costs typically incurred by employees:

- Bicycles;
- Books;
- Caravans;
- Cars;

- Clothing;
- Computers;
- Entertaining-related expenditure;
- Loose tools;
- Personal security costs;
- Taxis;
- Tool boxes;
- Vehicles.

E5   Energy-saving technology

Full (100 per cent) first-year allowances are available for expenditure on new (unused) plant or machinery that meets criteria set by the Treasury with regard to energy efficiency.

Accountants and tax advisers should be ready to raise the possibility of these enhanced allowances in appropriate cases, but will generally need to rely on suppliers to show which assets meet the specified technical criteria.

How the rules work

As with **Environmentally beneficial technology** (see below) the statutory path to claiming these allowances is rather convoluted.

Section 45A of CAA 2001 first explains that the expenditure must be on energy-saving plant or machinery that is unused and not second-hand. It must not be excluded by s. 46 (general exclusions – e.g. for cars or for expenditure incurred in the final chargeable period).

The CAA 2001 legislation then states that certain conditions must be met "when the expenditure is incurred, or ... when the contract for the provision of the plant or machinery is entered into". Those conditions are twofold:

- first, the plant or machinery must be "of a description specified by Treasury order"; and
- second, it must meet "the energy-saving criteria specified by Treasury order for plant or machinery of that description".

The Treasury Order in question is SI 2018/268, the *Capital Allowances (Energy-Saving Plant and Machinery) Order* 2018 (which replaced SI 2001/2541 (as frequently amended) from 22 March 2018). This Order refers to (and defines) both the "Energy Technology Criteria List" and the "Energy Technology Product List". These lists are not reproduced within the Order itself, but rather are updated from time to time and published separately.

The Treasury Order then imposes three further conditions for claiming the enhanced allowances:

- first, the plant or machinery must fall within a technology class specified in the energy technology criteria list;
- second, it must meet the environmental criteria set out in that list; and
- third, for plant or machinery falling within any technology classes specified in art. 3(2), it must be of a type specified in (and not removed from) the energy technology product list (or it must have been accepted for inclusion in that list). This is subject to modified rules, detailed below, for solar thermal systems, for automatic monitoring and targeting equipment, and for certain heat pumps.

Technology criteria list

The technology classes on the criteria list are as follows at the time of writing (taken from the website https://etl.beis.gov.uk in June 2018). Most of the following categories are then broken down into sub-categories, with different criteria applying to each:

- air-to-air energy recovery devices;
- automatic monitoring and targeting;
- boiler equipment;
- combined heat and power;
- compressed air equipment;
- heat pumps;
- heating, ventilation and air conditioning (HVAC) equipment;
- high speed hand air dryers;

- lighting;
- motors and drives;
- pipework insulation;
- refrigeration equipment;
- solar thermal systems;
- uninterruptible power supplies;
- warm air and radiant heaters; and
- waste heat to electricity conversion equipment.

Taking lighting as an example, there are then three listed sub-categories, namely higher efficiency lighting units, lighting controls, and white light emitting diode lighting units. For each of these, different criteria are specified that must be met if the enhanced allowances are to be given.

Guidance: http://tinyurl.com/oqskeeg (shortened link)

Requirement to be on technology list

The technology classes listed at art. 3(2) are as follows at the time the Order came into effect (22 March 2018). For each of the following categories, therefore, the item will qualify only if it is listed on the official technology product list. It will be seen that the list is similar, but not identical, to the criteria list above:

- air-to-air energy recovery equipment;
- automatic monitoring and targeting equipment;
- boiler equipment;
- compressed air equipment;
- heat pumps;
- heating, ventilation and air conditioning (HVAC) equipment;
- high speed hand air dryers.
- motors and drives;
- refrigeration equipment;
- radiant and warm air heaters;

- solar thermal systems; and
- uninterruptible power supplies.

Continuing with the example of lighting from above, it will be seen that that category is *not* included on this second list. The lighting will still only qualify for enhanced allowances if the *criteria* are met, but the *particular product* does not have to be included on the official product lists.

To give a contrasting example, refrigeration equipment has numerous sub-categories, including "evaporative condensers". To qualify for enhanced allowances, these must meet the specified energy-saving criteria. However, the category of refrigeration is also included in the list of technology classes immediately above. As such, enhanced allowances will be due only if the particular product is included on the energy technology product list. By checking the official product list at the https://etl.beis.gov.uk site, it will be seen that there are well over 2,000 listed products under the heading of "evaporative condensers" (more than four times the number of just a few years ago) from a small list of manufacturers. The lists are updated monthly, so go out of date rapidly.

Reference may be made to the relevant website (details as below) to check the current list of categories at any given time.

Exceptions

For solar thermal systems, either the solar thermal system or the solar collector included in the system must be listed.

For automatic monitoring and targeting equipment, component based fixed systems are subject to a certification process (see SI 2018/268, art. 3(4)), rather than having to be included on the energy technology product list.

A different rule similarly applies in the case of certain heat pumps. Air source split and multi split (including variable refrigerant flow) heat pumps need not (since August 2014) be included on the energy technology product list.

Law: CAA 2001, s. 45A to 45C
Guidance: https://etl.decc.gov.uk; www.hmrc.gov.uk/tiin/tiin684.pdf; CA 23140

Restrictions for feed-in tariff and renewable heat incentive schemes

ECAs are restricted where the expenditure attracts tariff payments under either the Feed-in Tariff or the Renewable Heat Incentive schemes. This was explained by HMRC as follows shortly before the introduction of the change in 2012:

> "From April 2012 (or April 2014 for CHP installations) ECAs will not be available in respect of expenditure on plant or machinery when it generates electricity or heat (or produces biogas or biofuels) that attracts tariff payments under either of the FiTs or RHI schemes. ECAs may still be claimed (subject the other conditions of the ECA schemes) in respect of expenditure on such equipment as long as no tariffs are paid.

> Any ECAs given, in respect of expenditure incurred from April 2012 (or April 2014 for CHP installations), will be withdrawn if FITs or RHI tariffs are paid subsequently."

Law: CAA 2001, s. 45AA

Guidance: www.hmrc.gov.uk/tiin/tiin684.pdf

E6   Enhanced capital allowances

The expression "enhanced capital allowances" is not a statutory term. It is, however, widely used to refer to the **First-year allowances** that are available for certain "green" expenditure.

Typically, the expression is used to refer to either **Energy-saving technology** or **Environmentally beneficial technology**. The mechanics for claiming the enhanced allowances are explained under each of these headings.

Some effort is required to understand how the rules work, but the cash flow benefits can make this very worthwhile. This is especially true as some of the assets in question would otherwise qualify only for the "special rate" allowances at eight per cent.

Example

A company is spending £100,000 on a hot water boiler that will in principle qualify for allowances at eight per cent. It investigates the option of buying a boiler that meets the necessary criteria to qualify for enhanced allowances. Although the boiler is more expensive, the fuel savings are expected to cover the additional costs over the first five years of ownership.

The company, which is profitable and which is paying tax at 20 per cent, then looks at the tax position. Assume that it is a member of a group and that all available annual investment allowances have been exhausted elsewhere.

If enhanced allowances are claimed, the first year tax saving on expenditure of £100,000 will be £19,000 (£100,000 x 100% x 19%).

With standard allowances, the first year tax saving for the same level of expenditure will be just £1,520 (£100,000 x 8% x 19%). It takes nine years to gain just *half* of the tax relief.

The cash flow advantages from the earlier tax saving may be enough to justify the investment in the more expensive technology.

See also First-year tax credits.

Law: CAA 2001, s. 45A, 45H

Guidance: www.hmrc.gov.uk/capital_allowances/investmentschemes.htm

E7   Entertaining-related expenditure

Plant or machinery used for providing business entertainment is treated as not used for the purposes of the qualifying activity. As such, it does not qualify for plant and machinery allowances.

The concept of "entertainment" is defined to include all kinds of hospitality, but does not include anything provided for employees (or directors), unless the provision for employees is merely incidental to the provision of the entertainment for others. Equipment for a staff sports room, for example, would not be excluded by these provisions.

The disallowance does not apply where the person's trade consists in the provision of entertainment for others, as long as the asset in question is provided for payment or with the object of advertising to the public generally.

Law: CAA 2001, s. 269
Guidance: CA 27200

E8   Environmentally beneficial technology

Full (100 per cent) first-year allowances are available for expenditure on new (unused) plant or machinery that meets criteria set by the Treasury with regard to environmental issues. The items in question are mostly to do with saving water. (See **Energy-saving technology** for equivalent, but different, rules applying for that category of expenditure.)

Accountants and tax advisers should be ready to raise the possibility of these enhanced allowances in appropriate cases, but will generally need to rely on suppliers to show which evidence meet the specified technical criteria.

How the rules work

The statutory path to claiming these allowances is rather convoluted.

Section 45H of CAA 2001 first explains that the expenditure must be on environmentally beneficial plant or machinery that is unused and not second-hand. It must not be long-life asset expenditure and must not be excluded by s. 46 (general exclusions – e.g. for cars or for expenditure incurred in the final chargeable period).

The CAA 2001 legislation then states that certain conditions must be met "when the expenditure is incurred, or ... when the contract for the provision of the plant or machinery is entered into". Those conditions are twofold:

- first, the plant or machinery must be "of a description specified by Treasury order"; and
- second, it must meet "the environmental criteria specified by Treasury order for plant or machinery of that description".

The Treasury Order in question is SI 2003/2076, the *Capital Allowances (Environmentally Beneficial Plant and Machinery) Order* 2003, as amended on various occasions. This Order refers to (and defines) both the "water technology criteria list" and the "water technology product list". These lists are not reproduced within the Order itself, but rather are updated from time to time and published separately (see wtl.defra.gov.uk/product_search_landing.asp).

The Treasury Order then imposes three further conditions for claiming the enhanced allowances:

- first, the plant or machinery must fall within a technology class specified in the water technology criteria list;
- second, it must meet the environmental criteria set out in that list; and
- third, for plant or machinery falling within any technology classes specified in art. 3(2), it must be of a type specified in (and not removed from) the water technology product list (or it must have been accepted for inclusion in that list). This is achieved by manufacturers who can demonstrate to Defra that the criteria have been met.

Currently, the technology classes specified in art. 3(2) almost exactly mirror those on the technology list, though they are presented in a different order. This is all best explained with an example.

One of the technology types included on the water technology criteria list is the category of efficient taps. This is sub-divided into four types of qualifying "sub-technology" (automatic shut-off taps, electronic taps, low flow screw-down/lever taps, and spray taps). Taking electronic taps as an example, the official website specifies the criteria that must be met for such taps to qualify (e.g. the maximum flow rate in litres per minute).

So an electronic tap that meets all the technical criteria has fulfilled the first two of the three conditions above (technology class and environmental criteria). However, "efficient taps" are also included in SI 2003/2076, art. 3(2). As such, the assets will only qualify for enhanced allowances if they are of a type specified in the product list. Elsewhere in the tax legislation, the concept of "type" allows a rather wider interpretation. In this context, however, the meaning seems to be that the specific asset must be included on the product list.

The product list can be searched generically or by specified manufacturer. If, for example, a particular manufacturer is being considered, the site shows the qualifying model numbers for electronic taps made by that manufacturer. If expenditure is incurred on one of those models (at a time when they are included on the list), enhanced allowances will be due. Products are added to and removed from the list on a monthly basis.

Qualifying categories of expenditure

Categories on the criteria list at the time of writing in 2018 (unchanged from a year previously) are as follows:

- cleaning-in-place equipment;
- efficient showers;
- efficient taps;
- efficient toilets;
- efficient washing machines;
- flow controllers;
- greywater recovery and reuse equipment
- leak monitoring and control equipment;
- meters and monitoring equipment;
- rainwater harvesting equipment;
- small scale slurry and sludge dewatering equipment;
- vehicle wash water reclaim units;
- water efficient industrial cleaning equipment;
- water management equipment for mechanical seals; and
- water reuse.

The list at SI 2003/2076, art. 3(2) (i.e. of assets that must specifically feature on the official product list) includes all of the above. **Water re-use systems** are treated differently as explained at that heading.

Law: CAA 2001, s. 45H; SI 2003/2076

Guidance: CA 23140; wtl.defra.gov.uk/product_search_landing.asp

E9   Escalators

Escalators are integral features and will qualify for plant and machinery allowances. The cost will be allocated to the special rate pool and writing-down allowances will therefore be available at the lower rate only. (See under **Lifts** for a discussion of the interaction between the integral features rules and items included in list C.)

No allowances are normally due for the cost of "shafts or other structures in which lifts, hoists, escalators and moving walkways are installed". See **Alterations to buildings** for a possible exception to that rule.

Law: CAA 2001, s. 21 (list A, item 5), s. 23 (list C, item 1), s. 33A(5)(d)

F1   Farm expenditure

There are no special statutory rules relating to plant or machinery allowances for farmers. In 2010, however, HMRC issued guidance on plant and machinery allowances for the pig industry. According to the introduction to the document, its aim is to "illustrate the range of assets on which the pig industry might claim plant and machinery capital allowances".

In practice, this guidance is of wider value than just for the pig industry or indeed for farmers in general. Naturally, though, it will be of greatest interest for those for whom it was intended.

Guidance: R&C Brief 03/10 (see **Appendix 4**)

F2   Farrowing crates

These are included by HMRC in their list of assets that can qualify for plant and machinery allowances at the standard rate.

Guidance: R&C Brief 03/10 (see **Appendix 4**)

F3   Fascia boards

The claim for the cost of fascia boards was allowed by the commissioners in *Wimpy* and this treatment was approved by the High Court and by the Court of Appeal. As Fox LJ put it:

> "There were also in issue fascia boards which the commissioners accepted were plant since they advertised the business and were merely attached to the building but did not form part of it."

In the same case, Lloyd LJ similarly commented:

> "As for the fascia boards, the commissioners found that they qualified as plant. 'They are [they said], in effect, advertising signs which are attached to the building for display purposes

but do not become part of it'. There is no criticism of that finding."

Case: *Wimpy International Ltd. v Warland* [1989] BTC 58

F4   Fencing

The HMRC view is that fences are not plant. In the *Football League* letter (see **Appendix 2**), HMRC comment that "fencing [at a football stadium] is not plant or machinery but may come within the 1975 safety legislation and so qualify under CAA 2001, s. 32".

Those safety legislation rules have now been repealed, but is the HMRC view correct? In other words, what is the correct treatment of fencing if considered on ordinary principles? The matter was touched on in the 2011 *Brockhouse* case, where it was initially argued that plant and machinery allowances should be given on the cost of the fencing: "the fencing expenditure was incurred, it is not part of the premises and is providing a function rather than being merely structural".

Sadly (from the point of view of testing the matter in court) that line of argument was not pursued and the point was therefore not tested. Instead, the case was argued on the basis of there being a special security threat (see **Personal security**), an argument that was rejected on the facts of the case. (HMRC do accept in principle that fencing may qualify as a security asset, but the conditions for the personal security rules to apply are very tight.)

In *Abbott Laboratories*, concerned with industrial buildings allowances, the findings of fact included the statement that "the cost of the factory was £1,222,625, which included the entire factory, the roadways and the boundary fence, but not the cost of the land and plant and machinery". On the face of it, that statement draws a distinction between fencing on the one hand, and plant and machinery on the other. However, it is not as simple as that as the factory would certainly have contained fixtures which, by definition, are plant and machinery. So not much weight can be attached to that comment.

In *Anduff*, the cost of the fencing was not included by the commissioners in the expenditure they held to qualify as plant and machinery. The reason for the exclusion was that the fencing did not play any part "as a tool of Anduff's trade". On the facts of that case, the fencing did not qualify, but the case does not give a clear ruling on the treatment of fencing in general.

So there are several case law decisions that touch on the question of whether fencing should qualify as plant, but none that address the matter full on. Fencing is not a building, though, and it is at least arguable that it is not a structure (though HMRC do not accept that argument, and a long fence might possibly be closer to being a structure).

If it can be argued that fencing is not a structure, the matter would come down to case law principles and to deciding whether a fence is the premises within which a qualifying activity is carried on, or whether it is apparatus used for that trade. It may be that some fencing would properly be treated as not qualifying, whereas other fences might qualify: for example, the author has been involved in a discussion with HMRC regarding a racing stable where there was a perimeter fence marking the overall boundary but also paddock fencing creating individual units in which the horses could graze. It is at least arguable that the paddock fencing functions as apparatus rather than merely as premises.

Certainly, it is suggested that HMRC could be pressed for their reasoning if rejecting outright a claim to treat fencing costs as qualifying plant and machinery expenditure. It is likely to require a Tribunal hearing, however, if the generic HMRC view – whereby all fencing is categorised as a fixed structure – is to be challenged.

Finally, it is possible that some types of fencing would be rescued by list C at s. 23 even if it has to be conceded that the fencing constitutes a structure in the first place. It is possible, for example, that a sophisticated fence could form part of a burglar alarm system.

The author has also been asked about knee rail restraint fencing, used outside car sales showrooms to prevent vehicle theft. The showroom may contain cars worth a seven-figure sum, and the prevention of theft is therefore a vital consideration. There seems every reason to think that ordinary case law principles would lead to a conclusion that such fencing constitutes plant rather than premises, in that it is acting as apparatus (to prevent theft) rather than as a mere part of the premises from which the business is conducted. It would still be necessary to convince HMRC that such fencing is not a structure (to prevent problems with s. 22) or possibly, though more awkwardly, that it falls within item 4 at list C (as storage or display equipment). See also **Car hoops**.

Law: CAA 2001, s. 22, 23, 32

Cases: *Abbott Laboratories Ltd v Carmody* (1968) 44 TC 569; *Attwood v Anduff Car Wash Ltd* [1997] BTC 454; *Brockhouse (t/a A6 Aquatics) v HMRC* [2011] UKFTT 380 (TC)

Guidance: CA 21230, 22240, 22270

F5   Fibre optic cabling

This is included by HMRC in a list of "typical examples of plant or machinery" that would qualify for annual investment allowances.

Guidance: CA 23084

F6   Films, tapes and discs

Special rules apply to the production of films. In the simplest terms, income and expenditure is generally treated as revenue in nature, even where film costs would normally be capitalised. The following HMRC guidance serves as a reminder of the limitations of the special rules:

> "The requirement to treat capital expenditure as being on revenue account only applies where the expenditure is on creation of the film, and would otherwise be treated as expenditure on creation of an asset. The revenue treatment of expenditure does not apply to the purchase of capital items, such as cameras and lighting equipment. Expenditure on these items remains capital expenditure and capital allowances will be available as appropriate."

Law: FA 2006, Sch. 4; CAA 2001, s. 23(2); ITTOIA 2005, s. 143

Guidance: http://webarchive.nationalarchives.gov.uk/20140109143644 /http://www.hmrc.gov.uk/films/guidance/taxation.pdf

F7   Finance costs

Business financing costs are not expenditure "on the provision of plant or machinery" and do not qualify for allowances. In *Ben-Odeco*, the company incurred a substantial sum of money on bank charges and interest, in connection with the construction of an oil rig.

Lord Russell summarised the point succinctly by saying that "the effect of the expenditure was the provision of finance and not the provision of plant".

The same principle would appear to apply to disallow the cost of mortgage valuation fees.

Case: *Ben-Odeco Limited v Powlson* (1978) 52 TC 459
Guidance: CA 20060

F8   Fire alarm systems

Fire alarm systems are included in list C at s. 23 and will clearly qualify as plant and machinery in normal circumstances. The associated wiring will likewise qualify, whether in a new building or an existing one. The qualifying costs will include bells, break glass points, control panels, smoke detectors, etc.

Fire alarm systems do not need to be classified as integral features, as confirmed by HMRC:

> "The term [electrical system] does not include other building systems intended for other purposes, which may include wiring and other electrical components. For example, communication, telecommunication and surveillance systems, fire alarm systems or burglar alarm systems. These other systems are all separately identified in S24 (3) List C of CAA01."

The guidance from HMRC goes on to confirm that the cost of a ducting system within a building or structure will follow the tax treatment of the system or systems that the ducting supports. So ducting for general electrical work will be classified as integral features, and will accordingly attract a slower tax rate. Ducting for a fire alarm system will qualify as plant and machinery in its own right and will attract the higher rate.

Law: CAA 2001, s. 21 (list A, item 6), s. 23 (list C, item 10)
Guidance: CA 21200

F9   Fire escapes

On the face of it, fire escapes cannot qualify as plant, at least if they are classified as stairs, as they seem to be caught by item 1 of list A at s. 21. It is difficult to argue that they are saved by item 10 at list C ("Fire alarm systems; sprinkler and other equipment for extinguishing or containing fires") or by any other item in the list.

Nevertheless, the waters are muddied by the *Capital Allowances (Leases of Background Plant or Machinery for a Building) Order 2007*. Article 2 of that Order lists "examples of the kinds of plant or machinery that may be regarded as falling within the definition of background plant or machinery for a building". The Order applies for the purposes of the long funding lease rules, but it operates on the basis that the items to which it refers are plant or machinery.

The list includes "protective installations such as lightning protection, sprinkler and other equipment for containing or fighting fires, fire alarm systems and fire escapes". Most of these are fairly uncontroversial (though there are possible arguments about **Lightning conductors**) but the inclusion of fire escapes is something of a surprise.

Where there are apparent statutory contradictions, a closer look at the context of the legislation may be required. The particular statutory restriction refers to "walls, floors, ceilings, doors, gates, shutters, windows and stairs". The inclusion of gates does not permit an interpretation that relates only to items on the inside of the building. Nevertheless, list A applies only if the asset in question is "in, or connected with, the building". It is suggested that the restriction would apply to an ordinary staircase within, for example, a hotel, even if the staircase is for use only in an emergency. However, there is a possible argument that the context of the restriction means that it would not apply to an external fire escape, such as might be used (for example) to escape from upper floors in a boarding school. The statutory position is not ideal but it is clear that s. 21 has to be interpreted in a way that takes account of the reference to fire escapes in SI 2007/303.

HMRC make no specific mention of the point in their guidance in the *Business Leasing Manual*, other than to re-state the statutory wording.

Law: CAA 2001, s. 21, 23; SI 2007/303, item j
Guidance: BLM 21330

F10   Fire safety systems

Some care is needed with the treatment of fire safety systems. They are specifically included as assets that are "treated as buildings" in list A at s. 21 (item 6). The starting point is therefore that these items do not qualify as plant and machinery.

The effect of that restriction is, however, mitigated by certain items in list C. In particular, item 10 refers to "fire alarm systems; sprinkler and other equipment for extinguishing or containing fires", so anything falling within these categories is protected from the exclusion and may qualify as plant. In principle, any associated equipment will qualify (including, for example, smoke detectors, hose reels, control panels, dry risers), as will alarm systems and sprinklers.

Anything constituting machinery will qualify in its own right, by virtue of item 1 at list C.

Any electrical system, including lighting, not qualifying in its own right will qualify under the category of integral features.

Law: CAA 2001, s. 21 (list A, item 5), s. 23 (list C, item 10), s. 33A
Guidance: CA 21200

F11   First-year allowances

First-year allowances (FYAs) offer immediate tax relief for the whole cost of qualifying assets. Unlike **Annual investment allowances**, there is no cap on the amount of expenditure that may qualify for these allowances. See also **First-year tax credits** at the next heading below.

Historically, FYAs have been given at various different rates. The trend, however, has been to reduce the categories of qualifying expenditure but to give a full write-off allowances for items that do qualify. Currently, all FYAs are given at 100% in the year in which the expenditure is incurred.

Categories of expenditure qualifying for FYAs are as follows:

- energy-saving plant or machinery;
- cars with low CO_2 emissions;
- zero-emission goods vehicles;

- plant or machinery for gas refuelling stations;
- plant or machinery for electric vehicle charging points;
- plant or machinery for use wholly in a ring fence trade;
- environmentally beneficial plant or machinery;
- plant or machinery for use in designated assisted areas.

Various "general exclusions" apply to restrict allowances in some circumstances, e.g. for most leased assets and most cars. More specifically, first-year allowances are not normally available:

- for the chargeable period in which the qualifying activity is permanently discontinued;
- for cars (as defined at s. 268A) – except that this does not apply to low emission cars qualifying for FYAs by virtue of s. 45D;
- for expenditure that would be long-life asset expenditure but for the transitional provisions at Sch. 3, para. 20;
- for plant or machinery for leasing;
- in certain cases where a change is made with a specific view to obtaining FYAs (again, see below);
- where any of the following applies:
  - s. 13 (use of asset provided originally for other purposes);
  - s. 13A (use of asset provided originally for long funding leasing); or
  - s. 14 (use of qualifying plant or machinery received as a gift).

These general exclusions are covered in greater depth in *Capital Allowances*, also available from Claritax Books.

Law: CAA 2001, s. 39ff.

F12   First-year tax credits

First-year tax credits are available for companies (only) that are loss-making and that have incurred expenditure on "energy-saving" or "environmentally beneficial" plant and machinery. If a company is not able to use its losses against its own profits (or against the profits of a group company), it may surrender the loss and receive a cash payment, rather than carrying the loss forward against future profits. The expression "payable enhanced capital allowances" has also been used to describe this form of relief.

A payment received under these rules is not treated as taxable income of the company concerned.

The scheme of first-year tax credits was set to end from 1 April 2018. In the event, the scheme has been extended for a further five years but the amount of the tax credit reduced from 1 April 2018, reflecting the fact that corporation tax rates today are lower than those in force when the tax credit scheme was introduced.

From 1 April 2018 (but subject to transitional rules for periods spanning that date), the amount of the tax credit is set at two thirds of the corporation tax rate for the chargeable period in question, rounded up to the nearest second decimal place.

With a CT rate of 19%, the two-thirds figure therefore becomes 12.67%. Companies will need to decide whether they prefer to claim the two-thirds figure for an immediate cash benefit at just 12.67%, or to carry the loss forward such that they may obtain later tax relief at the full 19%.

Example

Anyco Ltd makes a loss of £20,000, wholly attributable to first-year qualifying expenditure, in its accounts for the year to 31 May 2019. It is entitled, on the facts, to surrender the loss and it chooses to do so. It is therefore able to claim a credit of £2,534 (£20,000 at 12.67%).

For earlier periods, the credit was calculated as a fixed 19% of the surrendered loss (not linked to the corporation tax rates then applying). The topic of first-year tax credits is covered in much greater depth in *Capital Allowances*, also available from Claritax Books.

Law: CAA 2001, Sch. A1, para. 2

F13   Fish tanks and ponds

"The provision of fish tanks and ponds" is included at list C and such items can therefore potentially qualify as plant.

If used for the purposes of a qualifying activity, perhaps as a display in a reception area or as a container for fish to be sold at a garden centre, it seems entirely reasonable to view a fish tank as an item of plant.

A pond is a more doubtful item of plant on case law principles. However, the inclusion of the category in list C presumably means that circumstances were envisaged in which a claim could be made for the cost of a fish pond (or possibly of a pond generally, depending on whether or not the word "fish" is to be applied to "tanks" only or to "tanks and ponds").

Law: CAA 2001, s. 23 (list C, item 30)

F14   Fixtures

Meaning

Much confusion arises over the concept of "fixtures" but an understanding of the issues is essential for many capital allowances claims.

In accounting language, the term "fixtures" may be applied to any number of small items of plant or machinery, whether or not they are in fact "fixed" in any sense to the property. Indeed, it is not uncommon to see, in a set of accounts, the heading "fixtures and fittings" used to describe only the moveable chattels owned by a business.

For capital allowances purposes, by contrast, a fixture has a specific statutory definition, namely "plant or machinery that is so installed or otherwise fixed in or to a building or other description of land as to become, in law, part of that building or other land". Take, for example, a central heating system: this is affixed to the property and a person buying the property would expect to acquire the system as part of the property price. In the business accounts, the cost of the central heating system would probably be shown under the heading of "property" rather than under "fixtures and fittings". Nevertheless, plant and machinery allowances are due for the cost of the system. It follows that if allowances are claimed only on items shown in the accounts as fixtures and fittings, tax relief is being under-claimed.

(If the property comes to be sold, incidentally, the cost of the central heating system will still qualify as part of the cost of the property for the purposes of calculating any capital gain, even though tax relief has been received by way of capital allowances.)

HMRC guidance (at CA 26025) explains that the term "fixture" has the same meaning for the capital allowances fixtures legislation as it does for property law. The guidance then continues as follows:

> "Property law distinguishes between chattels and fixtures. A chattel is an asset which is tangible and moveable. A chattel may become a fixture if it is fixed to a building or land. For example, before it is installed in a building as part of a central heating system, a central heating radiator is a chattel. Once installed, it becomes a fixture.
>
> The courts have developed two tests for determining whether an asset is a fixture or a chattel:
>
> - the method and degree of annexation,
> - the object and purpose of annexation.
>
> The first test is not conclusive. Some degree of physical affixation is required before a chattel becomes a fixture. If the asset cannot be removed without serious damage to, or destruction of, the building or land, that is strong evidence that it is a fixture. But it is neither a necessary nor a sufficient condition.
>
> The second test is now accorded greater significance by the courts than the first. The courts look at the purpose and intention of the asset and its affixation. If, when viewed objectively, it is intended to be permanent and effect a lasting improvement to the property, the asset is a fixture. If the attachment is temporary and is no more than is necessary for the asset to be used and enjoyed, the asset remains a chattel.
>
> Where a property is leased, property law distinguishes between tenant's fixtures and landlord's fixtures. A tenant's fixture is one installed by the tenant which may be removed by the tenant during or at the end of the lease. For example shop fittings are frequently installed on this basis. This distinction is not relevant for the fixtures legislation. The rules on fixtures apply to both tenant's and landlord's fixtures."

Fixture or chattel

HMRC's SDLT manual gives some examples of items that will normally be treated as fixtures rather than as moveable chattels:

- fitted kitchen units, cupboards and sinks;
- agas and wall mounted ovens;
- fitted bathroom sanitary ware;
- central heating systems;
- intruder alarm systems.

By contrast, the following items will, according to that guidance, "normally be regarded as chattels":

- carpets (fitted or otherwise);
- curtains and blinds;
- free standing furniture;
- kitchen white goods;
- electric and gas fires (provided that they can be removed by disconnection from the power supply without causing damage to the property);
- light shades and fittings (unless recessed).

The treatment of fitted carpets is arguably not clear cut. There is certainly a possible argument that carpet tiles that are glued in place should be treated as fixtures. The point is considered in some depth in the *Botham* case.

SDLT is included as part of the purchase price when buying fixtures, and would be included when making an apportionment using the agreed formula (see **12.8.2**).

Case: *Botham v TSB plc* (1996) 7P&CRD1
Guidance: SDLTM 04010

Ownership

A further difficulty in relation to fixtures is with the whole question of ownership. Plant and machinery allowances are in principle only due if, as a result of the person incurring expenditure, that person owns the plant or machinery in question (s. 11(4)).

In the context of leased property, this can cause problems, as brought to light in the *Costain Property Investments* case. In simplified terms, a tenant might incur expenditure on fixtures, but these might thereby become legally part of the property and might therefore belong to the landlord. The landlord has no entitlement to allowances as he did not incur the expenditure and the tenant has no entitlement as he does not own the assets.

Following that case, new rules were introduced to ensure that allowances were due to one party (and only one party) in such circumstances. These are now found in Chapter 14 of Part 2 of CAA 2001.

Claiming allowances for fixtures

As can be seen from the statutory wording given above, a fixture is *by definition* plant and machinery. This then leads back to s. 21, which states that "expenditure on the provision of plant or machinery does not include expenditure on the provision of a building" and that "building" includes any asset incorporated in the building. It even also includes an asset of a kind normally incorporated in a building.

If that were the end of it, these provisions would merely be circular and self-cancelling: something fixed into the building cannot be plant or machinery, and an item that is not plant or machinery cannot be a fixture. In reality, the restrictions in s. 21 are subject to the many exceptions at s. 23, encompassing (inter alia) the whole of list C and also all integral features. Nearly every property contains substantial numbers of fixtures, covering everything from boilers and radiators, to electrical and water systems, to toilets, carpets and lifts.

Changes in Finance Act 2012

The capital allowances rules for fixtures were changed from April 2012, with further changes applying from two years later. Broadly, these have the effect that a valuation must be agreed at the time a property is sold for any fixtures that have been the subject of a capital allowances claim. Since April 2014, a claim must be made for all fixtures if the property owner is entitled to claim. Failure to claim and to agree a formal transfer value – normally by means of an election between the two parties to a sale and purchase agreement –

will deny all future owners the chance to claim allowances on the items in question.

The details of these rules are beyond the scope of this book, but are covered in depth in *Capital Allowances* 2018-19, written by the same authors and also available from Claritax Books.

Law: CAA 2001, s. 11, 172ff.
Case: *Stokes v Costain Property Investments Ltd* [1984] BTC 92
Guidance: CA 26000ff.

F15   Flag poles

In *Cadogan Gardens*, flag poles in the grounds of a hotel were accepted as plant. This was subject to a caveat that the Inspector of Taxes was "not conceding that all of these items would necessarily be machinery or plant in all circumstances".

That case preceded the legislation restricting claims for **Structures**, however. No claim would be possible now for a flag pole if HMRC could argue that it was a fixed structure.

Law: CAA 2001, s. 22
Case: *Lupton v Cadogan Gardens Developments Limited* (1971) 47 TC 1

F16   Floodlighting

One of the categories of integral features is "an electrical system (including a lighting system)". As such, it is now clear that plant and machinery allowances can be given for the cost of floodlighting. If allowances are given under the integral features rules, writing-down allowances will be given at the lower "special rate".

If floodlighting could be seen as part of a burglar alarm system, then it would seem that allowances could be given in the main pool instead of as integral features (list C, item 11).

In the *Football League* letter, reproduced at **Appendix 2**, floodlighting was listed as an item that "would normally qualify as plant or machinery". However, that may have been by virtue of the now partially repealed item 2 at list C, which previously referred to electrical and lighting systems that were provided mainly to meet the particular requirements of the qualifying activity. On the other hand, it may be that the floodlighting was considered to qualify simply on general principles.

The provision of towers to support floodlights is mentioned at item 26 and it is therefore possible that a legitimate plant and machinery claim could be made in connection with such expenditure.

See also **L7** re enhanced capital allowances for certain lighting costs.

Law: CAA 2001, s. 23 (list C, item 11), s. 33A

F17   Floors and flooring materials

As a general principle, floors do not qualify as plant (list A, item 1 at s. 21).

List C includes many items that are exempt from the s. 21 restriction, but the first 16 items at list C do not provide an exemption for "any asset whose principal purpose is ... to provide an interior ... floor ... which ... is intended to remain permanently in place".

HMRC guidance on this aspect is given at CA 22080 as follows:

> "The [integral features] rules also specifically clarify that the new definition does not extend to any asset whose principal purpose is to insulate or enclose the interior of a building, or to provide interior walls, floors or ceilings which are intended to remain permanently in place. ... So if, for example, a business installs a new, permanent false ceiling in its premises, in order to conceal new wiring and service pipes, expenditure on that ceiling would not qualify for PMAs.

> On the other hand, if a business installs in its premises a plenum floor or plenum ceiling, the principal purpose of which is to function as an integral part of the heating or air conditioning system (for example, the plenum floor or plenum ceiling may form the fourth side of a duct or channel through which stale air is extracted and treated air is discharged), that expenditure would qualify for PMAs as part of an 'integral feature' of the building or structure."

Raised floors

The HMRC view is that allowances should be denied for floors generally, including raised floors. This appears to be a justifiable approach as raised floors were denied allowances in the *Wimpy* and *Associated Restaurants* cases.

Temporary floors

The HMRC guidance also contains the following instructions to tax officers:

> "You should give plant and machinery allowances on a temporary floor put down solely to enable the room to be used for dancing and on a plenum floor, which is a floor that forms part of the reticulation system of a heating or air conditioning system. For example, it may form the fourth side of a duct of channel through which stale air is extracted for treatment. Other floors covering heating and ventilation systems and computer cabling are not plant just as suspended ceilings are not plant."

Sports flooring

HMRC accept that the "special floor" of a **Squash court** qualifies as plant.

Slatted floors

HMRC accept (R&C Brief 03/10) that "slatted flooring areas (as internal parts of a slurry system)" will qualify as plant.

Mezzanines

The treatment of mezzanine floors can be complicated. On the one hand, the HMRC view is given very simply that plant or machinery claims for mezzanine floors should be refused. In the same section of guidance (CA 22070), however, a slightly less adamant approach is taken:

> "In the cases of *Hunt v Henry Quick Ltd* and *King v Bridisco Ltd* 65 TC 108 the companies claimed plant or machinery allowances on mezzanine floors used for storage installed in warehouses. The Commissioners found that the mezzanine

floors were movable temporary structures used for storage. The mezzanine floors had not become part of the premises. The kind of expenditure incurred in these cases is covered by the reference to 'storage equipment' at s. 23 CAA. The fact that a mezzanine floor is not part of the premises is irrelevant. S. 21 defines buildings as including assets which are not incorporated in a building but are of a kind normally incorporated in a building.

An asset is either a floor or a large shelf (storage equipment) and will rarely, if ever, be both and so the claim either fails or it succeeds in full."

One of the leading cases in dealing with mezzanine flooring is that of *Bridisco* (and the *Henry Quick Ltd* case heard with it). In each case, the mezzanine flooring was held to be plant. In *Bridisco*, the mezzanine floors comprised free-standing raised platforms on steel pillars with steel beams supporting wooden flooring. Each steel pillar was bolted to the floor of the warehouse by means of welded plates to ensure rigidity and safety. Ancillary lighting was added. The floors were accepted as plant in both cases, but more clearly so in *Bridisco*. Factors influencing that decision included:

- the fact that there were four different mezzanine floors installed at different times;
- they covered only 60 per cent of the floor area;
- one, and part of another, had been moved to a different warehouse;
- fork-lift trucks, used elsewhere, could not be used on the mezzanine floors;
- staff were allowed to use the mezzanines only for storage and retrieval of goods.

In *Wimpy*, the cost of mezzanine floors was disallowed on the facts:

"The raised and mezzanine floors were installed to create variety in the seating areas, to give visual interest and to provide more seats. The mezzanine construction is a steel frame suspended from the upper structure with a timber infill. The commissioners held it was part of the premises. The floors would have to be removed at the termination of the lease.

The raised floors serve to break up what would otherwise be a large open seating area and make the premises more interesting for the customers.

They were designed in conjunction with the double staircase so that they formed landings at the entrance to the staircase and helped to reduce the apparent height of the ceiling from ground floor level. They are substantial structures made by concrete beams on a steel framework put together on the site. They are not bedded into the underlying concrete and could be dismantled leaving a level floor exposed.

The commissioners decided that the raised areas, like the mezzanine, while they are in position form part of the premises in which the business is conducted and were not plant. Similarly, the balustrading which is held in place by brackets and the function of which is the safety of customers and staff in using the areas in question. The commissioners held that they were necessary additions to the raised and mezzanine floors for those purposes and were not plant."

As these cases predated the changes introduced in 1994, some care is needed. It would now be necessary to show, as a statutory requirement, that the floors were exempt as storage equipment (item 4 at list C) or on some other statutory basis. It may obviously be helpful to describe the assets in question as storage facilities rather than as floors if such description is justifiable on the facts.

Alterations to existing buildings

In certain circumstances, the costs of a floor may be incidental to the installation of plant or machinery in an existing building. In this case, allowances may be due under the rules for **Alterations to buildings**.

This was the outcome in the *Wetherspoon* case, as explained in the following quotation from the Upper Tribunal decision:

"In order to feed the relevant trade-specific equipment, which we take to have been installed plant or machinery, a lowered drain duct had to be created in the floor, and in order that the floor should slope towards the drain, the existing floor had to be removed and replaced by a slightly inclined floor. It seems to us that, on the basis that our understanding is that the drainage duct actually feeds water and spilt beer into trade-specific fluid extraction equipment ... , all these costs were properly allowable under [CAA 2001, s. 25]."

In the same case, allowances were permitted under s. 25 for the cost of strengthening the kitchen floor where this was needed to support the extra weight of the commercial equipment (cookers, freezers, dishwashers, etc.). The Tribunal rejected the HMRC suggestion that the floor was strengthened to support the weight of people moving around in the kitchen area.

Slate floors

A claim was made in *McMillin* that part of the flooring costs should be treated as expenditure on plant and machinery. This was on the basis that the flooring was an integral part of the system for heating the furnished holiday cottages in question. The claim related to slate floors on the ground floor, on the basis that energy consumption was reduced when stone flooring was used. The claim never came near to succeeding, however: the main purpose of the slate was to provide a floor and any part the floor may have played in the heating system could only have been secondary. Even if such a secondary purpose existed, allowances were precluded by list A.

Wipe clean floors

In *Wetherspoon*, the First-tier Tribunal regarded it as "unreal" to treat the cost of a wipe-clean floor as incidental to the installation of WCs and urinals. This view was not disturbed by the Upper Tribunal.

Floor coverings

For main coverage of this, see **Carpets** above.

In the *McMillin* case referred to above, the cost of screed laid under the flooring was initially disallowed by HMRC but they gave in on the point before the appeal and the Tribunal accepted that treatment.

Laminate floors

It may be necessary to decide whether laminates are part of the flooring as such or whether they are a covering to the floor, akin to a carpet.

A key point will be to consider the nature of its function and how it is affixed. If it is the primary flooring material or if it is glued in place, HMRC might well resist a claim. However, if it performs the same function as a carpet, and can simply be lifted up without any permanent effect on the underlying flooring, then it is difficult to see why it should be treated differently from a carpet.

Law: CAA 2001, s. 21 (list A, item 1), s. 23 (list C, item 4), s. 23(4)

Cases: *Wimpy International Ltd v Warland* [1989] BTC 58; *Associated Restaurants Ltd v Warland* [1989] BTC 58; *Hunt v Henry Quick Ltd* [1992] BTC 440; *King v Bridisco Ltd* [1992] BTC 440; *McMillin v HMRC* [2011] UKFTT 65 (TC); *J D Wetherspoon plc v HMRC* [2012] UKUT 42 (TCC)

Guidance: CA 21230, 22070, 22130; R&C Brief 03/10 (see **Appendix 4**)

F18   Flow controllers

"Flow controllers" are one of the technology classes specified in the water technology criteria list. As such, the equipment may qualify for first-year allowances as **Environmentally beneficial technology** when all necessary conditions are met, as explained in that section.

Two types of equipment may qualify under this heading. In each case, the specific item must be included on the water technology product list.

The first category is for control devices, used to shut off flow at predetermined times or in particular situations. According to the official guidelines, these "may be time, condition sensitive, programmed, or manually controlled at a central unit".

The second category is for flow limiting devices, which "are designed to produce a constant flow of water through a product such as a tap or tap outlet, over a range of pressures".

Law: CAA 2001, s. 45H; SI 2003/2076, art. 3(2)(a)

Guidance: CA 23135; wtl.defra.gov.uk/product_search_landing.asp

F19   Fly killers

Fly killers (in a hotel kitchen, for example) will generally qualify for plant and machinery allowances, whatever the type (e.g. electronic or adhesive strips).

F20   Football grounds

Businesses involved with football have more guidance than most other occupations when it comes to plant and machinery. The (then) Inland Revenue's letter to the Football League back in 1991 listed out many relevant assets that would typically qualify as plant and machinery. Although the list predates the statutory rules (now at s. 21ff.) those rules were intended to mark a line in the sand to prevent further (perceived) shifts in what would constitute plant or machinery – they were not meant to change any of the practice from the time. The key part of the *Football League* letter is reproduced at **Appendix 2**.

The treatment of the football stand itself is considered under **Sports facilities** below.

Guidance: CA 21230 (see **Appendix 2**)

F21   Furnished holiday lettings

Plant or machinery allowances are only given where the person incurring the expenditure is carrying on a qualifying activity. The list of qualifying activities includes both UK and EEA furnished holiday lettings (FHL) businesses.

The distinction between these businesses and what the legislation calls "ordinary" property businesses is important for various reasons.

First, the restrictions for expenditure on a **Dwelling-house** apply to ordinary property businesses but not to furnished holiday let businesses. This means that an FHL business can potentially claim for fixtures and other plant or machinery in the property that would not qualify in a different residential property.

Conversely, the relief for **Replacement of domestic items** is not available for FHL properties.

Law: CAA 2001, s. 15, 35

Losses

Losses arising from the carrying on of a qualifying furnished holiday lettings (FHLs) business are subject to various restrictions. In particular, it is not possible to offset losses from such an activity against an individual's total net income, or against corporate profits arising from other activities. Such losses may therefore only be carried forward against profits from the same qualifying activity.

Law: ITA 2007, s. 127(3A); CTA 2010, s. 65(4A), 67A(5)

Single activity

If a person (or partnership, or body of persons) makes more than one such commercial letting of furnished holiday accommodation, all such lettings are treated as a single qualifying activity for the purposes of claiming capital allowances. Accommodation that is let may qualify as holiday accommodation only in part. If so, just and reasonable apportionments must be made to determine the correct calculation of capital allowances.

Law: CAA 2001, s. 17

Rotated assets

Special rules may apply where plant or machinery is used in rotation for a variety of property-related activities.

The special rules apply where a person ceases to use plant or machinery for one such activity but continues to use it for another, the expenditure having originally been incurred for the purposes of that other activity. The way the rules work was explained in the *Explanatory Notes* to the 2011 *Finance Bill* as follows:

> "Where a person carrying on a property business of any of the four types listed ... uses plant or machinery in rotation between different types of property business, whilst still retaining ownership, that person is treated as if the plant or machinery was first acquired at the date it started to be re-used for the first property business after ceasing to be used in the second property business."

In these circumstances, the person is treated as incurring notional expenditure on new plant or machinery for the purposes of the ongoing activity. The figure to use for the notional expenditure is the lower of market value at the date of cessation and the amount of the actual expenditure.

There is a potential pitfall here in that the cessation of use for the earlier activity will mean that a disposal value must be brought into account at market value. In the context of a disposal of fixtures in the property, it will not be possible to control the disposal value by means of a fixtures election under s. 198 as the disposal will not fall within items 1 or 9 of the table at s. 196 (and the condition at s. 198(1) is therefore not met). A market value disposal will therefore be required and the recipient business may well be denied allowances on the grounds that the property is a dwelling-house (s. 35 – see above).

Law: CAA 2001, s. 13B

F22   Furniture and furnishings

Furniture and fittings are included in list C at CAA 2001, s. 23. As such, they may qualify as plant even though affixed to a building.

HMRC comment that "fixtures and fittings are plant if they are of a permanent and durable nature" and they go on to instruct their staff to "treat furniture including carpets, curtains and linoleum and items like cutlery, crockery, glassware, linen, kitchen utensils and protective clothing in the same way".

See also **Pictures** for a discussion of assets that are in an employee's home.

Law: CAA 2001, s. 23 (list C, item 5)
Guidance: CA 21200, 27100

G1   Garden offices

Questions are often posed on accounting and taxation forums, asking whether allowances can be claimed for the cost of a shed or other outbuilding, typically used by a self-employed individual as an office for his or her business.

Normal principles apply here, and the starting point is undoubtedly that the shed or other building is likely to be disqualified by sections 21 and 22, dealing with buildings and structures respectively.

It will therefore be necessary to consider the various exemptions within section 23 to determine which items may potentially qualify as plant or machinery. Such items will then need to be subject to the usual case law principles to determine whether or not they qualify.

Assuming that the outbuilding is used entirely for business purposes, a claim will in principle be possible for heating, lighting, security alarms, WC and basin, office equipment and furniture, etc. If there is private use, a claim can still be made but will need to be restricted proportionately.

Law: CAA 2001, s. 21, 22, 23

G2   Gas refuelling stations

Subject to the usual general exclusions, first-year allowances are given for expenditure incurred up to 31 March 2021 on certain plant or machinery for a gas refuelling station. The plant or machinery must be "unused and not second-hand".

Qualifying expenditure must be on plant or machinery installed at a gas refuelling station for use solely for or in connection with refuelling road vehicles with natural gas, biogas or hydrogen fuel. This is defined to include:

- any storage tank for natural gas, biogas or hydrogen fuel;
- any compressor, pump, control or meter used for or in connection with refuelling vehicles with natural gas, biogas or hydrogen fuel; and
- any equipment for dispensing natural gas, biogas or hydrogen fuel to the fuel tank of a vehicle.

The provisions do not extend the normal definition of plant and machinery, so the premises in which the plant is installed would (in principle) not qualify as plant or machinery in their own right.

There is no statutory requirement for the refuelling station to be open to the public, or to be used for cars. HMRC confirm, for example, that FYAs would be due under this heading for an operator of a fleet of commercial vehicles who installs a gas refuelling station.

For these purposes, "biogas" is defined to mean "gas produced by the anaerobic conversion of organic matter and used for propelling vehicles". It is a non-fossil fuel that can act as a substitute for natural gas.

"Hydrogen fuel" is defined as "a fuel consisting of gaseous or cryogenic liquid hydrogen which is used for propelling vehicles".

Law: CAA 2001, s. 45E (as amended)
Guidance: CA 23155

G3   Gas systems

Mains services of gas are treated as part of the building (s. 21, list A, item 2). If they are to qualify for plant and machinery allowances, it is therefore necessary to find a statutory justification.

Gas systems provided mainly to meet the particular requirements of the qualifying activity, or to serve particular plant and machinery used for such purposes, are included in list C at CAA 2001, s. 23. As such, they may qualify as plant even though affixed to a building.

The legislation therefore recognises a distinction between mains services on the one hand, and gas systems on the other. In some cases, it may also be appropriate to consider the rules for **Alterations to buildings**.

It will also be necessary to distinguish between trade-specific gas systems as above and another category that will need to be classified as "integral features". The latter category (still eligible for **Annual investment allowances** but otherwise attracting writing-down allowances only at the lower "special rate") will encompass any "space or water heating system, a powered system of ventilation, air cooling or air purification, and any floor or ceiling comprised in such a system". By contrast, a restaurant that installs an oven can claim the installation cost as part of the cost of the oven, attracting standard rate allowances.

If an item falls into both categories, the HMRC view seems to be that it must be treated as an integral feature. As such, a gas central heating system would be covered by the integral features rules, whereas a gas driven turbine that was specific to the needs of the trade would qualify for standard rate capital allowances.

If it is necessary to consider whether a gas system is a "single entity" or whether allowances should be given on the basis of dividing it into its constituent parts, readers should refer to **Electrical installations and equipment** above. The point was considered in the *Cole Brothers* case.

Law: CAA 2001, s. 21 (list A, item 2), s. 23 (list C, item 2), s. 25
Case: *Cole Brothers Ltd v Phillips* [1982] BTC 208
Guidance: CA 21170

G4   Gates

The starting point is that gates do not qualify as plant or machinery. List A at s. 21 includes, as one category of assets treated as buildings, "walls, floors, ceilings, doors, gates, shutters, windows and stairs".

List B at s. 22 contains a further exclusion, in a more specific context. This is for "a dam, reservoir or barrage, including any sluices, gates, generators and other equipment associated with the dam, reservoir or barrage".

Such restrictions are subject to the relieving provisions of s. 23. It is possible that a claim for gates will be allowed if they constitute machinery (item 1 at list C), if they are decorative assets in the context of a hotel or similar trade (item 14), if they form part of a dry dock (item 23) or under various other possible provisions. The item 1 and item 14 exceptions would be subject to any HMRC argument that the principal purpose of the gates is to enclose the interior of a building (see s. 23(4)). The author's view is that such an argument would fail, as the principal purpose of the gate is not to enclose the interior but precisely to break through the enclosing exterior so as to allow ingress and egress.

CA 21230, based on the Revenue's earlier *Football League* letter (see **Appendix 2**), indicates that automatic exit doors and gates at a football ground "would normally qualify as plant or machinery". As machinery, such items would normally qualify in any other environment as well.

Law: CAA 2001, s. 21 (list A, item 1), s. 22 (list B, item 4), s. 23 (list C, various items)
Guidance: CA 21230

G5   Gazebos

The question of whether a gazebo in a pub garden was an item of plant was considered in the recent case of *Andrew*. The taxpayer was successful in the claim but various particular facts influenced the outcome and it does not follow that a gazebo would qualify in all circumstances. The arguments, and the reasoning of the Tribunal, were clear, so the case provides a useful precedent.

The argument essentially turned on whether the gazebo merely formed part of the *premises in which* the pub trade was conducted, or whether it could properly be described as *apparatus with which* the trade was conducted.

HMRC argued that the gazebo was part of the premises, and relied on the reasoning of *Fitch's Garage* and of *St John's School*. For the taxpayer, it was argued that the gazebo provided seating to which the covering was incidental. It was "a movable piece of wood garden furniture purchased as a decorative asset for the enjoyment of customers who may sit there to enjoy the views of the South Downs".

The Tribunal considered whether the gazebo was caught by s. 22 by virtue of being a "structure". However, s. 22(3) defines a structure as a "fixed structure of any kind". The Tribunal found as a fact that it was not a fixed structure as "it could be moved and looking at it gave the impression that it could be moved". As it provided only limited shelter or security, it was not properly described as a building either. The reasoning of the Tribunal was then as follows:

> "25. We have no doubt that if the gazebo was simply a polygonal bench surrounding a table then it would be plant: it would be a permanent asset provided for the comfort of customers during their stay in the pub and such provision would be a function of the conduct of the pub trade. It would not matter whether the bench were used or intended to be used by customers to sit, eat, read, talk, wait, or smoke: its provision would be part of the way the publican discharged the function of his trade, and it would not have been premises in which they were conducted.
>
> 26. If on the other hand the gazebo was simply a fixed roof on pillars to which customers could resort to smoke outside the

pub building it would seem more likely that it could properly be described as part of the premises within which the customer is given licence to put himself where the giving of such licence was part of the trade. In such a case the gazebo, like the roof of the pub, is housing to which customers are given access rather than some further benefit or comfort whose provision is part of the publican's trading function."

After considering the issue in this way, the Tribunal reached its conclusion as follows:

"On this basis we conclude that the gazebo is plant: it does not look like part of the garden, rather it looks as if it rests upon it; it is attached simply by its own weight and not in any permanent way; without it the gardens of the pub would still be complete; it is movable and possibly may be moved; it provides some shelter but remains open on all sides to wind and some rain. Overall the gazebo looks to us more like an embellishment of the garden, and, rather than something which simply performs the function of housing the business, it provides facilities for its customers to sit and eat and drink."

The Tribunal went on to make the following important distinction:

"This is not saying that, because the gazebo performs another function as well as housing, it is plant – that approach was eschewed by the Court of Appeal in *Wimpy*, rather it is saying that regarded as a whole it is more appropriate to call it apparatus than to call it premises."

The case was distinguished from *Fitch's Garage* on the basis that the gazebo did not simply house the delivery of food but provided services that were a function of the business.

As the gazebo was considered to be neither a building nor a (fixed) structure, it was not necessary to consider whether or not it was a decorative asset. Nevertheless, the Tribunal noted its view that it would be wrong to describe the gazebo as such. The Tribunal left open the question of whether – if the gazebo had been more correctly described as a building – it would have been right to exempt it under the category of "moveable buildings intended to be moved in the course of the qualifying activity".

At the time of updating this text in 2018, the HMRC manuals remain silent on the question of whether or when they will accept that a gazebo qualifies as plant.

Law: CAA 2001, s. 21-23
Case: *Andrew v HMRC* [2010] UKFTT 546 (TC)

G6   Generators

It is thought that generators used for the purposes of a qualifying activity will almost invariably qualify as plant or machinery.

There is a statutory restriction preventing allowances for "a dam, reservoir or barrage, including any sluices, gates, generators and other equipment associated with the dam, reservoir or barrage" (list B, item 4 at s. 22). However, the inclusion of generators in the list seems pointless, given that generators are surely machines and are therefore exempted by virtue of item 1 in list C at s. 23. It then becomes necessary to consider the tax treatment on normal case law principles and the cost of a generator will thus qualify for allowances.

The only possible exception would seem to be if it were impossible to quantify the particular proportion of an overall cost of building a dam etc. that related to the generator.

If a generator forms part of a general electrical or lighting system, it will need to be treated as special rate expenditure by virtue of the rules for integral features. (Before the introduction of those rules, HMRC accepted that allowances were due for "a standby generator and the emergency lighting and power circuits it services".)

Law: CAA 2001, s. 22 (list B, item 4), s. 23 (list C, item 1), s. 33A
Guidance: CA 21180

G7   Golf courses

In the context of the now repealed rules for industrial buildings allowances, HMRC took the view that a golf course was not a structure (and that it could not therefore qualify for IBAs):

> "Land which retains its character as land is not a structure, even if it has been cultivated or modified in some way. For

example, grass tennis courts, grass football pitches, grass bowling greens and golf courses are not structures."

Nevertheless, it seems unlikely that there could ever be a successful claim that an entire golf course would constitute an item of plant. On ordinary principles, the course would be treated as the premises on which a game is played rather than the apparatus used for playing it.

A claim was made in the *Family Golf* case that the cost of new putting greens should qualify as plant. The special commissioner did not accept the argument, though, and concluded that the greens were part of the place whereon the taxpayer's trade was carried on. The greens were an important adjunct to the carrying on of the business, but so was the rest of the golf course. The course would be incomplete without the greens, and the fact that they could be separately identified was not material.

The treatment of a "crazy golf" course might well be different. Many of the individual obstacles placed on the course would seem to qualify without any problem and it is conceivable that a claim could be justified for the entire cost of the course. The facts about the underlying land and the nature of the course will be crucial in determining the decision.

Taking a wider perspective, every golf club will have qualifying expenditure on particular parts of the whole. The club house will contain both integral features (e.g. general electrics, heating, water) and standard plant and machinery (e.g. toilets, basins, driers). The pro shop will again have a wide range of qualifying expenditure. Outside, claims may be possible for irrigation costs, external lighting and more.

Synthetic turf

In a very different tax context, the treatment of synthetic grass used for golf was considered in some depth in the Customs Duty case of *Huxley v HMRC*. The technical issue was whether the assets in question should be classified as "other golf equipment" (as argued by the taxpayer) or as "carpets and other textile floor coverings" (according to the HMRC view).

According to HMRC, "a playing surface for golf cannot properly be described as being part of the equipment". Again, "the equipment needed for golf is golf balls and golf clubs. It cannot be said that grass is equipment for golf, nor is artificial turf."

The taxpayers countered this view, as follows:

> "HMRC say natural grass is not gold equipment and, therefore, synthetic grass is not golf equipment. However, natural grass is not generally regarded as equipment because it is [a] natural thing and because of its associated objective characteristics ... and not because it is a surface."

Care is needed in applying the very different principles of Customs Duty in a corporation tax or income tax context for capital allowances purposes. However, the conclusion of the Tribunal was that the products in question could mostly be classified as other golf equipment. One particular principle enunciated by the Tribunal was as follows:

> "That the products are used in place of natural grass does not in our view mean that they should be categorized in the same way as natural grass."

The Tribunal also had "some difficulty" in seeing that the products were "floor coverings".

Cases: *Family Golf Centres Ltd v Thorne* (HMIT) (1998) Sp C 150; *Huxley (UK) Ltd v HMRC* [2016] UKFTT 606 (TC)
Guidance: CA 31110

G8   Goodwill

No capital allowances are available for the cost of goodwill. Goodwill is not plant or machinery, and does not fall within any of the other categories of expenditure for which allowances can be given.

HMRC define goodwill quite widely, for example to include a **Customer list** (other than the probably negligible costs that relate to the physical provision of the list itself).

Guidance: CA 10020, 21210

G9   Grain silos

In statutory terms, a grain silo is almost certainly a structure, such that no allowances would normally be due. However, list C at s. 23 includes, at item 28, an exemption for "silos provided for temporary storage". This allows such assets to be considered on the basis of normal case law principles.

HMRC guidance to Revenue staff reads as follows (with one minor correction):

> "Treat a grain silo as plant where, together with its attendant machinery, it performs a function in distributing the grain so that [it] acts as a transit silo rather than a warehouse."

This is based on the *Schofield v Hall* case, where a grain silo was held to be an item of plant or machinery on the grounds that it functioned as apparatus within the trade. The factual summary referred to the function played by the silos "of reception and distribution, cooling and turning over, and, if necessary, fumigation, in connection with the Company's trade of grain importing". The commissioners also noted that "storage played only a trifling part".

In the Court of Appeal, Lowry C J commented:

> "I have no difficulty in comparing the silo with a series of mechanically operated hoppers so placed and constructed as to facilitate with the aid of gravity the rapid reception, distribution and discharge of grain. The silos, with their operating crews, in fact take the place of very large numbers of men equipped with sacks, shovels and bogeys and occupied in transferring grain from the holds of ships to the holds of other ships and to lorries. I cannot see why, in order to qualify as plant, a structure must be seen to replace other plant as distinct from superseding manual effort."

So the only case law found that a grain silo qualified as plant or machinery. Nevertheless, it is probably fair to see it as a borderline decision. Given the statutory framework that has come into place since the decision was heard, a silo would now qualify only if it meets the "temporary storage" condition (or somehow falls within one of the other exemptions at s. 23).

Law: CAA 2001, s. 22 (list B, item 7), s. 23 (list C, item 28)
Case: *Schofield v R & H Hall Ltd* (1975) 49 TC 538
Guidance: CA 22050

G10   Green technology

Green technology is obviously a growing category of expenditure and is considered in this book under numerous different headings.

The inconsistent tax treatment was brought out in a question and written answer in Parliament on 1 December 2017. The Exchequer Secretary, Andrew Jones, was asked about the capital allowances treatment of various specific types of technology, and replied as follows:

> "Capital Allowances are tax reliefs available for qualifying expenditure by businesses which comply with the conditions of the schemes.
>
> The rate of Capital Allowances available for:
>
> (a)   Solar power is 8%
>
> (b)   Gas CHP is 100%
>
> (c)   Solar thermal is 100%
>
> (d)   Battery storage technologies is 18%
>
> (e)   Biomass boilers is either 100% or 18%
>
> (f)   Heat pumps is 100%."

Guidance: www.theyworkforyou.com/wrans/?id=2017-11-23.115 378.h

G11   Greenhouses

The HMRC view is that "most glasshouses are not plant or machinery". By way of support for this assertion, HMRC refer to the *Seymours* case, in which "a planteria, which was effectively an unheated glasshouse, was held not to be plant".

A greenhouse is almost certainly a building or structure. A very small greenhouse might possibly escape that definition if it is not a "fixed structure" (per s. 22(3)(a)).

There is an exemption from the statutory restriction for "any glasshouse constructed so that the required environment (namely, air, heat, light, irrigation and temperature) for the growing of plants is provided automatically by means of devices forming an integral part of its structure" (list C, item 17). HMRC have provided detailed guidance on how they apply that provision, as follows:

Accept that a glasshouse and its attendant machinery are inter-dependent and form a single entity which functions as plant in a grower's business if the following conditions are satisfied:

"(1)   The structure and the equipment were designed as one unit to operate as a single entity.

(2)   It incorporates extensive computer controlled equipment, without which the structure cannot operate to achieve the optimum artificial growing environment for the particular crops involved.

(3)   The equipment was permanently installed during the construction of the glasshouse.

(4)   The equipment includes computer systems which control:

- boiler and piped heating systems,
- temperature and humidity controls,
- automatic ventilation equipment,
- automatic thermal screens or shade screens."

The idea that the equipment should be "computer controlled" is an HMRC interpretation of the rules, but the statutory requirement is merely that the growing environment should be "provided automatically by means of devices forming an integral part of its structure".

HMRC list the types of equipment that are likely to qualify, including:

- "equipment for carbon dioxide enrichment of the glasshouse atmosphere (for example for tomatoes or cucumbers),
- hydroponic culture (for tomatoes and capsicums),

- mobile benching or transport tables (for pot plant production),
- lighting to control day length or to supplement natural light (for pot and cut chrysanthemums and plant propagators)".

In practice, HMRC take the view that "a glasshouse that qualifies as plant is likely to be used for year round growing of high value crops".

Back in 1998, HMRC published details of an agreement that had been negotiated with the National Farmers' Union (NFU). The text featured in a *Tax Bulletin* of June 1998 but there is still (at the time of writing in 2018) a reference to it in the HMRC manuals:

> "An agreement was made with the NFU that sophisticated greenhouses, which qualify for allowances as machinery and plant ... are not long-life assets. It says that such glasshouses built to current designs have a useful economic life not exceeding 25 years and will not therefore be long-life assets for the purposes of Capital Allowances. The agreement includes only expenditure incurred up to 31 December 2005 because designs and technology will not stand still. If glasshouses are developed before then that have a useful economic life exceeding 25 years, they will necessarily be outside this agreement."

Law: CAA 2001, s. 23 (list C, item 17)
Case: *Gray v Seymours Garden Centre (Horticulture)* [1995] BTC 320
Guidance: CA 22090, 23785

G12   Greywater recovery and reuse equipment

This is one of the technology classes specified in the water technology criteria list. As such, the equipment may qualify for first-year allowances as **Environmentally beneficial technology** when all necessary conditions are met, as explained in that section.

According to the official website:

> "Greywater recovery and reuse equipment is purpose-designed equipment containing one or more treatment processes with associated storage, pumping and control

systems that accept and treats greywater from baths, showers, washbasins or laundry. After appropriate treatment, greywater may be used for purposes that do not require water of potable water quality, such as toilet flushing, garden watering or laundry use."

Currently, there is just one type of equipment that may qualify under this heading, namely "standardised greywater recovery and reuse units". These are described on the official site as follows:

"Standardised greywater recovery and reuse units are packaged and/or site-assembled domestic greywater treatment equipment, where all prefabricated components are factory or site-assembled by one manufacturer and tested as a single unit. This does not include bespoke greywater systems or individual components of systems."

Law: CAA 2001, s. 45H; SI 2003/2076, art. 3(2)(h)
Guidance: wtl.defra.gov.uk/product_search_landing.asp

G13   Guns

In a capital gains tax context, HMRC have accepted that guns are machinery. Applying a dictionary definition of machinery as "an apparatus for applying mechanical power, consisting of a number of interrelated parts, each having a definite function", HMRC guidance now in the *Capital Gains* manual continues as follows:

"In our article in Tax Bulletin Issue 13, October 1994, we set out our views on the various types of asset which we regard as "machinery" and those included antique clocks. However, in our view there has to be a subtle difference between clocks and shotguns. Once you have wound up a clock, it continues to tick more than once, whereas with a shotgun once you have pulled the trigger, you only get one discharge out of the barrel. That said, we accept that you then have to go on and consider what happens if you have an automatic weapon or machine gun which effectively fires continuously.

While we take the view that the matter is not free from doubt, we would generally accept the argument that all types of gun should be treated together under the general description of 'machinery' ... ."

Guidance: CG 76905

G14   Guttering

It is thought that gutters will normally be excluded from a claim for plant or machinery allowances, being assets that form part of a building.

HMRC do accept, however, that allowances will be due for "gutters and associated piping for carrying rain water harvested for business uses".

Guidance: R&C Brief 03/10 (see **Appendix 4**)

G15   Gymnasium

In *St John's School*, a gymnasium and a school laboratory were held not to be plant; neither the laboratory nor the gymnasium had any function to perform other than to shelter the pupils. As such, the building was "only the structure within which the function of educating the boys was carried on".

Law: CAA 2001, s. 21
Case: *St. John's School (Mountford and Another) v Ward* (1974) 49 TC 524

H1   Hand dryers

These commonly found items will qualify for plant and machinery allowances in all normal circumstances.

In some cases, high speed hand dryers, as widely used in public and office washrooms, will attract 100 per cent first-year allowances under the scheme for **Enhanced capital allowances** (ECAs).

The official ECAs guidance includes the following description:

"High speed hand air dryers are products that are specifically designed to dry human hands by moving air past the hands in a manner that removes water from the hands by physical displacement and/or evaporation."

The guidance goes on to give the following technology description:

> "They use an electric blower to produce one or more jets of air that are used to dry hands placed under, or into, the hand air dryer unit. Some models heat the air jets prior to use with electrical heating elements or by passing it over the electric motor that drives the blower."

Investments in these devices will only attract ECAs if the specific product is named on the energy technology product list, having satisfied the eligibility criteria.

Law: SI 2018/268, art. 3(2)(g)

Guidance: https://www.gov.uk/energy-technology-list

H2   Hand rails

HMRC accept in principle that hand rails qualify as plant and machinery. In the document relating to the implementation of the provisions of the *Disability Discrimination Act*, HMRC wrote as follows:

> "Where businesses replace existing handrails with special handrails to ease access for disabled people, the expenditure would normally be accepted as a repair and would be deductible in full.
>
> Where new handrails are installed for the specific purpose of helping customers with mobility impairments, the cost would constitute capital expenditure but would qualify for PMAs."

In the reorganisation of the HMRC website, this appears to have been removed but there is no reason of principle as to why these principles would no longer apply.

H3   Hanging rails

These were accepted as plant in *Cadogan Gardens*, in the context of a hotel.

Case: *Lupton v Cadogan Gardens Developments Limited* (1971) 47 TC 1

H4   Harbours, wharfs, piers, marinas, jetties

Harbours are included in list B at s. 22, alongside a range of similar assets ("a dock, harbour, wharf, pier, marina or jetty or any other structure in or at which vessels may be kept, or merchandise or passengers may be shipped or unshipped").

As such, harbours are in principle excluded from the definition of plant and machinery and no allowances are due. HMRC guidance confirms that plant and machinery allowances will not be given "on the provision, construction or acquisition" of such assets.

There is an exception, however, given at item 24 in list C at s. 23. This is for "the provision of any jetty or similar structure provided mainly to carry plant or machinery". Inclusion in this list does not guarantee that such assets will qualify for plant and machinery allowances but the point can be considered on ordinary case law principles.

The scope of the restriction must be carefully considered. In a real case run by one of the authors of this book (Jake Iles of Six Forward), around £1.7 million had been spent on – in broad terms – a new marina. More detailed analysis revealed, however, that this included around £500,000 on floating pontoons, attached to piles in the marina. In accordance with clear HMRC guidelines (see **Pontoons**), it was possible to claim allowances for this substantial element of the overall expenditure, as well as a further £300,000 for other identifiable elements of plant and machinery.

See also **Docks (including dry docks)** above.

Law: CAA 2001, s. 22 (list B, item 5), s. 23 (list C, item 24)
Guidance: CA 22020

H5   Hard standings

"Hard standings" are included in list B at s. 22 (alongside such related items as roads, vehicle parks, etc.). As such, they are excluded from the definition of plant and machinery and no allowances are due.

HMRC guidance confirms that plant and machinery allowances will not be given "on the provision, construction or acquisition" of such assets.

Law: CAA 2001, s. 22 (list B, item 2)
Guidance: CA 22020

H6   Hearses and funeral vehicles

Particular issues arise in relation to vehicles owned by those working in the funeral business. The vehicles are undoubtedly plant, so there is no doubt that allowances are due, but it is not so easy to determine whether the vehicles constitute cars.

This will affect, for example, the question of whether annual investment allowances (AIAs) are available (see, generally, **Cars**). It will also determine whether or not writing-down allowances have to be given at the special rate, rather than the standard rate. The amounts of money involved can be significant, as both hearses and limousines can cost well over £100,000 per vehicle.

As far as hearses are concerned, the author's view is that these fall clearly outside the definition of "car". A hearse is not of a type commonly used as a private vehicle and it is also unsuitable for such use. As a result, it would appear to qualify for AIAs without too much debate. Furthermore, if AIAs are for any reason unavailable, any writing-down allowances should be given at the standard rate.

The treatment of funeral limousines is less clear cut. It might once more be argued that these are not of a type commonly used as private vehicles, but are they unsuitable for such use? (Both tests must be met if AIAs are to be given.) Assuming that the proprietors of the business do not in fact use the vehicle for any private purpose, it might be hoped that HMRC would take a reasonable line in the context of a funeral business.

The suitability argument would turn mainly on cost and practicality. The fuel consumption is obviously very poor, though that in itself is not a strong argument as the same could be said of many vehicles that are undoubtedly used privately. A weightier argument is perhaps that the vehicle would simply be too long for many day-to-day purposes. If there are any particular features built into the design, they may also help to take the vehicle over the line so that it falls outside the definition of "car" for capital allowances purposes.

If the owner wishes to claim AIAs – or standard rate writing-down allowances – for the cost of a funeral limousine, it will be advisable to include a full disclosure of the nature of the vehicle, thus protecting against a possible discovery assessment, should HMRC take a different view.

Law: CAA 2001, s. 38B, 45D, 46(2), 104AA, 268A

H7   Heat pumps

Heat pumps transfer heat from external sources, normally air or water or underground. Such equipment will qualify for plant and machinery allowances in all normal circumstances. In some cases, the equipment will attract 100 per cent first-year allowances under the scheme for **Enhanced capital allowances** (ECAs). According to the official ECA site:

> "In many applications, heat pumps offer a more efficient way to provide heat. They are particularly useful in areas with no natural gas supply or where only low levels of heat are needed, such as underfloor systems."

The following categories of equipment are specified for the purposes of claiming ECAs. As a general rule, investments in these devices will only attract ECAs if the specific product is named on the energy technology product list, having satisfied the eligibility criteria. Variations of this rule are indicated under the appropriate headings below. The quotations are all taken from the official ECAs guidance or from the energy technology criteria list.

Air source: air to water heat pumps

The descriptive wording from the energy technology criteria list (as revised in 2016) is as follows:

> "An air to water heat pump uses an electrically driven refrigeration system to transfer heat from outside air into a water-based heating system. They can be used to provide space heating in a wide range of buildings, and some products also are able to provide heat to deliver domestic hot water

and /or cooling by reversing the refrigerant flows around the product."

Air source: gas engine driven split and multi-split heat pumps

The details of this sub-category were revised in 2018.

"Air-source gas engine driven (GED) split and multi-split heat pumps use a gas-fired internal combustion engine driven refrigeration system to transfer heat from air outside a building to the air inside it. They can be used to provide space heating in a wide range of buildings, and some products also are able to provide cooling by reversing the refrigeration flows around the product. (These products are known as reversible gas engine driven 'air-cooled' air conditioning units)."

Air source: packaged heat pumps

The descriptive wording from the energy technology criteria list (as revised in 2016) is as follows:

"Air source packaged heat pumps use an electrically operated refrigeration system to transfer heat from air outside a building to the air inside it. They can be used to provide space heating in a wide range of buildings, and some products also are able to provide cooling by reversing the refrigeration flows around the product. (These products are known as reversible 'air-cooled' air conditioning units)."

The guidance also includes the following additional information:

"Air source heat pumps are products that are specifically designed to transfer heat from the air in one space to the air into another space by means of a refrigeration cycle."

'Packaged' type heat pumps are single factory assembled units that incorporate all the elements of the refrigeration system and air distribution mechanisms for space heating."

Air source: split and multi-split heat pumps

"Multi-split units consist of an outdoor unit connected to one or more indoor units and transfer heat from the outdoor air to the space being heated. The system can also be designed to run in reverse, providing low-energy cooling."

Ground source and surface water source heat pumps

This category was formerly (until 2016) known as "ground source brine to water heat pumps".

"Ground source and surface water source brine/water to water heat pumps use an electrically operated refrigeration system to transfer heat from the ground or surface water into a water-based heating system. They can be used to provide space heating in a wide range of buildings, and some products may be also able to provide cooling by reversing the refrigerant flows around the product."

The following fuller descriptions are given on the energy technology criteria list:

"Ground source heat pump systems are specifically designed to transfer heat from the ground to a water-based heating system by means of a refrigeration cycle.

Surface water heat pump systems are specifically designed to transfer heat from surface water to a water-based heating system by means of a refrigeration cycle.

In a brine to water heat pump, the heat is collected from the ground or surface water by circulating a solution of water and anti-freeze (known as 'brine') through a buried or submerged, closed-loop, ground heat exchanger.

In a water to water heat pump, the heat is collected from ground water (aquifer) or surface water by circulating the water through a direct, open-loop heat exchanger."

Heat pumps for domestic hot water heating

This category was formerly (until 2016) known as "CO2 heat pumps for domestic hot water".

"Heat pumps for domestic hot water heating are products that are specifically designed to transfer heat from the ambient air, ground, or water into a system for heating domestic hot water by means of a refrigeration cycle."

Heat pump dehumidifiers

The following description is given on the energy technology criteria list:

> "Heat pump dehumidifiers are widely used to improve personal comfort, to protect building fabric and stored goods or materials, and to dry industrial products. They work by circulating the moist air over the evaporator of the refrigeration system. This reduces the temperature of the air, which causes the water vapour to condense. The resulting condensate can be then drained away."

Heat pump driven air curtains

> "Heat Pump Driven Air Curtains are products that are specifically designed to be fitted above a doorway or similar opening, and to produce an air curtain that is specifically designed to reduce the infiltration or transfer of air from one space to another, and that is heated and/or cooled by a heat pump that transfers heat by means of a refrigeration cycle."

The following fuller descriptions are given on the energy technology criteria list:

> "Air curtain heaters are used to reduce losses by disrupting the natural convection between two adjacent areas, or spaces, in a building that are at differing temperatures thereby reducing the amount of heating or cooling needed to maintain the temperature of a space. They are typically used in commercial premises for situations where an open door is required to allow uninterrupted access or where traffic through the doorway is so high that the door is open for extended periods.
>
> Heat pump driven air curtains use a heat pump to heat or cool the air curtain expelled by the product. This reduces the need to heat the air with electricity or heat derived from other fuels."

Water source: split and multi-split heat pumps

> "Multi-split units consist of an outdoor unit connected to one or more indoor units and transfer heat from the outdoor air to

the space being heated. The system can also be designed to run in reverse, providing low-energy cooling."

The following fuller descriptions are given on the energy technology criteria list:

"Water source heat pumps are products that are specifically designed to transfer heat from water (in an internal water loop) into the air within the space to be heated by means of a refrigeration cycle.

Water source split and multi-split heat pumps use an electrically operated refrigeration system to transfer heat from an internal water loop into the air within the space to be heated. They can be used to provide space heating in a wide range of buildings, and some products also are able to provide cooling by reversing the refrigeration flows around the product."

According to the official criteria list, investments in water source split and multi-split (including variable refrigerant flow) heat pumps only qualify for ECAs if the specific product identified by the outdoor unit and the matching indoor unit(s) is named in the ETL Heat Pump Master List, having met some qualifying criteria that are more complex than for other products.

Law: SI 2018/268, art. 3(2)(e)

Guidance: https://www.gov.uk/energy-technology-list

H8   Heating, ventilation and air conditioning equipment

These items will qualify for plant and machinery allowances in all normal circumstances. This will include boilers and boiler flues, radiators, circulating pumps, supply and return pipework, convector heaters, and so on.

Heating, ventilation and air conditioning (HVAC) zone controls will attract 100 per cent first-year allowances under the scheme for **Enhanced capital allowances** (ECAs), where the relevant conditions are met. The individual items must be included on the energy technology product list.

According to the official ECAs guidance:

> "Heating, ventilation and air conditioning (HVAC) systems control the temperature, humidity and quality of air in buildings to a set of chosen conditions. To achieve this, the systems need to transfer heat and moisture into and out of the air as well as control the level of air pollutants either by directly removing them or by diluting them to acceptable levels.
>
> By considering HVAC systems as individual elements rather than as an interacting system, it would be easy to overlook a major area of energy wastage that one component might impact on another. For example, it would be wasteful to increase heating inside a building whilst the cooling system is fighting to reduce temperatures. It is therefore useful to look at how each element of an HVAC system complements the other and fine tune each part to save energy and money."

Four categories of product are covered, as below. In each case, the descriptive wording is taken from the official ECA site and/or from the energy technology criteria list.

Active chilled beams

This category was added in 2014 and revised in 2015.

> "Active chilled beams incorporate an integral (primary) air supply and cooling coil(s) to provide cooled air into occupied spaces without the use of an integral fan, in order to achieve comfortable working conditions. The primary air supply enhances and controls the induction of air from the occupied space through the cooling coil."

Building environment zone controls

> "Building Environment Zone Controls (formerly known as HVAC controls) can help a company save energy by matching actual demand to the operational requirement in each zone."

Close control air conditioning

> "Close control air conditioning equipment is used to control temperature (and optionally humidity) in rooms and

enclosures containing heat generating equipment, such as servers, computers or telecommunications devices, and in some types of manufacturing process (e.g. clean rooms). The equipment typically operates continuously and has a much higher unit floor area cooling load requirement than conventional air conditioning."

Evaporative air coolers

This category was added in 2018. The scheme covers both direct and indirect coolers.

"An evaporative air cooler is a device that cools air through the evaporation of water."

"Evaporative air coolers can be direct or indirect. With direct evaporative air cooling, outside air is blown through a water-saturated medium and cooled by evaporation. The cooled air is circulated by a fan. With indirect evaporative air cooling, a secondary air stream is cooled by water. The cooled secondary air stream passes through a heat exchanger, where it cools the primary air stream. The cooled primary air stream is circulated by a fan."

See also Air conditioning systems.

Law: SI 2018/268, art. 3(2)(f)
Guidance: https://www.gov.uk/energy-technology-list

H9   Hoists and associated structures

Hoists are included in list C at CAA 2001, s. 23, both specifically and as falling within the general category of machinery. They clearly fall within the definition of plant and machinery in normal circumstances.

The structure within which a hoist operates will not normally qualify. List A at s. 21 includes "shafts or other structures in which lifts, hoists, escalators and moving walkways are installed".

However, allowances will normally be due for the cost of a structure containing a hoist where installed in an existing building. The treatment is analogous to that of **Lifts and lift shafts** and is considered in depth under that heading.

Law: CAA 2001, s. 21 (list A, item 5), s. 23 (list C, items 1, 6)
Guidance: CA 21190

H10   Horses

HMRC accept in principle that a horse may be plant for capital allowances purposes, on the basis that the animal may function as apparatus with which the trade is carried on. This would be the case, for example, if the horse is used for the purposes of a riding school.

The earliest case law on the meaning of plant, *Yarmouth v France*, confirmed that a cart-horse was properly treated as plant, being part of the "goods and chattels, fixed or moveable, live or dead" kept for permanent employment in the business.

The treatment of farm animals in general, where the creatures are kept as trading stock, is considered under **Animals** above.

Case: *Yarmouth v France* [1887] 4 TRL 1
Guidance: CA 21220

H11   Hot and cold water systems

These will now almost invariably qualify as integral features. Qualifying costs will include boilers, circulating pumps, calorifiers, pipework, etc.

The starting point is still that "mains services, and systems, for water, electricity and gas" are among the categories of assets that are statutorily treated as being buildings (list A, item 2). Without other provisions, such items would therefore fail to qualify as plant and machinery.

By virtue of s. 23 and s. 33A, the bar on claiming allowances is removed. The definition of "integral features" includes "a cold water system" and also "a space or however, water heating system". The whole of the plumbing system in a property can therefore qualify for plant and machinery allowances at the lower ("special") rate applying for integral features.

There is no statutory definition of "cold water system" but HMRC say that:

> "the term takes its ordinary meaning: a system for taking water from the point of entry to the building or structure and distributing it through the building or structure, as required".

To the extent that an item falls within list C at s. 23, it may be possible to claim allowances in the main pool. The former reference to space or water heating systems in list C has been removed. The list still includes, however, gas systems provided mainly to meet the particular requirements of the qualifying activity and also gas systems that are provided mainly to serve particular plant or machinery used for the purposes of the qualifying activity.

This raises the possibility that a claim might be possible for allowances at the standard rate. The HMRC view is that the integral features rules always take priority (see, for example, the wording at CA 22330) but it seems to the author that this is not clear cut. The point is discussed more fully under **Lifts and lift shafts**.

HMRC make it clear that the integral features rules would not necessarily apply to water industry undertakings:

> "The inclusion of cold water and electrical systems in the classification of integral features of a building or structure does not mean, for example, that the water processing and supply systems of the water industry, or the electricity generating and supply systems of an electricity undertaking, count as the cold water or electrical system respectively, 'of a building or structure'."

Some such assets will now qualify for first-year allowances if they constitute **Environmentally beneficial technology**. According to HMRC:

> "many businesses may now be able to claim 100 per cent first-year allowances (FYAs), when their expenditure on these systems includes specific items on the 'Green Technology' ECA list".

Law: CAA 2001, s. 21 (list A, item 2), s. 23 (list C, items 2, 3), s. 33A; SI 2003/2076, art. 3

Guidance: CA 21200, 22310-22330

H12   Human body

Unlike animals, the human body cannot qualify as plant or machinery. As Lord Greene put it in *Norman v Golder*:

> "Your own body is not plant ... I have never heard it suggested by anybody that the taxpayer's own body could be regarded as plant. In fact the point has only, I think, to be stated."

The decision would override, for UK tax purposes, the case of an Egyptian belly dancer who won her case for tax relief on her belly on the grounds that it was a depreciating asset. It was argued that "a belly is plant and equipment used by the taxpayer to carry on business".

Case: *Norman v Golder* (1945) 26 TC 293

Guidance: www.independent.co.uk/news/business/people-business-1162806.html

I1   Industrial cleaning equipment

"Water efficient industrial cleaning equipment" is one of the technology classes specified in the water technology criteria list. Such equipment constitutes plant and machinery and will qualify for first-year allowances as **Environmentally beneficial technology** when all necessary conditions are met, as explained in that section.

According to the official website:

> "Industrial cleaning equipment is often used where it is most suitable to use a dedicated tool due to the scale or nature of the surface to be cleaned. However, cleaning and rinsing processes often use high volumes of water and therefore present a good opportunity for savings."

Three types of equipment may qualify under this heading. In each case, the specific item must be included on the water technology product list.

The three categories of equipment that can qualify are as follows:

- scrubber/driers (walk-behind machines);
- scrubber/driers (ride-on machines);
- steam cleaners.

Where the criteria for first-year allowances are not satisfied, normal principles must be applied. On the face of it, such equipment will qualify as plant and machinery and allowances will be given in the main pool.

Law: CAA 2001, s. 45H; SI 2003/2076, art. 3(2)(m)
Guidance: wtl.defra.gov.uk/product_search_landing.asp

I2   Inland navigation

Inland navigations ("including a canal or basin or a navigable river") are included in list B at s. 22. As such, they are excluded from the definition of plant and machinery and allowances are not due.

HMRC guidance confirms that plant and machinery allowances will not be given "on the provision, construction or acquisition" of such assets.

Law: CAA 2001, s. 22 (list B, item 3)
Guidance: CA 22020

I3   Inspection pits

Car servicing businesses, and a variety of other industries, use inspection pits for examining heavy assets. These can be substantial, measuring several metres in all directions. Some such pits may have removable lids, perhaps of concrete.

On the face of it, such pits are "incorporated into the building" and therefore caught initially by s. 21. If this analysis is correct, allowances can only be due if one of the exceptions in s. 23 is in point. The expenditure is not on integral features, and the other provisions of s. 23(2) do not appear to help. As such, it would be necessary to rely on list C, where the most promising mention is item 4 (manufacturing or processing equipment).

As such, it only seems possible to consider a claim if it can be argued that the pit is part of the company's "manufacturing or processing equipment". If we merely rely on the label, that seems improbable – can a pit really be described as equipment? As so often, however, it may be necessary to search for the underlying reality behind that label. As one reader has kindly pointed out following a site visit:

"I found that the 'inspection pits' where service operatives can stand are in fact pre-fabricated steel troughs which incorporate the steel guides upon which the guide mounted vehicle jack is located. It seems that these pre-formed 'pits' are located in an excavated void and the concrete slab is poured up to the edges, level with the jack guides."

This helpful description makes it easier to justify the conclusion that the steel troughs are part of the processing equipment. Each case will obviously depend on the detail and on its own merits, but it may be possible to argue that the restrictions of section 21 are overcome.

Even if that argument could be sustained, it would still be necessary to consider the matter on ordinary case law principles. In such a case, there would certainly be room for discussion.

In *Barclay Curle*, which concerned a dry dock, Lord Upjohn commented as follows:

"In the old days the garage proprietor would have an inspection pit where his men could examine and repair the underside of a motor car. Nowadays he has a platform on to which the car is run and is then lifted up by mechanical means so that the men can perform the same operation; it fulfils precisely the same function as the old inspection pit. The moving platform is plainly machinery or plant, but then I would think it clear that the inspection pit, equally functional and even more integrated into the garage as a whole, does not qualify as plant for a capital allowance ... ."

In the event, the House of Lords decision about the dry dock was close, but they did find (by a majority of 3-2) that the dock should qualify as an item of plant. Lord Upjohn was therefore in a minority and, in any case, the comments were merely *obiter*, which are therefore not legally binding. Nevertheless, a lower court might take note of what was said and HMRC might certainly wish to refer to these words. It is probably the case, however, that inspection pits today are much more sophisticated than the scenario envisaged by Lord Upjohn, who perhaps had in mind little more than a hole in the ground.

It might be possible to look at the lid as a separate item from the pit itself. As it is removable, it can reasonably be argued that it is not "incorporated in the building". HMRC might still maintain that it is in reality a floor, in which case it will still be caught (by virtue of being "in" the building and within list A) but a case could probably be made that it is not in reality a floor, given its primary use of functioning as a removable cover for the pit.

Law: CAA 2001, s. 21, 23

Case: *CIR v Barclay, Curle & Co Ltd* (1969) 45 TC 221

I4   Integral features

Expenditure on integral features, incurred for the purposes of a qualifying activity, qualifies for plant and machinery allowances. This is still subject to other statutory restrictions (for assets in a dwelling house, for example) but it removes the need to show that the assets in question would qualify as plant or machinery on ordinary case law principles. The rules relating to integral features also override any restrictions in s. 21 (buildings) or s. 22 (structures) (s. 23(1), (2)).

The concept of integral features was introduced in 2008. There were several effects of the rules but two particular features stand out. First, some expenditure that did not previously qualify for allowances is now unambiguously eligible. Second, some expenditure that did previously qualify continues to do so but now only as "special rate" expenditure, which means that writing-down allowances are given at a slower rate.

The statutory definition of integral features currently encompasses five categories of expenditure, as follows:

"(a)   an electrical system (including a lighting system),

(b)   a cold water system,

(c)   a space or water heating system, a powered system of ventilation, air cooling or air purification, and any floor or ceiling comprised in such a system,

(d)   a lift, an escalator or a moving walkway,

(e)   external solar shading."

(Note that the concept of integral features is not synonymous with that of **Special rate expenditure**. To give one example, **Solar**

panels are designated as special rate expenditure but are not integral features.)

Various special rules, beyond the scope and intention of this book, apply in relation to the replacement of integral features.

Integral features may qualify for **Annual investment allowances**, but writing-down allowances are given more slowly than for the main pool. It follows that the question may arise of whether a particular asset has to be classified as an integral feature or whether it may be possible to claim standard rate allowances.

This is usually a straightforward distinction. HMRC accept, for example, that the concept of an "electrical system" does not encompass the specific electrical items that are included in list C at s. 23. So, for example, a burglar alarm system will not be treated as part of the electrical system but, as it is clearly plant or machinery on ordinary principles, it will be eligible for standard rate allowances by virtue of being included as item 11 at list C.

Nevertheless, there are cases where the interaction between the two different parts of the legislation does not seem to be satisfactory. A lift, for example, is clearly machinery but is also listed as one of the classes of integral feature. This is considered in detail under **Lifts and lift shafts** below.

Law: CAA 2001, s. 23, 33A
Guidance: CA 22310, 22330

I5   Invalid carriages

An invalid carriage is treated as a car for capital allowances purposes (but not for the purposes of calculating a benefit in kind, where an additional exemption applies).

Law: *Road Traffic Act* 1988, s. 185(1); CAA 2001, s. 268A
Guidance: CA 22020

J1   Jet aircraft

Jet aircraft will clearly qualify as plant or machinery when used for transporting people or goods for the purposes of a qualifying activity. The question may arise, however, as to whether such aircraft should be treated as long-life assets.

In the past, HMRC took the view that the cost of jet aircraft over a certain size should be treated as long-life expenditure. The HMRC view has been moderated for expenditure incurred from July 2014. The current HMRC guidance includes the following:

> "The useful economic life of a jet aircraft may be more than 25 years depending on how it is used.
>
> Useful economic life of a jet aircraft will depend on the pattern of use by the owner. The owner's own assessment of the likely useful life should be taken into account when considering whether a jet aircraft has a useful economic life of at least 25 years or not.
>
> CA23720 tells you that the definition of useful economic life is the same as that used in accounting standards in certain circumstances. Where an owner of jet aircraft draws up accounts under UK GAAP or IFRS, you should consider their estimate of the useful economic life of new aircraft used in their company and consolidated accounts (if these are different then you should find out why).
>
> If a company's accounting estimate of the useful economic life of the fuselage is at least 25 years then you should treat the jet aircraft as a long life asset.
>
> If a company's estimate of the useful economic life of the fuselage of a new jet aircraft is less than 25 years and the residual value is based on scrap then you should normally accept that the jet aircraft is not a long life asset.
>
> If a company's estimate of residual value of the fuselage is based on a second-hand sale of the aircraft then you should ask for more facts to establish whether it is reasonable to expect that the total useful life (including the use by subsequent owners) of the aircraft is at least 25 years."

Where accounting policies cannot determine the matter, HMRC will look for other evidence, including industry data and regulatory requirements. HMRC will also wish to discuss with the owner any assessments made "of the likely life of the aircraft in use and what is likely to be done with the aircraft after it ceases to be used in the current owner's qualifying activity".

(This guidance was provided to the authors early in 2017 but, at the time of writing, the *Capital Allowances Manual* has not yet been updated to reflect it.)

Law: CAA 2001, s. 91
Guidance: CA 23781*ff.*

K1   Kennels

The question of whether dog kennels are plant was considered in *Carr v Sayer*, which concerned both normal and quarantine kennels. (The case also looked at whether industrial buildings allowances might be available – no longer a relevant consideration.)

The case considered both movable kennels and immovable ones. The former were described as "temporary, movable kennels which are of wooden construction with mesh runs". The immovable ones were "specifically constructed as quarantine kennels and ... permanently fixed to the premises". Finding the former to be plant but the latter not to qualify, the judge explained his reasoning as follows:

> "I recognise that the consequence of this is to draw a stark contrast in the present case between the temporary movable kennels and the permanent immovable kennels. The former are plant, and the latter are not. I do not find this odd. Both perform a similar function, of housing and segregating the animals. But the latter, unlike the former, have been constructed in such a way that they are on the buildings or premises side of the boundary line drawn by the legislation.
>
> I add this, I also recognise that there may be cases where a structure, used for housing animals or birds, is so small or made of such ephemeral materials that, despite being fixed, it will be difficult to see clearly on which side of the boundary line the structure stands. That is not this case. As already noted, the fixed kennels are stoutly made and are of an ordinary single-storey size."

The case predated the statutory rules introduced from 1994 but in the author's opinion, this outcome would remain correct today. The movable kennels were not fixed structures but were plant and machinery. The fixed kennels would be treated as fixed structures and no allowances would be due.

HMRC do not accept that there is anything in list C that would override a finding that a kennel was a fixed structure:

> "The list does not operate by analogy: for example item 33 which refers to fixed zoo cages does not apply to any other form of animal shelter such as kennels or stables."

Law: CAA 2001, s. 22
Case: *Carr v Sayer* [1992] BTC 286
Guidance: CA 22030

K2   Kitchen fittings and worktops

These items will normally qualify as plant without problem, even though the author was advised in 2016 that a Valuation Office surveyor asked why a claim had been made for the kitchen fittings in the staff room of a car dealership.

Although initially barred from qualifying by virtue of s. 21 (as the items in question are incorporated in the building), such assets are clearly rescued from that prohibition by virtue of the categories included at list C at s. 23. Item 4 at list C includes display equipment and also counters, checkouts and similar equipment. Item 5 includes a range of specific kitchen equipment and also includes furniture and furnishings. Other items there may also be relevant. So there is no statutory bar on claiming, and the items in question will then qualify on ordinary case law principles – apparatus used for the business – without any problem.

HMRC guidance at www.gov.uk/capital-allowances/what-you-can-claim-on states that "You can claim for fixtures, eg: fitted kitchens". And the *Capital Allowances Manual* at CA 23084 specifies that typical examples of plant or machinery include various specified items but also "other building fixtures, such as shop fittings, kitchen and bathroom fittings".

In short, claiming for these items should be straightforward and any resistance on the part of HMRC should be robustly countered.

Law: CAA 2001, s. 21, 23
Guidance: CA 23084

K3   Knives and lasts

Knives and lasts have been found by the House of Lords to be plant. One issue to be considered was whether they were durable enough to be so classified. As they had an average life of three years, that test was satisfied. Lord Reid commented:

> "Subject to [that] one point, I have no doubt that these knives and lasts are plant in the ordinary sense of the word. It is true that they are numerous, small and cheap. But one trader may have to use a few large articles while another may have to use a large number of small articles, and I see no good ground for distinguishing between them as regards investment allowance."

HMRC now apply a two year test for plant and machinery, but anything with a shorter life is likely to be deductible as revenue expenditure. Even that two year test may be open to challenge in some circumstances, however, for Lord Jenkins in that same case made the following observation:

> "The upper knives are given a life of only 12 months, but the intention, no doubt, is to keep and use them for so long as they are serviceable, and I cannot regard the circumstance that they wear out in that relatively short period as investing them with so transitory a character as to take them out of the category of plant to which they would otherwise belong."

Case: *Hinton v Maden & Ireland Ltd* (1959) 38 TC 391
Guidance: BIM 35415, CA 21100

L1   Land

The cost of acquiring land can never qualify for plant and machinery allowances (s. 24). For the purposes of that restriction, land does not include buildings or structures. Nor does it include any asset that has become legally part of the land by virtue of being affixed to it.

In view of that piece of legislation, no weight can now be attached – as far as land as such is concerned – to the earlier comments of Lord Templeman in the *Yard Arm* decision, where he stated that land could rank as plant if operating as the means by which a trading operation is carried out.

Buildings and structures are not affected by the restriction of s. 24. Although in principle these are still barred from allowances, by virtue of s. 21 and s. 22 respectively, there are exceptions (such as the dry dock or the grain silo) which can still qualify by virtue of list C and other exceptions at s. 23.

See also **Alteration of land** above.

Law: CAA 2001, s. 21-24
Case: *Benson v The Yard Arm Club Ltd* (1979) 53 TC 67

L2   Land remediation relief

Overview

Land remediation relief – or "relief for expenditure on contaminated or derelict land" to give it its statutory name – is a separate form of tax relief, and not part of the capital allowances regime. It potentially offers relief at 150%, consisting of a standard deduction for the full cost of the expenditure incurred, plus an additional deduction of 50%.

The relief is available for corporation tax only. A claim may not be made by individuals or partnerships, except that a corporate member of a partnership may elect for its share of the qualifying expenditure.

The details of the relief fall outside the remit of this volume. Nevertheless, it is helpful to be aware of the essentials of the relief so that it may be considered alongside any capital allowances claim.

Law: CTA 2009, s. 1147
Guidance: CIRD 60050

Types of expenditure

The relief is typically available for the cost of removing asbestos, radon, arsenic, Japanese knotweed, oil and other fuels, landfill gases, and sulphates. That list is not exhaustive.

Relief is dependent on the remediation work being carried out but, subject to that, may include the cost of measuring the level of contamination in the first place.

A company may surrender a loss in return for a cash payment (tax credit).

Guidance: CIRD 60015

Interaction with capital allowances

No relief is available under the land remediation relief rules if relief has been given, or could be given, by way of capital allowances (whether under the plant or machinery regime or otherwise).

Law: CTA 2009, s. 1147(8)
Guidance: CIRD 60085

L3   Landscaping

Where a new property, such as an office building or a hotel, is constructed, costs are typically incurred on landscaping the area to create a pleasant environment.

These landscaping costs are unlikely to constitute expenditure on plant or machinery, even on ordinary principles. Furthermore, the project is likely to constitute **Alteration of land** and to be disallowed on that basis.

In short, landscaping costs are unlikely to qualify for allowances.

Law: 22(1)(b)

L4   Leakage detection equipment

"Leakage detection equipment" is one of the technology classes specified in the water technology criteria list. As such, the equipment may qualify for first-year allowances as **Environmentally beneficial technology** when all necessary conditions are met, as explained in that section.

Three types of equipment may qualify under this heading. In all cases, the specific item must be included on the water technology product list. The two categories of equipment that can qualify are as follows:

- pressure reducing valve controllers;
- early leak warning devices.

Law: CAA 2001, s. 45H; SI 2003/2076, art. 3(2)(b)
Guidance: wtl.defra.gov.uk/product_search_landing.asp

L5   Letter boxes

Although no allowances are due for doors, there is no guidance on whether or not a letter box should qualify as plant or machinery.

As regards the flap through which letters may be posted, the author's view is that there is a possible analogy with the treatment of door handles, regarding which HMRC have written as follows:

> "A door handle would normally be an integral part of the door to which it is affixed, with the result that it would not qualify for PMAs. Any subsequent replacement of the door handle would then count as a repair of the door. However you should not in practice refuse a PMA claim where this is the treatment adopted in the computations. Some mechanical handles can in any event constitute machines in their own right."

If there is an actual box into which post from outside is dropped through a flap, then there is a somewhat stronger case for arguing that this box is separate from the door and that allowances should be given.

See also **Door furniture.**

Law: CAA 2001, s. 21 (list A, item 1)
Guidance: CA 21200

L6   Lifts and lift shafts

The cost of "a lift, an escalator or a moving walkway" now qualifies for plant and machinery allowances under the rules relating to "integral features". This renders irrelevant the various earlier case law discussions on whether or when lifts or their wiring would qualify as plant or machinery.

It seems possible to argue that the lift can in fact qualify under general principles, thus attracting a faster rate of write-off, on the grounds that a lift is undoubtedly a machine. The statute does not appear to give precedence to one interpretation or the other but as the mention of lifts at s. 33A is so specific, it is thought that a court would take the view that the "integral features" rules take priority.

Certainly, this is the line taken by HMRC who have written to the author as follows:

> "I don't think we would argue with you that a lift is machinery. However we take the view that the legislation is clear that lifts are integral features and expenditure on integral features has to be allocated to the special rate pool.
>
> So in our view the person making the claim does not have a choice, it may be qualifying expenditure on machinery but more specifically it is qualifying expenditure on a lift which is an integral feature and that qualifying expenditure has to be allocated to the special rate pool."

On the other hand, allowances are given for integral features "as if" the expenditure were on plant or machinery (s. 33A(2)). That could be read as suggesting that the integral features rules should apply only to assets that do not already constitute plant or machinery.

HMRC state that expenditure on the provision of wiring for a lift should be treated as part of the cost of the lift itself.

The treatment of a lift shaft is different. This is clearly incorporated in the building and, initially, allowances are thus denied by virtue of s. 21. List A specifically refers to "shafts or other structures in which lifts, hoists, escalators and moving walkways are installed". There is nothing in list C at s. 23 to rescue the expenditure incurred on a lift shaft.

In an existing building, as opposed to one that is being newly built, the cost of a lift shaft will nevertheless be allowed as incidental to the installation of the lift itself (s. 25). The principles are discussed in detail at **Alterations to buildings** above, but HMRC specifically accept the point in relation to lift shafts.

Where allowances are claimed by virtue of s. 25, the capital allowances rules operate as if the incidental expenditure were expenditure on the provision of the plant or machinery. The cost of the lift shaft, where it qualifies by virtue of this provision, is thus treated as part of the cost of the plant or machinery itself. It follows that the cost of the lift shaft will in such a case be treated as expenditure on integral features and will accordingly be allocated to the special rate pool (if indeed that is the way in which the expenditure on the lift itself is treated).

It is debatable whether or not a chair lift falls within the definition of "lift" in this context. A chair lift is clearly machinery, and therefore qualifies for allowances on that basis, but it is not certain

Law: CAA 2001, s. 21 (list A, item 5), s. 25, 33A
Guidance: CA 21190

L7   Lighting

Plant and machinery allowances are available, as integral features, for the whole of "an electrical system (including a lighting system)". This therefore overrules the general restriction for "mains services, and systems, for ... electricity" (s. 21, list A, item 2).

The key issue now is likely to be the rate at which writing-down allowances can be given for lighting costs. There is no statutory definition of "a lighting system" and there may be circumstances in which it could be argued that lighting qualifies in its own right without being part of any lighting system. According to HMRC:

> "An electrical system (including a lighting system) is not defined for the purposes of the legislation, so the term takes its ordinary meaning: a system for taking electrical power (including lighting) from the point of entry to the building or structure, or generation within the building or structure, and distributing it through the building or structure, as required. The system may range from the very simplest to the most complex."

The interaction between the **Integral features** rules and the general rules for giving plant and machinery allowances is not always clear cut: a lift, for example, is clearly machinery and yet is specifically an integral feature. In the case of emergency lighting, it may be possible to argue that it forms part of a fire alarm system. If so, it falls within item 10 of list C at s. 23, and there is an argument that allowances would be due at the standard rate.

If lighting meets the criteria to be classified as **Energy-saving technology**, full first-year allowances may be available. Currently, these can be given for the following categories of expenditure. The descriptive quotations are from the official ECAs website and/or from the energy technology criteria list.

Efficient white lighting units

"Products that are specifically designed to provide efficient, high quality, illumination."

Categories covered include:

- amenity, accent and display lighting units;
- general interior lighting units;
- exterior area lighting units;
- exterior floodlighting units.

These are important assets that are bought by many different types of business, so the following descriptive wording (from the energy technology criteria list) is provided in full to illustrate what each of these headings includes:

- "**Amenity lighting** is decorative lighting intended to enhance the appearance of a building or outdoor area in order to promote the activities of a business. It can include 'mood' lighting of hotels, bars and restaurants and other leisure activities; and decorative lighting for public areas of buildings and parts of buildings or the surrounding grounds (where such lighting is necessary to the enhancement of the business function). It does not include lighting to provide general illumination or circulation, or building lighting that would be present regardless of the type of business being carried out

- **Display lighting** comprises lighting intended to highlight displays of exhibits, merchandise and other associated uses. It includes for instance spot or projector lighting in shops, theatres, galleries and studios

- **Accent lighting** comprises lighting that is intended to provide additional light over a specific small area in order to carry out or promote the activities of a business. This may include lighting required for a particular task (e.g. medical or dental examination, supplementary lighting for fine machining work or critical inspection work). It does not cover general lighting for an entire room or a large part of a room

- **General interior lighting** covers all other interior lighting
- **Exterior area lighting** covers all exterior lighting which is intended to provide downward light onto horizontal or near horizontal surfaces, including roadways, car parks, paths, stairs, ramps, gardens and other open spaces. This includes illuminated bollards and post- top lanterns
- **Exterior floodlighting** covers exterior lighting that is intended to light vertical or near vertical surfaces, including floodlighting of buildings, monuments and statues."

Lighting controls

"Lighting controls manage electric lighting levels within specific areas, as and when required to match changes in daylight or occupancy, or individual activities."

Categories covered include:

- time controllers that automatically switch off lighting, or dim it down, at predetermined times;
- presence detectors with associated controllers that monitor occupancy or movement of personnel, and automatically switch off lighting, or dim it down, when the area is unoccupied;
- daylight detectors with associated switching controllers that monitor daylight availability, and automatically switch off lighting when daylight is sufficient to illuminate the area;
- daylight detectors with associated dimming controllers that monitor daylight availability, and automatically dim lighting, by reducing its power consumption, to the level needed to sufficiently illuminate the area;
- central area and network control units that provide the facility to manage the overall operation of electric lighting installations that include some or all of the categories of lighting controls above.

White LED lighting modules for backlit illuminated signs

This sub-category was added in 2018. It covers certain products that "provide white light by means of solid state lighting to illuminate signage". The technology is used, both internally and externally, in combination with appropriate control gear.

Former sub-categories

The following sub-categories have been removed in recent years:

- high efficiency lighting units (removed 2018);
- white LED lighting units (removed 2018).

No product list

Unlike most energy-saving technology, there is no requirement that specific lighting products must be named on the energy technology product list. However, technical "eligibility criteria" are specified for each of the above categories, and allowances may only be claimed if it is confirmed that these criteria were met at the time of purchase. According to the official ECA guidance, "businesses looking to purchase lighting products should seek confirmation of compliance for the products they intend to purchase to the ETL [energy technology list] criteria from the product manufacturer / supplier".

Law: CAA 2001, s. 21, 33A
Guidance: https://www.gov.uk/energy-technology-list; CA 22320, 22330

L8   Lightning conductors

Lightning protection appears to qualify as plant. This is based on the wording of the *Capital Allowances (Leases of Background Plant or Machinery for a Building) Order* 2007. Article 2 of that Order lists "examples of the kinds of plant or machinery that may be regarded as falling within the definition of background plant or machinery for a building". The Order therefore applies for the purposes of the long funding lease rules, but the clear implication is that the items it contains are plant or machinery.

The list includes "protective installations such as lightning protection, sprinkler and other equipment for containing or fighting fires, fire alarm systems and fire escapes".

221

A note of caution is perhaps needed in that the restrictions in s. 21 should still be borne in mind: even if an asset is plant on general principles, it is possible that the legislation will exclude it. However, analysis of the rules suggests that this is not the case: a lightning conductor is not "in the building" and the author would argue that it is also not "incorporated in the building". Nor is it included in list A. In any case, the restrictions in s. 21 apply "for the purposes of this Act" and their effect is therefore to say that certain assets do not qualify as plant or machinery at all for capital allowances purposes. The inclusion of such items within SI 2007/303 would therefore appear to lead to a statutory contradiction if s. 21 excluded lightning protection. This point is considered in greater depth under **Fire escapes**.

Law: SI 2007/303, item j
Guidance: BLM 21330

L9   Line markings

The author was asked whether line markings in a car park could be claimed on the basis that they constitute directional signage.

On balance, it seems unlikely that such a claim would be permitted. This is because the lines do not seem to constitute plant or machinery, being part of the setting in which the trade is conducted, rather than apparatus with which it is carried on.

The treatment of paint on walls was considered in the *McMillin* case (see **Painting and decorating**), where the Tribunal ruled:

> "We find that none of the information supplied shows that the paint has a function beyond that of covering the walls and making them easier to clean and the paint is not therefore so obviously plant that it can escape the premises test. We find that the paint has not retained a separate identity from the walls onto which it has been painted. It has in effect become part of the premises and is excluded from plant and machinery allowances."

There is, of course, some difference between paint on walls – where the function is merely to cover them and to make them easier to clean – and painted lines where the function is more clearly related to the trade of operating the car park, whether that function is to mark out the parking spaces or to indicate direction of travel. However, it is thought that a Tribunal would once more conclude that the paint, once applied, becomes part of the premises.

Arguably, the painting of lines could be said to constitute **Alteration of land**, though that is not how that phrase is typically interpreted. Again, it is possible that the lines simply become part of the "park for vehicles" and would thus be caught also by item 2 of List B at s. 22.

Law: CAA 2001, s. 22
Case: *McMillin v HMRC* [2011] UKFTT 65 (TC)

L10   Linkspans

Linkspans are a type of drawbridge, typically used at ferry terminals for loading vehicles onto the vessel. HMRC instructions to tax staff are to treat linkspans as items of plant.

Guidance: CA 21215

L11   Long-life assets

The long-life asset rules operate to slow down the rate at which plant and machinery allowances are given for certain assets that are expected to have a long useful life.

Originally, the mechanics of giving slower tax relief formed part of the long-life asset provisions themselves. Since April 2008, however, long-life assets are treated as just one form of **Special rate expenditure**; allowances are therefore now given according to the rules applying to such expenditure. As such, the main function of the long-life asset rules is now simply to identify certain assets that must be allocated to the special rate pool.

Plant or machinery is treated as a long-life asset if:

- it is new, and can reasonably be expected to have a useful economic life of at least 25 years; or
- it is second hand, but could reasonably have been expected when new to have a useful economic life of at least 25 years.

The useful economic life begins when the asset is first brought into use by any person.

Law: CAA 2001, s. 101, 102

L12   Loose tools

Capital allowances will not normally be needed for expenditure on loose tools as such expenditure will be written off as a revenue cost.

HMRC generally apply a "two year test" for expenditure to be capitalised, so if tools have a useful life of at least two years, it is arguably open to the taxpayer to claim capital allowances in lieu of a revenue deduction. Indeed, there is some case law authority for arguing that only one year is needed, as discussed under **Knives and lasts** above.

The statutory relief for replacing tools – formerly at ITTOIA 2005, s. 68 and (coincidentally) CTA 2009, s. 68 – was repealed in 2016. However, relief will still normally be available in one way or another: capital allowances where the cost is capital in nature, or as a simple trading deduction (i.e. on normal principles) where it is not. Residential landlords may now be able to claim relief by way of the **Replacement of domestic items** relief.

Case: *Hinton v Maden & Ireland Ltd* (1959) 38 TC 391
Guidance: CA 21100

M1   Machinery

Plant and machinery allowances are given, under Pt. 2 of CAA 2001, for "capital expenditure on the provision of plant or machinery". The significance of the word "or" is that an item properly defined as being machinery does not also have to be plant.

List C at s. 23 includes, as the first item, a category of "machinery (including devices for providing motive power) not within any other item in this list". So any machine used for the purposes of a qualifying activity is not affected by the restrictions relating to buildings and structures, and will in principle qualify for allowances.

This therefore raises the question of what constitutes machinery, which is in practice given a fairly broad definition (but see below). HMRC guidance states the following:

"Machinery includes machines and the working parts of machines. A machine usually has moving parts. Assets like motor vehicles and lathes are machines. Computers and similar electronic devices are also machinery. You may find machinery in places where you might not expect it. For example, door handles with moving parts are machinery."

In the Capital Gains Manual, HMRC comment that "antique clocks and watches, such as 'Tompion' clocks, are regarded as machinery for Capital Gains Tax purposes". There is no reason why that should not also apply for capital allowances purposes.

Earlier HMRC guidance said that "a machine is any apparatus which applies mechanical power" and also stated that machinery would include "trawlers, fishing vessels, tankers and other vessels propelled by engines" and "railway locomotives and tramway engines ... irrespective of the method of propulsion". By contrast, any "vessels propelled by sail or oars" would not be machinery (though they might, presumably, be plant).

So far, so good. However, the author has recently been made aware of a case in which HMRC have sought to impose a narrower definition of what constitutes machinery. The case concerned a sophisticated (but fairly standard) system for controlling tickets for a transport undertaking. The type of assets in question will be familiar enough to anyone who travels by train or underground in the UK, with a unit on the side to accept or read tickets, and a connected mechanism that opens to allow access to the platforms, etc.

In the case in question, the units were designed, constructed and installed as a single entity, and it is the author's clear view that each unit constitutes a single item of machinery, which might be called an automated ticket gate, or automated ticket barrier, and which qualifies in full as plant or machinery. (So even if they are initially barred by virtue of s. 21 as "gates", though that is not necessarily an appropriate description, the author's clear view is that they are rescued by item 1 at List C as machinery.)

HMRC argued that the units in question did not constitute just one asset each, but that every unit was in reality a collection of assets, each of which had to be considered on its own merits. It followed, according to HMRC, that the card reader (for example) would qualify but the actual "gates" (i.e. the flaps that move out of the way to allow passengers to pass) would not. It is suggested that this is a completely flawed analysis and that it is wholly inappropriate to break down an overall piece of machinery into its constituent parts in this way, and to say that some parts qualify but others do not.

Sadly, from a technical point of view, the matter was not resolved. In the writer's opinion, HMRC completely failed to provide robust arguments in defence of their position. For its own particular reasons, however (which were broader than simply taxation considerations), the taxpayer was not keen to pursue the matter to Tribunal. As HMRC conceded some considerable ground on the allocation of percentages between what they considered to be qualifying or non-qualifying elements, the amounts of tax at stake were reduced and the costs and delays of an appeal were too high to justify.

Law: CAA 2001, s. 23 (list C, item 1)

Guidance: *Tax Bulletin* 13 (October 1994), CA 21010, CG 76904

M2   Manufacturing equipment

"Manufacturing or processing equipment" is included in list C at s. 23. As such, it may qualify as plant even though affixed to a building. In practice, such equipment would almost invariably qualify.

Law: CAA 2001, s. 23 (list C, item 4)

M3   Manure storage

In the guidance issued to the pig industry, HMRC included a reference to a "concrete pad surrounded by low-level barriers for temporary storage of manure". This was listed as an example of expenditure on outdoor items that would qualify for plant and machinery allowances.

Guidance: R&C Brief 03/10 (see **Appendix 4**)

M4   Members of Parliament

Allowances are restricted for Westminster MPs and for members of the Scottish Parliament, the National Assembly for Wales or the Northern Ireland Assembly.

Expenditure incurred by such individuals will not be qualifying expenditure for plant and machinery purposes if:

- it is incurred "in or in connection with the provision or use of residential or overnight accommodation"; and
- the purpose of the expenditure is to enable the member to perform his or her duties at or near the place where the body sits, or the constituency or region that the member represents.

Law: CAA 2001, s. 34

M5   Meters

"Meters and monitoring equipment" in relation to water consumption are one of the technology classes specified in the water technology criteria list. As such, these may qualify for first-year allowances as **Environmentally beneficial technology** when all necessary conditions are met, as explained in that section.

Three types of equipment may qualify under this heading:

- flow meters;
- water management software;
- data loggers.

In each case, the specific item must be included on the water technology product list.

Law: CAA 2001, s. 45H; SI 2003/2076, art. 3(2)(c)
Guidance: wtl.defra.gov.uk/product_search_landing.asp

M6   Milking parlours

With the demise of agricultural buildings allowances, it becomes more relevant to consider what farming expenditure would qualify for plant and machinery allowances.

A milking parlour will normally be a building or fixed structure which will not qualify as plant or machinery (though it will undoubtedly contain many individual items for which a claim can be made, including the electrical and water supplies, which will qualify as integral features).

227

The only relieving provision in list C at s. 23 that could be appropriate in certain circumstances would probably be item 21: moveable buildings intended to be moved in the course of the qualifying activity. It is understood that the concept of the moveable milking parlour, for use in large remote areas, does exist. In such cases, it may be possible to argue that the asset qualifies as plant if there is a genuine intention to move it around.

Law: CAA 2001, s. 21-23, 33A

M7   Mirrors

In the *Wimpy* case, mirrors were held to be plant, albeit without great conviction:

> "We have to resolve the problem by considering the function of the wall panels and mirrors in the conduct of Wimpy's trade. The creation of atmosphere must, in the nature of things, be less important in Wimpy's trade than in an hotel or a restaurant where customers will be expected to linger over their meals, but we do not think that the concept is wholly incompatible with the conduct of a fast food restaurant."

In other words, reliance was placed on the special rules relating to "ambience" in a hotel or similar establishment. However, it should be noted that the mirrors in that case were effectively part of the wall panelling used to line all interior walls.

For ordinary free-standing mirrors, there seems to be no reason why they should not qualify as plant. They were accepted as such in both *John Good & Sons* and *Cadogan Gardens Developments*.

Cases: *Jarrold v John Good & Sons Ltd* (1963) 40 TC 681; *Lupton v Cadogan Gardens Developments Limited* (1971) 47 TC 1; *Wimpy International Ltd. v Warland* [1989] BTC 58

M8   Monitoring equipment (including telemetry)

In the guidance issued for the pig industry, HMRC listed various "building features that can qualify for WDAs at 20 per cent". Although the percentage has changed, this means that HMRC accept that such assets qualify for plant and machinery allowances, with writing-down allowances available at the standard rate.

One such listed item is for "monitoring systems (including telemetry) for monitoring temperature, humidity, lighting, water and food levels".

As regards first-year allowances, see also **Meters**.

Guidance: CA 21200; R&C Brief 03/10 (see **Appendix 4**)

M9   Motor cycles

Motor cycles are clearly plant and machinery. They used to be treated as cars for capital allowances purposes, but this is no longer the case.

As such, **Annual investment allowances** are available for motor cycles, failing which they will attract writing-down allowances at the standard rate.

Law: CAA 2001, s. 268A

M10   Motor homes

The question of whether a "motor home" is a car for tax purposes has been tested in the courts (*Morris v R & C Commrs*). The case was concerned with the question of whether the vehicle was a company car for employment tax purposes, but the principles are equally valid in this capital allowances context.

Mr Morris was a pharmacist and worked for his own company, which provided the director with a motor home that was used as a mobile office. The vehicle was also used to buy stock and was available to the director for his private use for leisure purposes.

The case considered both the construction of the vehicle and the question of whether it was commonly used as a private vehicle and suitable for such use. The court ruled that such a vehicle was correctly treated as a car for tax purposes.

The motor home was not of a construction primarily suited for the conveyance of things rather than people; it was not, in fact, well suited for carrying goods and the judge commented that that exemption could not possibly apply to a motor home. The fact that it was in fact used to buy and carry stock did not mean that the vehicle was primarily suited for the conveyance of goods or burden.

The court therefore had to consider whether the motor home was of a type commonly used as a private vehicle and suitable to be so used. The "obvious problem" here was that motor homes are sold mainly for the recreational market and are both commonly used as private vehicles and suitable for such use.

The vehicle was patently not a motorcycle (or, in the employment tax context, an invalid carriage), so it fell clearly within the statutory definition of "car" and was to be taxed accordingly.

Law: CAA 2001, s. 115
Case: *Morris v R & C Commrs* [2006] BTC 861
Guidance: EIM 23155

M11   Motors and drives

Such equipment will qualify for plant and machinery allowances in all normal circumstances. In some cases, the equipment will attract 100 per cent first-year allowances under the scheme for **Enhanced capital allowances** (ECAs).

The following categories of equipment are specified for the purposes of claiming ECAs. In each case, investments in these devices will only attract ECAs if the specific product is named on the energy technology product list, having satisfied the eligibility criteria. The descriptive quotations are from the official ECAs guidance and/or from the energy technology criteria list.

Converter-fed motors

This category was formerly labelled as "permanent magnet synchronous motors" but the category was revised in 2015. This category now incorporates integrated motor drive units (see next entry below).

The energy technology criteria list includes the following description of these converter-fed motors:

> "Converter-fed motors are products that are specifically designed to convert electrical power into mechanical power, and to rotate a drive shaft at a speed that is directly related to the non-sinusoidal multi-phase electrical power supplied to the motor.

Converter-fed ac motor drives consist of a motor, and a matched, electronic, variable speed drive (VSD) that is specifically designed to provide the multi-phase electrical power input needed to operate the motor, and to vary its speed in a controlled manner in response to an external signal."

Line operated AC motors

This category was formerly labelled as "single speed AC induction motors" but the category was revised in 2015. The energy technology criteria list includes the following description of these line operated AC motors:

"Line operated ac motors covers products that are specifically designed to convert standard three phase electrical power into mechanical power, and to rotate a drive shaft at a fixed speed that is directly related to the frequency of the electrical power supply."

The energy technology criteria list includes the following description of these motors:

"Line operated ac motors are used to drive plant and machinery throughout industry and commerce, and a wide range [of] 'general purpose' products are available in internationally agreed, standard designs with different rated power outputs, frame sizes, fixed operating speeds, and energy efficiency ratings."

Variable speed drives

The details of this sub-category were revised in 2018.

"The controllers or drives in this category are used when the speed of a motor is varied via the supply frequency.

They enable power to be more closely matched to demand and therefore save energy."

Former sub-categories

The following sub-categories have been removed in recent years:

231

- integrated motor drive units (removed 2016);
- switched reluctance drives (removed 2013).

Law: SI 2018/268, art. 3(2)(h)
Guidance: https://www.gov.uk/energy-technology-list

N1   Number plates

There is nothing in the capital allowances legislation that specifically deals with number plates. HMRC guidance to tax staff provides some useful pointers, however, as follows:

> "Do not accept a claim that expenditure on a car's (or van's etc.) registration number qualifies for PMAs in its own right.
>
> The physical number plate is a chattel that does not become plant or machinery unless and until it is attached to a car which is itself plant or machinery. Once it is attached it becomes part of the car and expenditure on it qualifies for PMAs as a part of the car.
>
> Expenditure on acquiring a right to a registration number is another matter. You are most likely to meet this in connection with expenditure on acquiring a "personalised" or "cherished" number. That does not qualify for PMAs. A personalised number plate gives intangible rights of enduring benefit – the right to use a certain combination of numbers and letters when registering the car. Those rights are not plant and so you should not give PMAs on the expenditure to the extent that it reflects the acquisition of the rights.
>
> However you should accept that the price of a car etc. that includes the cost of registering the car with a "normal" number can all be qualifying expenditure.
>
> You may get a capital allowance claim on a Hackney carriage (taxi) licence plate either on its own or, more usually, as part of the cost of the taxicab to which it is attached. The cost or value of the taxi licence plate represents both the actual licence plate itself, which is plant, and the right to trade, which is not. It is only the part of the cost that is attributable to the actual licence plate that qualifies for capital allowances as

expenditure on the provision of plant or machinery. This will be a nominal amount."

Guidance: CA 21250

O1   Overhead costs

Overhead costs are sometimes distinguished from the **Preliminary costs** of a project. Very broadly, the former term may be used to cover support activities where the cost is not known at the outset, whereas the preliminary cost category may cover lump sum payments, insurance and similar items that may be reasonably predicted at the outset. In practice, the distinction is not clear cut, however, and in *Wetherspoon* the term "overheads expenditure" was used to cover "the preliminaries costs and professional fees incurred".

Overhead costs should be apportioned in a reasonable way between the different categories of expenditure: those qualifying as standard plant or machinery, those qualifying as special rate expenditure (e.g. integral features) and those not qualifying at all.

In *Wetherspoon*, for example, the parties agreed that a cost of some £54,000 relating to site supervision and management "was a project overhead which should be apportioned equally to each and every item of main project expenditure".

See **Preliminary costs** for a more detailed discussion.

Case: *J D Wetherspoon plc v HMRC* (2007) Sp C 657

P1   Painting and decorating

The claim for the cost of painting and decorating, and of various other wall finishes, was rejected by the commissioners in *Wimpy* and this view was upheld in the High Court and then by all three judges in the Court of Appeal. Fox LJ commented as follows:

> "There was expenditure on plaster, paint, varnish and other wall finishes. All of it was incurred to put the premises, including the staff area, into decorative order for use. The commissioners rejected the claim that it was expenditure on plant. I agree with Hoffmann J, that the items were in the same

position as the artex claim and were rightly held not to be plant."

The cost of painting and decorating was also considered in *McMillin*, where the taxpayer argued that paint applied to the walls of her holiday cottages helped to keep the air clean as its organic nature was non polluting and dust free. This argument was rejected by the First-tier Tribunal, as follows:

"On balance we find that the claims made by the manufacturers do not support Mrs McMillin's claim that the paint cleans the atmosphere after it has been applied. The paint may be breathable and may sterilise the wall to which it is being applied but we do not find that a claim is being made that it sterilises the air after application. If, as Mrs McMillin suggests, the paint does indeed attract less dust onto the wall from the air then the possibility must remain that the dust in the room will remain in the atmosphere and/or be deposited on other surfaces.

We find that none of the information supplied shows that the paint has a function beyond that of covering the walls and making them easier to clean and the paint is not therefore so obviously plant that it can escape the premises test. We find that the paint has not retained a separate identity from the walls onto which it has been painted. It has in effect become part of the premises and is excluded from plant and machinery allowances."

Cases: *Wimpy International Ltd. v Warland* [1989] BTC 58; *McMillin v HMRC* [2011] UKFTT 65 (TC)

P2   Panelling

The correct tax treatment of wall panelling costs is not clear cut. The case law is contradictory and in some ways unsatisfactory and a further case may be needed to throw light on the appropriate factors to weigh in the balance.

The first question to be asked is whether panelling is caught by statutory restrictions which place a specific prohibition on "walls" (list A, item 1) and which also deny allowances for assets that are incorporated in a building or are of a kind normally so incorporated.

If it is accepted that panelling is caught by those provisions, it can only qualify for plant or machinery allowances if rescued by s. 23. This leads to the possibility that it might qualify as thermal insulation (see s. 28), as trade-specific sound insulation (list C, item 7), as moveable partitions (unlikely, but see item 13) or, most probably, as "decorative assets provided for the enjoyment of the public in hotel, restaurant or similar trades" (item 14).

The last of these possible exemptions from the statutory bar on claiming allowances has been considered in the courts. In *Wimpy*, the correct treatment of the panelling was considered to be borderline, but it was accepted as plant "under the general description of embellishments". The commissioners decided that even in a fast food restaurant, some heed could be paid to the creation of atmosphere. They could not ignore the evidence that the panels had been chosen to create the right environment for the trade in question.

The opposite conclusion, though, was reached in *Wetherspoon*, where the company was unable to persuade the commissioners that the wooden panelling had (despite being affixed to the property) retained a separate identity.

The author does not find it easy to follow the reasoning of the commissioners in *Wetherspoon*. They began, quite fairly, by saying that:

> "it seems to us that we are being asked whether the decorative panelling is more appropriately described as part of the premises in which the pub's trade is carried on or instead as an embellishment used to enhance the atmosphere of those premises."

They then introduced a novel test, by saying:

> "A factor ... which seems to us to be helpful to consider in the context of the decorative panelling is the extent to which the panelling can be regarded as an unexceptional component which would not be an unusual feature of premises of the type to which the Appellant is inviting the public. If an item is or becomes such an unexceptional component of the premises into which it is introduced, that, in our view, is a factor

tending to the conclusion that it does not retain a separate
identity for relevant purposes."

This test was purportedly based on the reference (in what is now s.
21(3)(b)) to assets of a kind normally incorporated into a building, a
reasoning that the author finds puzzling. Having posed that test, the
commissioners concluded as follows:

> "Because the decorative panelling in the Prince of Wales
> effectively turns the premises, or that part of them to which it
> is applied, from an unpanelled room into a room which is
> mainly panelled, we consider that it is an unexceptional
> component of the type of premises, in contradistinction, for
> example, to the fixed but not easily removable metal
> sculpture, which was held, in Scottish & Newcastle Breweries,
> to be plant.

> Balancing all the above matters, we conclude that the
> panelling is more appropriately described as having become
> part of the premises than as having retained a separate
> identity. Therefore it does not qualify as plant."

The author's difficulty with this may be summarised as follows. The
commissioners refer to an unexceptional component in "premises of
the type". So this seems to be saying that if decorative panelling may
often be found in a hotel, restaurant or similar premises, then it is
less likely to qualify as plant. Yet it cannot possibly be right to deny
the status of plant to assets that are trade-specific, when the whole
thrust of the case law and even the legislation is to say that an asset
used for the specific purposes of a trade is more likely to qualify as
plant.

The author finds the conclusion of the commissioners all the more
puzzling given that, earlier in their deliberations, they had
commented as follows:

> "We accept that the panelling was an embellishment to create
> ambience for the purposes of the Appellant's trade; this was
> not in dispute. The Revenue's case was that the panels were
> fixed to the wall and formed part of the premises."

Yet the fact that the panels were fixed to the wall and formed part of
the premises was not the right question to pose. The legislation
precisely recognises that certain assets may be affixed to the

property and yet qualify as plant or machinery if, for example, they are intended to create the appropriate atmosphere in the premises. Having found as a fact that the panelling was an embellishment to create ambience, the *statutory* bar on claiming allowances was removed.

The author does not assert that the conclusion in *Wetherspoon* was necessarily wrong, merely that the reasoning seems inadequate and that the case therefore provides a poor precedent on this particular issue. The author respectfully suggests that another case on similar facts could therefore lead to a different conclusion, or might at least provide a better analysis.

Law: CAA 2001, s. 21 (list A, item 1), s. 22, 23 (list C, items 7, 13, 14), s. 28
Cases: *Wimpy International Ltd v Warland* [1989] BTC 58; *J D Wetherspoon plc v HMRC* (2007) Sp C 657

P3   Partition walls

Partition walls qualify as plant in some circumstances, but care is needed.

Walls are specifically included in the extended definition of "building" in list A at CAA 2001, s. 21. As such, the starting point is that they do not qualify as plant or machinery. Even if a partition cannot specifically be said to be a wall, it may still be caught by s. 21 on the basis that it is "incorporated in the building".

List C at s. 23, however, does provide a possible statutory let-out as it refers to "partition walls, where moveable and intended to be moved in the course of the qualifying activity" (item 13). This would be subject to any HMRC argument that the principal purpose of the partition walls is to enclose the interior of a building or to provide an interior wall that is intended to remain permanently in place (see s. 23(4)). This therefore reinforces the requirement that the partition walls must be movable and intended to be moved, but taxpayers should also note the requirement that the principal purpose must be something other than to enclose the interior of the building.

This does not mean that moveable partition walls necessarily constitute plant but it gives them a chance to do so. It will therefore be necessary to consider the matter on first principles, guided by case law.

First principles lead to the question of whether the partitions are part of the premises within which the activity is conducted or whether they are an asset more akin to equipment used in the trade. In the *John Good* case, partitions were accepted as qualifying on the grounds that:

> "instead of having internal walls in its office building, needs to have, and does have, for the special requirements of its business, movable partitioning, by means of which it can, in response to changing volumes of business in its departments or to the cessation of departments or the emergence of new departments, rapidly and cheaply and without much interruption of business alter the sub-divisions of its office building".

In this case, the partitioning could "undoubtedly" be regarded as plant. This decision was commended by the House of Lords in the *Barclay, Curle* case. Partitions were also accepted as plant, though without any discussion of the issues, in *Cadogan Garden Developments*.

The HMRC view is that some moveable partitions are not plant. Advice to local tax officers is that they "should check to see if they need to possess mobility as a matter of commercial necessity before you accept the claim". Officers are also advised to check whether the partitions have ever in fact been moved (though the fact that they have not should not necessarily be considered fatal to the claim).

This serves as a reminder that there are two distinct requirements – not only must the partitions be moveable but there must be a commercial intention to move them.

The concept of being "moveable" is not defined: in one sense, any wall is moveable, but the legislation clearly envisages something less permanent than a normal wall. A key test is whether the partitions can be moved around without causing structural damage to the surrounding parts of the building.

If this hurdle is successfully negotiated, the second part of the test must also be considered. HMRC may ask for evidence of an actual intention to move the partitions in the course of the qualifying activity. Any evidence should be obtained and preserved, including in particular any discussions with the business installing the partitions in the first place. Given that there is a premium price to be paid for moveable partitions, as compared with a simple wall, it is reasonable to assume as a starting point that there may have been an intention to move the partitions at some point. But if the partitions have been disguised, perhaps by being papered over, this may be an indication that there is no intention to move them in the course of the trade.

For treatment of partitions in a particular context, see also **Toilet cubicles.**

Law: CAA 2001, s. 21 (list A, item 1), s. 23 (list C, item 13)

Cases: *Jarrold v John Good & Sons Ltd* (1963) 40 TC 681; *CIR v Barclay, Curle & Co Ltd* (1969) 45 TC 221; *Lupton v Cadogan Gardens Developments Limited* (1971) 47 TC 1

Guidance: CA 21120

P4   Partnerships

Capital allowances are potentially of great value to partners, especially professional partners or others who are paying tax at 45%. The detailed special rules applying to partners and partnerships are covered in depth in *Capital Allowances*, also available from Claritax Books and written by the same authors as this book. A few key points are covered here, however, by way of some particular issues to consider.

Partnerships claim allowances at partnership level, and claims by individual partners are not permitted. This would apply, for example, to a fleet of cars provided for the partners of a large firm.

The same principle applies if partners personally own an asset (e.g. a car) that is used for the purposes of the qualifying activity carried on by the partnership. The only exception is if the partner charges for use of the asset (e.g. rent), such that the partnership is able to claim a tax deduction for the amount paid. In this case, the individual partner can claim allowances to offset against the taxable income received.

Partnership changes are normally ignored for the purposes of claiming plant and machinery allowances, as long as at least one person carrying on the activity before the change continues to do so thereafter. The ongoing partnership continues to claim allowances as if anything done by former partners had been done by the present partners.

A partnership may claim annual investment allowances, but only if all the members of the partnership are individuals. It follows that partnerships with a corporate or trust member, or indeed with a partnership as a member, may not claim AIAs.

Any annual investment allowance, first-year allowance or writing-down allowance is made to the present partners. The allowance is calculated as if the present partners had at all times been carrying on the qualifying activity and as if everything done to or by their predecessors had been done to or by them.

Law: CAA 2001, s. 3, 38A, 263, 264, 557

P5   Parts of assets

Unless the context requires otherwise, references to an asset of any kind include a part of an asset. This principle applies to all assets, including buildings, structures, works or plant and machinery.

Law: CAA 2001, s. 571

P6   Paths

Paths are not likely to qualify as plant in any normal circumstances, as they are part of the premises, rather than apparatus.

However, HMRC accept that a full revenue deduction will be due "where a business incurs expenditure on its paths in order to remove obstacles that could present a danger to the disabled, for example on:

- replacing cracked or uneven paving slabs;
- cutting back protruding or overhanging objects, grass or other vegetation".

In the reorganisation of the HMRC website, this appears to have been removed but there is no reason of principle as to why these principles would no longer apply. See, generally, **Appendix 3**.

P7   Pavements

Pavements do not qualify as plant, as they are specifically listed as excluded assets in CAA 2001, s. 22. HMRC guidance confirms that plant and machinery allowances will not be given "on the provision, construction or acquisition" of such assets.

None of the exceptions in list C at s. 23 is likely to apply to pavements in normal circumstances, but for particular activities it is conceivable that some of them should be considered (e.g. ballast for a tramway).

Law: CAA 2001, s. 22 (list B, item 2)
Guidance: CA 22020

P8   Pen dividers

In the guidance issued for the pig industry, HMRC listed various "building features that can qualify for WDAs at 20 per cent". Although the percentage may change, this means that HMRC accept that such assets qualify for plant and machinery allowances, with writing-down allowances available at the standard rate.

One such listed item is for "moveable, adjustable pen dividers". If pen dividers are not moveable, it is likely that they will be disqualified as structures or as part of a building.

Guidance: CA 21200; R&C Brief 03/10 (see **Appendix 4**)

P9   Personal security

The legislation has a particular section dealing with assets provided for personal security. These may qualify for plant and machinery allowances but the provisions apply only in cases where there is an exceptional security risk. Numerous conditions must be met and it is clear that the legislation will rarely apply.

The following conditions are listed:

- the expenditure must be incurred by an individual, or partnership of individuals, in connection with the provision for, or for use by, the individual, or any of the individuals, of a security asset;

- the individual or partnership must be carrying on a relevant qualifying activity;
- the asset must be provided or used to meet a threat which is a special threat to the individual's personal physical security, and which arises wholly or mainly because of the relevant qualifying activity;
- the person incurring the expenditure must have the sole object of meeting that threat in incurring that expenditure;
- he or she must intend the asset to be used solely to improve personal physical security (though any incidental use is ignored, as is any protection also provided for members of the individual's family or household);

If expenditure has a dual purpose, the legislation does allow an apportionment so that relief may be given for "the proportion of the expenditure attributable to the intended use to improve personal physical security". According to HMRC, "the appropriate proportion is that attributable to the intended use to improve physical security".

The legislation cannot apply to a car, ship or aircraft. Nor does it apply to "a dwelling or grounds appurtenant to a dwelling" (for which purposes HMRC apply the CGT private residence principles). The rules can, however, cover "equipment, a structure (such as a wall) and an asset which becomes fixed to land". HMRC have indicated that "assets like alarm systems, bullet resistant windows, reinforced doors and windows, and perimeter walls and fences are the sort of assets that may qualify as security assets".

The capital allowances legislation is similar to that applying for employees. In the latter context, HMRC have updated their guidance but formerly stated that a deduction was due for individuals whose work exposed them "to a very real threat to their physical safety from terrorists, extremists and others who may resort to violence". In *Hanson*, a claim for security expenditure was allowed but the commissioners stated that the facts of the appeal and the appellant himself were unique (which could, however, be said of every appellant and probably of every appeal).

The tests were considered in the 2011 *Brockhouse* case, where it was initially argued that plant and machinery allowances should be given on certain fencing costs. The Tribunal was satisfied that the appellant's premises "had been subjected to criminal damage, vandalism and poaching". However, no evidence was submitted to demonstrate the degree of risk faced by Mr Brockhouse personally, or to show why that risk was out of the ordinary or exceptional. His case was not helped by a delay of some 11 years between the problems he had experienced and the erection of the fence. The Tribunal declared that the question of whether there was a special threat had to be determined objectively.

The *Brockhouse* appeal also failed on a second issue. On the facts before the Tribunal, the fence appeared had clearly been put in place for sole purpose of protecting the land and the stock, rather than to improve the appellant's personal physical security.

Law: CAA 2001, s. 33

Cases: *Lord Hanson v Mansworth (HMIT)* (2004) Sp C 410; *Brockhouse (t/a A6 Aquatics) v HMRC* [2011] UKFTT 380 (TC)

Guidance: CA 22270; EIM 21811

P10   Pictures

The author disagrees with the HMRC reasoning about whether pictures hung on an office wall qualify as plant or machinery. The HMRC assertion is that such items will qualify only in the context of a business that is selling "ambience" (such as a hotel). See, generally, **Decorative assets** above for a discussion of the principles involved.

The HMRC view has been expressed as follows:

> "A painting on an accountant's office wall that is owned by the accountant is not plant because selling atmosphere is not part of an accountant's business."

In the author's opinion, this shows a confused understanding of the case law, as is revealed by a further quotation from the HMRC guidance:

> "Decorative assets are likely to be caught by CAA 2001, s. 21 – S22 and not to be plant, except where they fall within item 14 of list C [at] CA 22030. This covers decorative assets provided for the enjoyment of the public in hotel, restaurant or similar trades. You should only accept that items of decor are plant if the taxpayer can show that:

243

- the trade involves the creation of atmosphere/ ambience and in effect the sale of that ambience to its customers, and

- the items on which plant or machinery allowances are claimed were specially chosen to create the atmosphere that the taxpayer is trying to sell."

In the case of assets that become part of the premises, these principles are correct. As part of the building, decorative assets may nevertheless qualify as plant and machinery by virtue of item 14 and of a correct application of case law principles.

But item 14 is only needed if the asset in question forms part of the premises in the first place. The picture hanging on the accountant's wall is clearly not a structure, and is therefore not caught by s. 22. Nor is a picture within list A at s. 21 (which includes such items as walls, floors and mains services). So it will only be caught by s. 21 if the picture is "incorporated in the building" (or "of a kind normally incorporated in a building").

For a picture that is simply hanging in a particular place, that can be moved around at the whim of the owner without having to involve any structural work on the building, it seems quite wrong to say that it is incorporated in the building. It thus seems equally wrong to deny it the status of plant or machinery. In the words of Lord Lowry in *Scottish and Newcastle*, "one might as well say that the tools and jigs of a wartime factory were part of the plant but that the apparatus used to convey 'music while you work' to those employed was not".

In such a case, it is therefore necessary to fall back on first principles as to what constitutes plant. The classic definition from *Yarmouth v France* therefore comes into play, whereby it was held that the term "plant" includes "all goods and chattels, fixed or moveable, live or dead, which [a business man] keeps for permanent employment in his business". There is no very clear distinction between pictures and mirrors, and the latter have been held to be plant.

HMRC may argue that the pictures are part of the "setting" and that they therefore fail to qualify as plant on general case law principles.

But here it is worth recalling more of what Lord Lowry had to say in *Scottish and Newcastle*:

> "My Lords, the [Revenue's] primary fallacy, in my opinion was to identify 'setting' inevitably with 'premises' or 'place'. ...

> And, even if one assumes that 'the setting' is the same thing as 'the premises', it is fallacious to say that articles used to adorn the setting thereby ceased to be apparatus used by the taxpayers for carrying on their business."

Reference may also usefully be made to the capital gains tax case of *Henderskelfe*. At the First-tier Tribunal, HMRC won that case concerning a very valuable picture, which was held not to be plant. However, the main reason for the decision was that "the Appellant executors did not have a business and in order to be 'plant' and fall within the exemption provided by Section 44 (1)(c) TCGA it is necessary for the asset to be owned by the business or at the very least leased formally to it". It was also argued that it lacked any degree of permanence as it could have been removed by the owner at any time.

The First-tier Tribunal decision was overturned by the Upper Tribunal. The judges were clear that the painting was being used for the purposes of the trade. On the rather peculiar facts of the case, HMRC had argued that the picture failed the test of being kept for permanent employment, but this too was rejected. Nor was there a problem, as had been suggested, with the concept of ownership.

The *Henderskelfe* case therefore concerned very different facts and technical issues from those where a painting is hung permanently in, for example, a business reception area. In the author's view, however, the painting in these more normal circumstances would also qualify as plant.

A different issue arises if the painting is not on the wall of the office but is displayed in the home of a director or employee. The HMRC line here may be much more justified where they assert that:

> "if the asset is not machinery, the company is only entitled to capital allowances if the asset functions as plant in its qualifying activity. For example, assets such as paintings and furniture provided for the director's home are unlikely to be

plant. They will not be apparatus with which the company's trade is carried on".

The HMRC view in this respect was followed without any hesitation in *Mason v Tyson*, where the judge found it "wholly unarguable" that the contents of a flat occupied by a businessman as a residence could be deemed a part of the profit-making apparatus of his business.

Law: CAA 2001, s. 21-23

Cases: *Yarmouth v France* [1887] 4 TRL 1; *Hinton v Maden & Ireland Ltd* (1959) 38 TC 391; *Jarrold v John Good & Sons Ltd* (1963) 40 TC 681; *CIR v Barclay, Curle & Co Ltd* (1969) 45 TC 221; *Mason v Tyson (HMIT)* (1980) 53 TC 333; *CIR v Scottish & Newcastle Breweries Ltd* [1982] BTC 187; *Wimpy International Ltd v Warland* [1989] BTC 58; *The Executors of Lord Howard of Henderskelfe (deceased) v HMRC* [2011] UKFTT 493 (TC); *Lord Howard of Henderskelfe (Deceased) v HMRC* [2013] UKUT 129 (TCC)

Guidance: CA 21130, 27100

P11   Pig tents or arks

In the guidance issued for the pig industry, HMRC listed various outdoor items that can qualify for plant and machinery allowances.

One such listed item is for "moveable pig tents or pig arks".

Guidance: CA 21200; R&C Brief 03/10 (see **Appendix 4**)

P12   Pig transportation crates

These are listed by HMRC as an example of non-fixtures that can qualify for plant and machinery allowances at the standard rate.

Guidance: CA 21200; R&C Brief 03/10 (see **Appendix 4**)

P13   Pipelines

Pipelines can probably always be described as structures, and would thus be caught by s. 22. There is a potential exemption, however, for "the provision of pipelines or underground ducts or tunnels with a primary purpose of carrying utility conduits".

In the context of talking about "milestone contracts", HMRC clearly imply that pipelines will qualify for capital allowances:

"Milestone contracts are often found where there is a large-scale construction project for buildings or for major items of machinery or plant such as oil pipelines."

Law: CAA 2001, s. 22, 23 (list C, item 25)
Guidance: CA 11800

P14   Pipework insulation

Pipework insulation can attract 100 per cent first-year allowances under the scheme for **Enhanced capital allowances** (ECAs).

Investments in pipework insulation will qualify only if the installation meets the specified eligibility criteria. However, individual products in this category do *not* have to be named on the energy technology product list.

Six categories of pipework insulation are covered by the ECA scheme, as follows:

- refrigeration pipework;
- chilled water pipework;
- non-domestic heating services;
- non-domestic hot water services;
- domestic heating and hot water services (but excluding insulation within individual dwellings);
- process pipework.

The official ECA site explains that:

"Distribution losses from a heating or cooling system can account for as much as 20% of the total energy used. Insulating the pipework effectively can reduce these losses.

It's also important to look out for leaks in valves and test points. These are often forgotten when insulating pipework, but can account for 5% of the energy used if not properly sealed."

Different criteria have to be met for each of the above categories, complying with various clauses of BS 5422:2009 ("Method for specifying thermal insulating materials for pipes, tanks, vessels, ductwork and equipment operating within the temperature range – 40°C to +700°C").

Law: CAA 2001, s. 45A

Guidance: https://www.gov.uk/energy-technology-list

P15   Planning costs

The cost of obtaining planning permission is not expenditure on plant or machinery.

Despite that general principle, the HMRC view for IBA purposes was that no attempt would be made to disallow a part of an overall figure if the builder's quotation included the cost of obtaining planning permission. It is possible that HMRC would take a similar line in relation to a plant or machinery claim.

Guidance: CA 31400

P16   Plant rooms

A room constructed to house plant or machinery will not normally qualify for allowances in its own right. Almost certainly, it will be a building or structure.

A plant room was allowed as plant by the commissioners in *Wimpy*, and the Revenue did not appeal. The reasoning given was as follows:

> "We think it right, on the evidence, to look at the plant and its housing as a single unit, on the lines suggested by Lord Donovan in relation to the dry dock in [*Barclay, Curle*]. The housing was erected not because the company wanted to enlarge the premises but because its trade of providing meals made it necessary to install that piece of machinery or plant and it could only be installed in a brick housing. In our opinion the whole unit constitutes plant."

That case pre-dated the statutory rules now at s. 21 and s. 22, however. On the face of it, the costs could only now be allowed if they were incidental to the installation of plant or machinery in an existing building: see **Alterations to buildings**. But this is not necessarily the case – the wording quoted above suggests that the plant room might be viewed in some instances as simply part of the plant itself.

Law: CAA 2001, s. 21, 22, 25

Case: *Wimpy International Ltd v Warland* [1989] BTC 58

P17   Police control rooms

At CA 21230, incorporating the *Football League* letter (see **Appendix 2**), HMRC have written as follows:

> "The letter states that expenditure on the fabric of a police control box will not qualify for capital allowances. We have now been advised that some local authorities take the view that they have the power under the Safety [of] Sports Grounds Act 1975 to require police control rooms to be installed. If that happens the expenditure will qualify under CAA 2001, s. 32."

However, s. 32 was repealed from April 2013, as one of many reliefs being removed to simplify the UK's tax system.

If relying on normal principles, a police control room would simply be a building. No allowances would be due on the cost as a whole, but there will be numerous assets within the building that will qualify for plant and machinery allowances.

Law: CAA 2001, s. 32

Guidance: www.hm-treasury.gov.uk/d/ots_capital_allowances.pdf

P18   Polytunnels

In 2012, HMRC changed their approach to the claiming of capital allowances for "polytunnels". According to HMRC, "a polytunnel is usually a metal framed semicircular tunnel covered in polythene that is used predominantly by the farming and horticulture industry".

The HMRC guidance now reads as follows:

> "If a polytunnel is a fixed structure it is excluded from plant or machinery allowances.

The exact use of the polytunnel can vary. As well as its use for growing plants, it may also be used to provide shelter for livestock, machinery or stores. In these cases it does not really matter whether the polytunnel is a fixed structure or not (although it is very likely to be fixed) because its primary, if not only, use is the provision of shelter and it will therefore comprise part of the premises or setting in which the qualifying activity is carried on.

However where the polytunnel is used for growing plants, whether or not it is a fixed structure will be crucial, because it is only possible to consider the function of a polytunnel in a qualifying activity where it is not a proscribed fixed structure.

Absent the prohibition in respect of fixed structures, it is accepted that in relation to the growing of plants a polytunnel does far more than just provide shelter from the elements. It can provide an enhanced growing environment for plants, not only increasing air and soil temperature and humidity, but also extending the crop growing season and protecting plants from insect infestations.

Neither 'fixed' nor 'fixed structure' is defined in the Capital Allowances Act. Anchor Intl (at [2005] STC 411 at 421) took the approach of applying the ordinary meaning to the term. Quite what the ordinary meaning of being 'fixed' amounts to is not entirely clear. There is a spectrum of potential definitions of 'fixed'. At one end of the spectrum 'fixed' could mean simply that the structure is set in place so that it does not move. At the other extreme it could mean that it is attached permanently in a certain place on the land such that it can never be moved intact.

Accordingly, it is necessary to look carefully at the facts of each case, including exactly how the polytunnel is to be used in the business.

In relation to strawberry and raspberry crops a key determinant will be the exact method of cultivation of the crops. Where strawberries and raspberries are grown in the ground then, as a matter of fact, the same ground cannot be continually reused. The maximum growing period for strawberries cannot usually be more than 4 years. For raspberries it can be slightly longer at 7 years. After the relevant period of time the crops must be planted elsewhere and the polytunnels will, therefore, be moved to the new location. HMRC will accept that, in such circumstances, the better view is that the polytunnels are not fixed structures, but are rather apparatus or plant, used in the qualifying activity.

However, where in relation to strawberries in particular, the crops are grown in raised beds (grow bags on trestle tables, for example) then there is no need or expectation that the crops will ever need to be grown elsewhere. In such situations it is far more likely that the polytunnels should properly be regarded as fixed structures and, as such, they will be unable to qualify for plant and machinery allowances.

In relation to other crops, similar careful consideration of the facts will be needed to determine whether or not the polytunnel is a fixed structure. For example, blackberries, gooseberries and black/redcurrants can be grown in the same location for ten years or more and in relation to such crops it is far more likely that the polytunnel will be a fixed structure."

Law: CAA 2001, s. 22
Case: *Anchor International Ltd v IR Commrs* [2005] BTC 97
Guidance: CA 22090; R&C Brief 32/12

P19   Pontoons

HMRC instructions to tax staff are as follows:

"Treat pontoons that float as plant, even if they are attached to a pile or other fixed structure. Do not treat fixed pontoons as plant.

Treat Linkspans as items of plant."

See **Harbours, wharfs, piers, marinas, jetties** above for details of a real life case concerning the interaction of this guidance with the statutory restriction for the cost of a marina.

Guidance: CA 21215

P20   Poultry houses

As a general rule, poultry houses will not qualify as plant or machinery. They will be the building or premises within which the trade is carried on, rather than apparatus used for the trade.

In *Lakeview Ltd*, it was held in the Irish High Court (not binding in the UK) that a prefabricated poultry house was plant as it played a part in the egg production process of the taxpayer. In *Anduff*, however, Peter Gibson LJ expressed "considerable doubt whether the premises test was properly satisfied in that case".

The HMRC view is that:

> "most poultry houses / chicken shacks are buildings or structures and so are excluded from plant or machinery allowances. They are not plant even if they are used in intensive poultry production and contain automated systems for ventilation, heating, food and water".

HMRC also take the view that "the fixed chicken cages inside a poultry house should not be accepted as plant".

The only exception will be where the poultry house is a moveable building and there is a genuine intention to move it in the course of the trade. In these circumstances, HMRC guidance suggests that a claim may be allowed.

See also **Chicken cages.**

Law: CAA 2001, s. 21, 22, 23 (list C, item 21)
Cases: *O'Srianian v Lakeview Limited* [1984] TL(I) 125; *Carr v Sayer* [1992] BTC 286; *Attwood v Anduff Car Wash Ltd* [1997] BTC 454
Guidance: CA 22110

P21   Preliminary costs

Meaning

It is probably helpful to begin by trying to define what is covered under this heading.

According to HMRC, preliminaries:

"are indirect costs incurred over the duration of a project on items such as site management, insurance, general purpose labour, temporary accommodation and security".

Formerly, the guidance stated that preliminary costs would "often include demolition works and site preparation, as well as the construction of a building".

In the first *Wetherspoon* hearing, the following comment was made by the special commissioner:

"Preliminaries generally refers to the building contractor's necessary costs which are not usually tangibly reflected in the finished works as opposed to costs directly related to the quantity of items of work, i.e. materials, tradesmen and site labour, tools and small plant. Costs concerned with the works as a whole are preliminaries being commonly referred to as the contractor's site-related overheads."

The same case defined preliminaries to mean "global costs covering several different items which are not readily attributable to specific items". On the other hand, it also made the point that :

"the expression 'preliminaries' is not a precise expression. Items which might be treated as preliminaries in one contract or tender might not be so treated in another. While some costs, such as portable toilets, are not capable of meaningful attribution to measured work, other costs may be capable of meaningful attribution, albeit with varying degrees of difficulty. All, however, will be integral parts of the construction costs of the measured work to the extent that they can be properly apportioned to such work. A cost properly attributable to one item of work cannot properly be apportioned among the whole."

Claiming allowances

Allowances will be due for a proportion of these preliminary costs, but the question arises of how that proportion should be calculated. This was considered at all three hearings of the *Wetherspoon* case (special commissioners, First-tier Tribunal, Upper Tribunal), where HMRC took a surprisingly hard line. The Upper Tribunal judges would have none of it, though, as is made clear in the following paragraphs:

"92. Preliminaries are, by their nature, items of overhead expenditure which cannot be, or which have not been, attributed to any single item in the building project. Some, like insurance, are inherently incapable of being so attributed. Others, like scaffolding, may be capable of specific attribution, but the time and cost involved in the process of specific attribution is often disproportionate to the amount at stake. Thus, apportionment of preliminaries between items which do, or do not, qualify for capital allowances is the only solution in relation to un-attributable preliminaries, and may be the sensible solution where attribution is uneconomic.

93. In the present case the parties were in dispute about a class of preliminaries which were 'trade specific', that is, attributed to particular types of building activity, such as scaffolding, electrical and photography of work in progress, but which had not at the time been attributed to specific items of work. They are set out at paragraph 34 of the First Decision, and hence acquired the label 'Para 34 items' during the appeal. JDW claimed to be entitled to apportion them for capital allowances between allowable and non-allowable works in the ratio derived from the respective aggregate specific costs of those two classes as a whole. We shall call that a pro rata apportionment.

94. HMRC maintained that a trader seeking capital allowances must specifically attribute all expenditure which is capable of attribution, however time-consuming or uneconomic that process may be. Accordingly HMRC maintained both before the Tribunal and on this appeal that no part of the Para 34 expenditure was allowable because it had only received a trade specific rather than item specific attribution, and because those items were not inherently incapable of specific attribution.

96. In order to meet a possible argument that pro rata apportionment might produce an excessive recovery for JDW, its expert Mr Phillippo spent 20 to 25 days work on an item by item attribution of the preliminaries at the Prince of Wales,

leading to his unchallenged conclusion that (on HMRC's case as to the allowable items of work) pro rata apportionment of preliminaries was worse for JDW than specific attribution: see paragraphs 105 – 106 of the First Decision.

97. The Tribunal's conclusion was that a pro rata apportionment of the para 34 items, and of any preliminaries where a detailed item by item attribution would be disproportionately time consuming or expensive, was a legitimate basis for claiming capital allowances for preliminaries, because it was a reasonable, common-sense solution which accorded with generally accepted accounting practice: see paragraphs 109 – 111 of the First Decision and paragraphs 106 – 112 of the Second Decision.

98. To the extent that this sensible conclusion involved any issue of law at all, we unhesitatingly agree with it. It cannot have been the intention of the legislature that a trader should have to spend more on the minute attribution of preliminaries to underlying items of work than either their cost or the value of the capital allowance thereby to be obtained. The question whether this commonsense approach was misapplied to the Para 34 items is plainly a matter of fact and degree with which it would be wrong for us to interfere, although our review suggests that the Tribunal's application to these items of their general approach to preliminaries was plainly correct. Accordingly HMRC's cross appeal on this point entirely fails."

HMRC guidance, now updated to reflect the above decision, is that "only the part, if any, which relates to services that can properly be regarded as on the provision of plant or machinery can be qualifying expenditure".

It is perhaps debatable whether that represents a correct re-statement of the *Wetherspoon* principles. In some instances, though, it will be clear that particular costs relate to parts of the overall expenditure that do not qualify (e.g. to a steel frame for a building) or that do qualify (e.g. to the hot and cold water system). In such cases, the preliminary costs should – as far as is reasonably possible – be allocated on an accurate basis between non qualifying items, items qualifying as integral features (or other special rate expenditure) and items qualifying as general plant or machinery.

Handling of plant

Expenditure included under the heading of preliminary costs may relate in part to supervising the provision or installation of fixtures or (possibly) other plant or machinery. To that extent, the costs will qualify as part of the cost of the items in question.

See also **Overhead costs and Professional fees.**

Cases: *J D Wetherspoon plc v HMRC* (2007) Sp C 657; *J D Wetherspoon v HMRC* [2012] UKUT 42 (TCC)
Guidance: CA 20070

P22   Pre-trading expenditure

A person may incur expenditure for the purposes of the trade, or other qualifying activity, before that trade or other activity has started. In such a case, the expenditure is treated as incurred on the first day on which the activity is in fact carried on.

This rule is disapplied for the purposes of determining entitlement to annual investment allowances (s. 38A(4)) or first-year allowances (s. 50).

Law: CAA 2001, s. 12

P23   Processing equipment

Processing equipment is included in list C at CAA 2001, s. 23. As such, it may qualify as plant even though affixed to a building. In practice, it may well also be machinery.

Plant or machinery allowances will be due for such equipment. Indirect confirmation, if needed, may be found by implication in the *Oil Taxation Manual.*

Law: CAA 2001, s. 23 (list C, items 1, 4)
Guidance: OT 26608

P24   Professional fees

A proportion of professional fees – for example where a property or large item of plant is bought – will be treated as expenditure on plant or machinery.

HMRC guidance in relation to these costs is as follows:

"Professional fees, such as survey fees, architects' fees, quantity surveyors' fees, structural engineers' fees, service engineers' fees or legal costs, only qualify for PMA as expenditure on the provision of plant or machinery if they relate directly to the acquisition, transport and installation of the plant or machinery and as such are part of the expenditure incurred on the provision of the plant or machinery.

Where preliminaries and professional fees are paid in connection with a building project that includes the provision of plant or machinery, only the part, if any, which relates to services that can properly be regarded as on the provision of plant or machinery can be qualifying expenditure for PMA.

Establishing the part which relates to such services needs to be determined on a case by case basis. There is no one correct answer for all cases. For some cases it may be necessary to carry out a detailed analysis of the individual costs to determine whether, or the extent to which each should properly be apportioned to particular plant or machinery expenditure. In other cases, it may only be possible to apportion the costs between items which do, or do not, qualify for PMA. (This is sometimes called 'the pro rata approach')."

The leading case is that of *Wetherspoon*, which considered the correct treatment of £4.8 million of professional costs. The parties in that case agreed that the structural engineer's fees should be allocated proportionally but disagreed about the treatment of the fees charged by the planning supervisor. In the end, the Tribunal adopted a fairly simple apportionment approach, completely rejecting the HMRC insistence on a detailed breakdown of all costs. This is discussed more fully under **Preliminary costs** above.

Not all professional fees and similar expenditure will qualify at all. For example, a person may incur legal costs when buying shares in a property-owning company and such costs would not qualify at all, whereas it may be appropriate to claim for a proportion of the legal costs for a property conveyance, including search fees.

Broadly speaking, the correct approach is that if a more accurate analysis can be obtained from a relatively small amount of work then that should be done, but a pro-rata apportionment is likely to be accepted where the work involved for a more accurate assessment is likely to be disproportionate.

If professionals are – at least to some degree – working specifically with fixtures then it may be helpful if they can invoice that part of their work separately, either with a particular invoice or at least with an itemised entry on the overall invoice. In cases of abuse (or perceived abuse), HMRC would not necessarily accept the purported breakdown, but it would provide a good starting point for any claim.

Case: *J D Wetherspoon plc v HMRC* (2007) Sp C 657
Guidance: CA 20070

Capital allowances advice

Many businesses will need to engage professional advisers to help with capital allowances claims. This is especially so in the context of property purchases, where valuation expertise may be needed for apportionments, and where specialist advice may be sought to deal with legal enquiries, fixtures elections, etc.

In strict statutory terms, the treatment of such costs may be open to some discussion. In practice, however, it seems likely that a revenue deduction can be claimed for such costs, following the principles established in a range of case law, and re-stated in the *Business Income Manual*:

> "In strictness, any additional fees incurred for computing and agreeing the tax liability on trading profits are not allowable. There is, however, a longstanding practice of allowing normal recurring legal, accountancy etc expenses incurred in preparing accounts, or agreeing the tax liability, see Statement of Practice SP 16/91 reproduced at EM3981. This has been approved by the courts as a reasonable response to the practical difficulties of apportionment, ..."

Elsewhere in the manual, HMRC confirm that tax staff "should allow the normal professional costs of preparing tax computations and supporting accounts". As capital allowances claims form an integral part of the overall income tax or corporation tax computations, there seems to be a clear acceptance that the costs are allowable.

Guidance: BIM 37850, 46450

P25   Public address systems

CA 21230, based on the Revenue's earlier *Football League* letter (see **Appendix 2**), indicates that public address equipment – microphones, amplifiers and loudspeakers – "would normally qualify as plant or machinery".

In practice, such equipment should invariably qualify as plant if used for the purposes of a qualifying activity.

Guidance: CA 21230

P26   Purchase consideration

Many incidental costs will be incurred when buying a property, and these are largely dealt with under their own headings. See, for example, **Finance costs, Professional fees**, **Stamp Duty Land Tax** and **Value Added Tax**.

Where appropriate, allowable costs will also need to be included in apportionment calculations.

Guidance: CA 21230

Q1   Quad bikes

As quadbikes have four wheels, they are not motorcycles. It follows that if they are road vehicles they will be treated as cars for capital allowances purposes (unless it can be argued that they are exempt on one of the other statutory grounds).

Law: *Road Traffic Act* 1988, s. 185(1); CAA 2001, s. 268A(1)(a)
Guidance: CA 23510

R1   Radiant and warm air heaters

Such items will qualify for plant and machinery allowances in all normal circumstances.

These heaters attract 100 per cent first-year allowances under the scheme for **Enhanced capital allowances** (ECAs), where the relevant criteria are met. As the official ECA site explains:

> "These heaters are more efficient than older boiler based systems, particularly in larger building spaces. If used in the

right way, they can completely eliminate traditional hot water systems that use far more energy."

Investments in these heaters will only qualify for first-year allowances if the specific products are named on the energy technology product list at the time of purchase. The lists are updated monthly.

The following three categories of equipment are specified for the purposes of claiming ECAs. The descriptive quotations are from the official ECAs guidance and/or from the energy technology criteria list.

Radiant heating equipment

"Radiant heating equipment covers products that are specifically designed to heat people or objects in the space below them by infrared radiation without heating the surrounding air directly, and optimising controllers that ensure radiant heating systems operate in an efficient manner."

Warm air heating equipment

"Warm air heating equipment covers products that are specifically designed to provide space heating by using the heat generated by a burner to raise the air temperature in the space(s) being heated, and optimising controllers that ensure warm air heating systems operate in an efficient manner."

See, more generally, **Central heating**.

Former sub-categories

The following sub-category has been removed in recent years:

- biomass fired warm air heaters (removed 2018).

Law: SI 2018/268, art. 3(2)(j)
Guidance: https://www.gov.uk/energy-technology-list

R2   Radiators

Radiators fixed into a property will form part of the **Central heating** system and allowances will be given as special rate expenditure.

HMRC use radiators to illustrate the difference between chattels and fixtures:

> "Property law distinguishes between chattels and fixtures. A chattel is an asset which is tangible and moveable. A chattel may become a fixture if it is fixed to a building or land. For example, before it is installed in a building as part of a central heating system, a central heating radiator is a chattel. Once installed, it becomes a fixture."

Guidance: CA 20625

R3   Rails, railways and railway assets

Railways are included in list B at s. 22. As such, they are in principle excluded from the definition of plant and machinery and no allowances are due.

HMRC guidance confirms that plant and machinery allowances will not be given "on the provision, construction or acquisition" of such assets.

Despite the general prohibition on allowances for railways, there is an exception for "the provision of rails, sleepers and ballast for a railway or tramway". This does not mean that such items automatically qualify as plant but the statutory distinction must be deliberate and so such items will presumably qualify as plant if functioning as such within a qualifying business.

Trains – both engines and carriages – will clearly be plant and machinery if used for the conveyance of goods or people as part of a qualifying activity.

Formerly, there was a specific prohibition on claiming first-year allowances for "railway assets" (including trains, carriages, a variety of other rolling stock and certain apparatus at railway stations and elsewhere). This restriction was removed from April 2013.

See also **Sleepers and ballast.**

Law: CAA 2001, s. 22 (list B, item 2), s. 23 (list C, item 31), s. 46(2), 95
Guidance: CA 22020

R4   Rainwater harvesting equipment

"Rainwater harvesting equipment" is one of the technology classes specified in the water technology criteria list. Such equipment constitutes plant and machinery and will qualify for first-year allowances as **Environmentally beneficial technology** when all necessary conditions are met, as explained in that section.

Three types of equipment may qualify for first-year allowances under this heading. In all cases, the specific item must be included on the water technology product list. The three categories of equipment that can qualify are as follows:

- monitoring and control equipment;
- rainwater filtration equipment;
- rainwater storage vessels.

Where the relevant criteria are not satisfied, rainwater harvesting and filtration equipment nevertheless qualify for plant and machinery allowances. HMRC have confirmed that such items are not treated as integral features (i.e. as part of a cold water system) but should instead be allocated to the main pool.

Law: CAA 2001, s. 45H; SI 2003/2076, art. 3(2)(f)
Guidance: wtl.defra.gov.uk/product_search_landing.asp; R&C Brief 03/10 (see **Appendix 4**)

R5   Ramps

Permanent ramps are unlikely to qualify for plant and machinery allowances.

HMRC have stated, however, that "businesses that buy moveable ramps that are not permanently fixed to the building are able to claim [plant and machinery allowances] on the cost of the ramp". That guidance was given in the context of the disability access legislation, but there is no reason why it should not apply generally.

See **Appendix 3** for more detail.

R6   Refrigerators and refrigeration equipment

These will qualify as plant or machinery in all normal circumstances. They feature twice in list C at s. 23. At item 5, there is a reference to "refrigerators and similar equipment" while item 9 refers to "refrigeration or cooling equipment". There is no obvious reason for that duplication.

In the context of furnished residential property, HMRC list fridges and freezers as "plant and machinery assets". Fridges and freezers were also included in the list of assets in the *Football League* letter that would normally qualify as plant. See also **Cold rooms and cold stores.**

In some cases, refrigeration equipment will attract 100 per cent first-year allowances under the scheme for **Enhanced capital allowances** (ECAs).

The following categories of equipment are specified for the purposes of claiming ECAs. As a general rule, investments in these devices will only attract ECAs if the specific product is named on the energy technology product list, having satisfied the eligibility criteria. This rule is varied only for the first heading below. Quotations are from the official ECAs guidance, either https://etl.decc.gov.uk/etl/site/etl/browse-etl/refrigeration.html or from the energy technology criteria list (best searched for as the address keeps changing).

Absorption and other heat driven cooling and heating equipment

"This category only covers products installed as part of a CHP scheme that has been awarded a certificate from the CHP Quality Assurance (CHPQA) programme. The absorption chiller's useful chilling effect must be driven by heat derived from the CHP plant."

Air blast coolers (formerly "forced air pre-coolers")

The details of this sub-category were revised in 2018.

These products "are specifically designed to cool water or process liquid by means of a heat exchanger, over which air is forced by a fan, prior to transfer to a refrigeration system".

In other terminology:

> "These are used in process cooling to remove heat from the circulating fluid, before it enters the mechanical refrigeration chiller. This means the chiller itself doesn't have to use as much energy cooling the fluid.
>
> The equipment consists of a finned tube liquid/air heat exchanger that cools any surrounding air that passes over it."

Air-cooled condensing units

> "An air-cooled condensing unit is a factory-assembled, packaged unit that consists of a refrigeration compressor, an air-cooled condenser and various ancillary components. This packaged unit does not contain a complete refrigeration system, but is designed to provide a convenient method for cooling a cold room or other equipment fitted with an evaporator that is controlled by an expansion valve."

The ECA scheme includes products in three temperature categories: high, medium and low temperature units.

Automated permanent refrigerant leak detection systems

> "Any leaks from a refrigerant system can reduce performance and damage the environment. These systems constantly monitor the atmosphere surrounding the system and trigger an alarm if they detect any gas escaping from the system."

As such, these are defined to encompass "products that are specifically designed to continuously monitor the atmosphere in the vicinity of refrigeration equipment and, in the event of detection of refrigerant, give an alarm".

Cellar cooling equipment

This category, of particular relevance to the hospitality industry, covers "refrigeration products that are specifically designed to maintain, by means of a refrigeration system, an indoor environment at a condition suitable for the storage of chilled beverages below 12°C, and free cooling units that ensure free cooling is utilised when the outside ambient temperature is sufficiently low".

ECAs are potentially available for "single split" systems, "dual split" systems (with an additional evaporator), and free cooling units.

Curtains, blinds, doors and covers for refrigerated display cabinets

These are various different means of reducing the infiltration of ambient air into refrigerated display cabinets. The ECA scheme covers the following categories of product, but the specific product must still be included on the product lists: strip curtains, blinds, transparent freezer covers ("bubble lids"), transparent sliding doors, and transparent hinged doors.

Evaporative condensers

The details of this sub-category were revised in 2018.

> "Condensers are used in a refrigeration or air conditioning system to condense any refrigerant gas discharged by the compressor.
>
> Energy-saving evaporative condensers use a combination of air and water to do this, which provides a more efficient way of removing heat."

As such, these:

> "are specifically designed to cool and condense high-pressure refrigerant vapour by means of a heat exchanger that has a wetted external surface across which air is blown by a fan".

Packaged chillers (tested for seasonal performance)

It was announced in an HMRC policy paper published on 14 July 2015 that this category was to be removed, but there appears to have been a reversal on this point as they remain on the energy technology criteria list and were subject to revision in 2016.

According to the official guidance, these chillers:

> "generate chilled water that can be used to provide space cooling in summer in large air-conditioned buildings. They can also be used to generate chilled water or other fluids for industrial process cooling. Reverse cycle packaged chillers are able to heat fluids and can be used to provide space heating in

winter, or for industrial process heating. Some air cooled packaged chillers also incorporate free cooling mechanisms that can be used to reduce the amount of electricity needed by the product to provide cooling at lower ambient temperatures."

These products "cool liquids by means of a refrigeration system that is packaged within a single factory assembled unit". In some cases, the same product may also be able to heat liquids.

The ECA scheme covers both air-cooled and water-cooled chillers.

Professional refrigerated storage cabinets

These widely used cabinets, formerly known as "commercial service cabinets", are "specifically designed to store, but not to display, chilled and frozen foodstuffs". A feature of them is that a door, lid or drawer must be opened to view or access the contents.

Refrigerated display cabinets

These familiar products are specifically designed to store and display chilled or frozen foodstuffs.

"Refrigerated display cabinets are used to maintain foodstuffs and drinks at chilled and frozen temperatures."

Refrigeration compressors

"Refrigeration compressors are products that are specifically designed to raise the pressure, temperature and energy level of a refrigerant vapour by mechanical means as part of a vapour-compression, economised vapour compression or transcritical CO_2 refrigeration cycle.

Economiser packages consist of a refrigeration compressor, an expansion device, and an economiser that is capable of increasing refrigerant sub-cooling and refrigeration cycle efficiency."

These products "range in size from those used in refrigerated display cabinets used in shops and supermarkets, to those used in large industrial refrigeration systems in breweries".

Refrigeration system controls

"Refrigeration system controls are products that are specifically designed to automatically optimise the operating temperatures, fan speeds and/or pressures within a distributed commercial refrigeration system in a manner that minimises the system's energy consumption, whilst maintaining the spaces or equipment being refrigerated within predefined temperature limits."

According to the ECA site at the time of writing (in 2018), the energy technology product list currently covers two categories:

- System management units or packages that are designed to optimise an entire refrigeration system, including the operation of refrigeration compressors, evaporators and condensers.

- 'Add-on' controllers that enable system management units or packages to optimise the operation of additional refrigeration compressors, evaporators and condensers.

Former sub-categories

The following sub-category has been removed in recent years:

- automatic air purgers (removed 2013).

Law: CAA 2001, s. 23 (list C), s. 45A; SI 2018/268, art. 3(2)(i)

Guidance: https://www.gov.uk/energy-technology-list; *Property Income Manual,* para. PIM 3200

R7   Removal costs

HMRC have given the following guidance in relation to the removal of plant or machinery:

"Plant is sometimes moved from one site to another. If the costs of removal and re-erection are not allowable as a deduction in computing profits you should treat those costs as expenditure on plant and machinery and give capital allowances on them."

In practice, HMRC will normally allow such costs as an ordinary trading deduction (rather than by way of capital allowances) unless the removal:

> "was essentially part of a scheme for expansion of the business, as distinct, for example, from a removal merely to re-site the machinery or plant to secure greater efficiency within the scope of an existing, even though increasing, trade".

Guidance: BIM 42530; CA 21190

R8   Replacement of domestic items

A new form of tax relief was introduced in 2016 to allow landlords of residential dwelling-houses to deduct costs incurred on replacing furnishings, appliances and kitchenware that are used by the tenants of the property. The relief has been generally referred to as "replacement furniture relief".

The relief replaced, for expenditure incurred from 1 or 6 April 2016, the former "wear and tear" allowance. It is available for individuals, companies and other entities (such as trusts or collective investment schemes). The item in question must be provided solely for the use of the lessee of the property. The stated intention behind the relief is "to give relief for the cost of replacing furnishings to a wider range of property businesses as well as a more consistent and fairer way of calculating taxable profits".

The background to the relief is that capital allowances are not normally given for expenditure incurred on plant or machinery for use in **Dwelling-houses**. There are exceptions, however, as discussed more fully under that heading.

The new relief is given for the capital cost of *replacement* items, so does not apply for the first expenditure on a particular type of asset. The relief is calculated as the cost of a like-for-like (or nearest modern equivalent) replacement asset. If the replacement item is an improvement on the old one, the deduction is limited to the amount of the expenditure that would have been incurred on one that was substantially the same. Any costs incurred in disposing of the old asset – and any incidental costs of purchasing the new one – may be added to the claim, but any proceeds from its disposal must be deducted. The rules are modified where the old item is part exchanged for the new one.

The relief is available for the cost of replacing a "domestic item". This is defined to mean "an item for domestic use (such as furniture, furnishings, household appliances and kitchenware)". The relief does not apply for **Fixtures**.

The relief is not given where capital allowances are available for the expenditure. This is of particular significance for furnished holiday let properties: capital allowances may be claimed for such properties, so the replacement furniture relief is not available. Nor is the newer relief available where the landlord derives rent-a-room receipts from the property and those receipts are brought into account in calculating the rent-a-room profits (per ITTOIA 2005, s. 793 or 797).

Law: ITTOIA 2005, s. 311A; CTA 2009, s. 250A

R9   Roads

In principle, roads do not qualify as plant, as they are specifically listed as excluded assets in CAA 2001, s. 22 (alongside such assets as pavements, car parks and runways). HMRC guidance confirms that plant and machinery allowances will not be given "on the provision, construction or acquisition" of such assets.

None of the exceptions in list C at s. 23 is likely to apply to roads in normal circumstances, but for particular activities it is conceivable that some of them should be considered (e.g. ballast for a tramway).

In particular cases, it may be possible to argue that the building of a road constitutes "the alteration of land for the purpose only of installing plant or machinery". This question could arise, for example, if modern power generating equipment is built in remote areas (see **Wind turbines** for a more general discussion). These can require major works on land, including the construction of new roads to remote areas where the equipment is to be sited. The question may arise in such cases of whether the roads are being built for the purpose *only* of installing the plant or whether they are also being built so that the new plant may be properly used.

In a different context, HMRC have stated that:

"the cost of levelling land in order to provide a stable base for a heavy machine would qualify, but the cost of levelling land in order to lay a hard standing or a foundation for a building would not qualify".

See **Alteration of land** for a fuller analysis of this issue.

Law: CAA 2001, s. 22 (list B, item 2), s. 23 (list C, items 22, 31)
Guidance: CA 22020; R&C Brief 03/10, para. 5 (see **Appendix 4**)

R10   Roofing costs

As a general principle, the cost of a roof does not qualify for plant and machinery allowances. It is clearly part of the cost of the building and is thus disqualified by virtue of s. 21.

Relief is available for the cost of insulating an existing building. In this context, HMRC have stated that tax officers should:

"treat capital expenditure on things like roof lining ... as expenditure on thermal insulation."

Such costs will be classed as "special rate" expenditure. See **Thermal insulation**.

Law: CAA 2001, s. 21, 28
Guidance: CA 22220

R11   Runways

Runways are included in list B at s. 22. As such, they are excluded from the definition of plant and machinery and allowances are not due.

HMRC guidance confirms that plant and machinery allowances will not be given "on the provision, construction or acquisition" of such assets.

Law: CAA 2001, s. 22 (list B, item 2)
Guidance: CA 22020

S1   Safes

Safes are mentioned in list C at s. 23. The effect of this is that they are not automatically disqualified from being plant and machinery by virtue of being incorporated in a building or of being a structure.

A safe being used for the normal purpose for which it is designed would seem to qualify clearly as an item of plant. If it is so big as to constitute a room in its own right, see **Strong rooms** below.

Law: CAA 2001, s. 23 (list C, item 12)

S2   Sanitary ware

Sanitary ware is included in list C at CAA 2001, s. 23 ("washbasins, sinks, baths, showers, sanitary ware and similar equipment"). In the *Football League* letter, the Revenue indicated that "toilet sanitary ware, sinks and basins, baths and showers whether for staff or public" would normally qualify as plant.

In practice, those categories can be expanded to include urinals, macerators, mirrors, towel holders, hand driers.

Such items will normally fall clearly within the definition of plant and machinery and will form an important part of the claim to be made by many businesses (such as care homes or hotels). Writing-down allowances will be due at the standard rate.

The mains water supply will now qualify under the heading of "integral features", thus attracting allowances at the lower rate. Hot water systems are treated in the same way, but HMRC guidance makes it quite clear that baths, wash basins, toilet suites etc. qualify in their own right, and not as integral features.

In *Wetherspoon*, it was held that timber partitions and doors to individual toilets in an existing building were incidental to the installation of plant as the toilets could not be properly used without them. See **Alterations to buildings**.

HMRC guidance to tax officers also states the following:

> "Treat temporary huts which are moved from one site to another and used by builders and contractors to provide canteen and toilet facilities or as storage sheds as site plant. They will then qualify for plant or machinery allowances."

Law: CAA 2001, s. 23 (list C, item 5)
Case: *J D Wetherspoon plc v HMRC* (2007) Sp C 657
Guidance: CA 21200, 22110

S3   Screens

Screens have been held to be plant in different contexts.

In *Leeds Permanent*, decorative screens were used as window displays to attract the attention of those passing in the street. These screens were held to be plant even though HMRC argued that attracting customers was "not of itself a sufficient business function to stamp an article as plant". In the High Court, it was held that the screens did not form part of the premises or setting as they were not "part of or inseparably annexed to" the office in question:

> "In my judgment, using the respective words of the three different Lords Justices in their conclusions, the screens here were part of the apparatus employed in the commercial activities of the Society's business and were not the structure within which the business was carried on. They were an adjunct to the carrying on of the business and not the essential site or core of the business itself. They were not used as premises but were part of the means by which the relevant trade was carried out."

In *Wimpy*, screens were installed between tables "to create a feeling of privacy as the customers sit at what appear to be separate tables". Some were fixed to the floor and others attached to the tables themselves, but the distinction was found to be immaterial. The screens were an integral part of the seating equipment in the restaurants and:

> "all such screens, like the tables and chairs, fulfil the function of apparatus in the trade and, in our view, plainly form part of the plant".

Thermal screens were originally one of the classes of asset qualifying for enhanced capital allowances but the category was removed in September 2006.

Cases: *Leeds Permanent Building Society v Proctor* [1982] BTC 347; *Wimpy International Ltd. v Warland* (HMIT)[1989] BTC 58

Guidance: CA 21120

S4   Seats

Seats will normally qualify as plant without problem, as long as they are used for the purposes of a qualifying activity. Seats specifically qualified in *Wimpy* and a dentist's chair was referred to in *Munby v Furlong* as an asset that would obviously qualify.

CA 21230, based on the Revenue's earlier *Football League* letter (see **Appendix 2**), comments that "most modern types of seats [at a football ground] are likely to qualify as plant or machinery, both plain plastic tip-up seats and more luxurious types of seat". On the other hand, HMRC specify that "seating which is no more than an integral part of the stand will not qualify".

Despite this view, seats forming part of a stand were specifically agreed as being plant in *Burnley* (a case heard some ten years before the letter to the Football League was sent):

> "The stand was designed to take seats and seats were fitted. It was a matter agreed between the parties to this appeal that for tax purposes these seats would in any event be regarded as 'plant' qualifying for capital allowances."

Case: *Brown v Burnley Football and Athletic Co Ltd* (1980) 53 TC 357
Guidance: CA 21230

S5   Security systems

Special rules apply, in very restricted circumstances, for assets used for personal security. See **Personal security**.

Apart from that category of expenditure, security systems will often qualify for plant and machinery allowances on ordinary principles. If they are incorporated into the building, it will be necessary to show that the possibility of a claim is kept open by s. 23. List C contains a number of promising headings, including machinery (item 1), storage equipment (item 4), computer, telecommunication and surveillance systems (item 8), burglar alarm systems (item 11), strong rooms and safes (item 12). Entry-phone systems would seem to fall clearly within the item 8 designation.

HMRC specifically accept that alarm and sprinkler systems should be treated as plant. Other items will have to be considered on their merits in the context of the qualifying activity, but all of the categories just listed will qualify as plant and machinery in most circumstances.

Law: CAA 2001, s. 23
Guidance: CA 21200

S6   Sewerage and drainage systems

Waste disposal systems are included in list A as items that do not qualify for plant and machinery allowances. On the other hand, sewerage systems provided mainly to meet the particular requirements of the qualifying activity, or to serve particular plant and machinery used for such purposes, are included in list C. As such, they may qualify as plant even though affixed to a building, a point confirmed by HMRC in the guidance given to the pig industry in 2010. In practice, it is thought that most businesses would claim for the sewerage systems for foul waste, but not for those dealing with storm water.

Any mechanical part of a waste disposal system would similarly be exempt from the statutory exclusion, by virtue of item 1 in list C.

Sewers were held, on the facts, not to qualify as plant or machinery in *Bridge House* but Salmon LJ commented that:

> "I do not wish, however, to be understood as deciding that sewers carrying trade effluent from a factory or even from a large hotel could in no circumstances be plant."

In *Wetherspoon*, the whole drainage system had to be amended because the existing system was inadequate for the proposed use. The special commissioners noted that it was "a statement of the obvious" that a large pub such as the one being discussed required substantial additional drainage for the kitchen and toilets. As such, the sewerage system costs were held to qualify as plant or machinery on the grounds that they were trade specific, or were incidental to the installation of plant or machinery.

When the *Wetherspoon* appeal reached the Upper Tribunal, further consideration was given to the drainage system. Trade-specific drainage to expel water and spilt beer from a basement cold store was confirmed as allowable under the rules for **Alterations to buildings**.

Any business may have its own trade-specific items falling generally within this heading. It is understood, for example, that a car dealership has successfully claimed for the costs of oil separators, petrol interceptors and silt traps. It is not necessarily the case, though, that such items will always be accepted, as they would appear to be caught initially by list A (as waste disposal or drainage systems), and it would therefore be necessary to find an appropriate let-out in list C (possibly item 4, though it is not a very good fit). They would only be rescued by item 2 if they constitute sewerage systems. This then raises the question of what "sewerage" actually is. Some dictionaries (e.g. Cambridge) refer to the carrying away of "waste water and human waste". Others (e.g. Collins) define sewers in terms of carrying away "surface water or sewage". If it is accepted that sewers are not restricted only or even primarily to human waste, but specifically also function to remove waste water and/or surplus surface water, then the distinction between drains and sewers becomes less clear.

A page on the *Citizens Advice* website comments on the distinction between sewers and drains. The fundamental distinction drawn there is between a drain that serves a particular building (and other buildings associated with it, such as a garage), and a sewer that collects water and other waste from the drains that serve more than one building. The site goes on to point out that most sewers are in public ownership and that some properties are not connected to sewers at all (as their drains may instead lead to a septic tank, to a cesspool or to some sort of treatment plant). A sewer may be privately owned where the site serves a number of properties (e.g. for a block of flats).

In terms of the legislation, however, it is not clear that this is the intended distinction. It creates an odd scenario if, for example, an owner can claim the cost of the pipework immediately adjacent to a new toilet (as part of the installation costs of the toilet), but not the drains within the building, but can then claim the costs when the drains meet up with those of another property to become a sewer. Clearly, some distinction is intended between the drainage systems of list A and the sewerage systems of list C. To add a further permutation, the costs of the drains within the property may be allowable under s. 25 (building alterations) for an existing property, but that could not help in the case of a new property.

Law: CAA 2001, s. 21 (list A, item 4), s. 23 (list C, item 2), s. 25

Cases: *Bridge House (Reigate Hill) Ltd v Hinder* (1971) 47 TC 182; *J D Wetherspoon plc v HMRC* (2007) Sp C 657; *J D Wetherspoon plc v HMRC* [2012] UKUT 42 (TCC)

Guidance: R&C Brief 03/10 (see **Appendix 4**); https://www. citizensadvice.org.uk/consumer/water/water-supply/sewerage/who-is-responsible-for-repairing-drains-and-sewers/

S7   Shares in plant and machinery

A person may own part of an asset, or a share in an asset. Unless the context otherwise requires, such a part or share is treated as an asset in its own right for the purposes of claiming plant and machinery allowances.

A share in plant or machinery is treated as used for the purposes of a qualifying activity so long as (but only so long as) the asset in question is used for the purposes of that activity.

Law: CAA 2001, s. 270, 571

S8   Sheds

The question of whether a shed can qualify as plant (it is obviously not machinery) is not necessarily clear cut. As always in cases of doubt, it is necessary to establish the exact nature of the asset and then to go back to first principles.

The first question is to ask whether a shed is a building. This is not absolutely clear but it is probably not normally appropriate to describe a shed as a building. So this then leads to the next question, of whether a shed is a fixed structure, to be caught potentially by CAA 2001, s. 22. HMRC acknowledge that the meaning of "fixed" in this context is unclear (see the discussion under **Structures** below). In practice, it is likely to be partly a question of scale – the author has heard a client refer to a vast warehouse covering many acres as a shed, but has also seen queries about tiny sheds being put in a corner of a garden as an overflow storage area.

If the shed is properly treated as either a building or a structure, allowances may be due only if the expenditure is rescued by list C at

s. 23. Possibly a shed could constitute "storage equipment (including cold rooms)" – the words in parentheses are not directly relevant to a shed but do suggest that the concept of "equipment" is to be given a wide meaning in this context. Again, list C will come to the rescue if the shed can be described as a moveable building that is intended to be moved in the course of the qualifying activity (see **Buildings (moveable)**.

If those statutory hurdles can be successfully negotiated, it is necessary to return to first principles and to ask whether the shed is the *premises within which* the qualifying activity is carried on, or whether it is *apparatus with which* it is carried on. If the shed is a large asset within which machinery is operated and people are constantly working, then it is in the nature of business premises and will not qualify as plant (unless, exceptionally, the whole building functions as a huge item of plant – which might be the case if a temperature-controlled warehouse used for storing food items were to be described as a shed). If the reality is that the shed is effectively a storage cupboard then allowances may properly be due.

If the shed fails to qualify in its entirety, allowances may nevertheless be due for some elements. The costs of an electrical or lighting system, for example, are allowable as **Integral features** where the items in question are provided for a building or structure.

Law: CAA 2001, s. 21-23, 33A

S9   Shelves

CA 21230, based on the Revenue's earlier *Football League* letter, indicates that racking, shelving, cupboards and furniture "would normally qualify as plant or machinery".

Free-standing shelves will qualify without problem if they are used for the purposes of a qualifying activity. If shelves are built in then they may initially be caught as being incorporated in the building (s. 21(3)) but the statutory restriction will be removed if the shelves can properly be described as storage or display equipment.

Law: CAA 2001, s. 21, 23 (list C, item 4)
Guidance: CA 21230 (see **Appendix 2**)

S10   Ships

Ships will almost invariably qualify as plant or machinery, even though the main case dealing with the matter found that a ship did not in fact qualify.

In the *Yard Arm* case, an old ship had been converted for use as a floating restaurant. As such, its function in the business was as premises within which the trade was carried on, rather than as apparatus. One judge commented that he could see "no distinction between a restaurant in the Thames and a fish and chip shop in Bethnal Green".

The judge went to make the valid point that "premises only become plant if they perform the function of plant".

Subject to that rather unusual scenario, ships may qualify as either plant or machinery. HMRC guidance may be found in the Capital Gains Manual, the principles including the following:

- large racing or ocean-going yachts, fitted with auxiliary engines, are machinery;
- smaller yachts or other vessels propelled only by sail are not machinery (but presumably they may well be plant);
- trawlers, fishing vessels, tankers and other vessels which are propelled by engines are machinery.

The key principle is that an item of machinery qualifies in its own right for capital allowances. If it is not machinery, it will be necessary to understand the role the asset plays in the business: if it functions as apparatus, as will normally be the case, it will be plant.

Formerly, there was a specific prohibition on claiming first-year allowances for ships (as defined). This restriction was removed from April 2013.

Law: CAA 2001, s. 46(2)
Case: *Benson v The Yard Arm Club Ltd* (1979) 53 TC 67
Guidance: CA 21100, CG 76909, 76910

S11   Shop fronts

HMRC take the unequivocal view that shop fronts are not plant or machinery. (The HMRC view is also that a new business replacing the shop front it has just acquired will be unable to treat the cost as a repair.)

On the other hand, HMRC do accept that showcases, associated with a shop front but distinct from the structure, are fixtures and fittings qualifying for plant or machinery allowances.

The treatment of shop fronts was considered in the *Wimpy* case. The cost was disallowed by the special commissioners, noting that the shop front is – in the English climate – a necessary part of the premises. This view was approved in the courts, especially by Fox LJ in the Court of Appeal.

If shop fronts are double glazed, it might be thought that a claim could be made on the basis that they constitute **Thermal insulation**. However, it would be necessary to show that the double glazing was first and foremost for the purposes of providing thermal insulation. It is likely that HMRC would argue that the primary purpose of a shop front is to display the goods, and that any insulation factor was merely secondary, in which case the special rules for thermal insulation would not apply.

Case: *Wimpy International Ltd v Warland* [1989] BTC 58
Guidance: CA 22110

S12   Short-life assets

Nobody is obliged to use the short-life asset rules. Nevertheless, the right to make an election is a useful one that can accelerate tax relief in certain circumstances. The election will typically be worth considering where annual investment allowances are not available to cover the costs incurred.

An election may be made for any asset where such treatment is not ruled out. There is no test as to whether the asset will in fact have a working life of a certain period.

Where an election is made, a nominated asset is removed from the main "pool" of plant and machinery. Capital allowances are then calculated instead on the asset in isolation, within a "single asset pool". Any tax advantage comes at the time the asset is sold or scrapped, at which point there may be an acceleration of the allowances that would otherwise have been given.

An election only has any beneficial effect if the asset is disposed of within a given period of (broadly) eight years, in each case counting from the end of the chargeable period. An election will normally be disadvantageous if the asset is sold, within approximately eight years, for more than its tax written-down value.

The rules are described and illustrated in greater depth in the companion volume to this book, *Capital Allowances*, also available from Claritax Books.

S13   Showers

Showers are included in list C at CAA 2001, s. 23. They will normally qualify without any difficulty as plant and machinery. Although integral features include "a cold water system", showers are separately identified in list C. HMRC have specifically confirmed that allowances for showers are given in the main pool rather than at the lower "special rate".

"Efficient showers" are one of the technology classes specified in the water technology criteria list. As such, the equipment may qualify for first-year ("enhanced") capital allowances as **Environmentally beneficial technology** when all necessary conditions are met, as explained in that section.

According to the official website:

> "Efficient showers deliver less water than ordinary showers without compromising shower performance. Through their unique design and/or particular way of delivering the water, efficient showers save not only water but also reduce energy consumption due to the amount of energy required to heat the water for a hot shower."

Four types of equipment may qualify under this heading. In all cases, the specific item must be included on the water technology product list.

The four categories of equipment that can qualify are as follows:

- aerated showerheads;
- auto shut-off showers;

- low-flow showerheads;
- thermostatically controlled showers.

A fifth category – flow regulators – was removed from 7 August 2013.

Law: CAA 2001, s. 23 (list C, item 5), s. 33A(5)(b), 45H; SI 2003/2076, art. 3(2)(i)

Guidance: wtl.defra.gov.uk/product_search_landing.asp; CA 23135; R&C Brief 03/10 (see **Appendix 4**)

S14   Shutters

As a starting point, shutters do not qualify for plant or machinery allowances (s. 21, list A, item 1).

Depending on the exact function and nature of the shutters, however, it may be possible to show that they are exempted from that exclusion. This will be the case if they can be described as furniture and furnishings (s. 23, list C, item 5) or if they fall into any of the other categories of list C. Possibilities include sound insulation (item 7), equipment for containing fires (item 10), decorative assets (item 14), advertising hoardings etc. (item 15).

If the shutters fall into one of the above exempt categories, the tax treatment must be considered on ordinary principles, including case law precedents. In *Cole Bros*, Oliver LJ made the following observation in the Court of Appeal:

> "I would have thought that the blinds fitted to shop windows to protect the goods displayed there from excessive sunlight were as much 'plant' as the heating system which prevents them from freezing."

Roller shutters operated by electricity are probably correctly treated as **Machinery** (given the wide definition of that term that HMRC accept for capital allowances purposes). In this case they will clearly qualify for allowances – they are exempt from any statutory restriction by virtue of item 1 in list C and, as machinery, they qualify in their own right without the need to refer to case law interpretations of what constitutes plant. HMRC might seek to argue that the shutters themselves should be seen as separate from the mechanism by which they are operated, but a more correct view would seem to be to treat them as a single item of machinery.

It is also conceivable that shutters may qualify as thermal insulation (s. 28) or even as part of the arrangements for personal security (s. 33).

See also **Active façades.**

Law: CAA 2001, s. 21 (list A, item 1), s. 23 (list C, various), s. 28, 33
Case: *Cole Bros Ltd v Phillips* (1981) 55 TC 188 (Court of Appeal)

S15   Signs

Signs used for various commercial purposes will normally qualify as plant without any problem. In the *Disability Act* document, reproduced at **Appendix 3**, HMRC stated simply that "the costs of permanent signage qualify" for allowances.

List C contains an entry that includes "signs, displays and similar assets".

In practice, many more minor signs will be written off as revenue expenditure.

Law: CAA 2001, s. 23 (list C, item 15)

S16   Silos and silage clamps

Silos and silage clamps may be structures, in which case they are initially caught by s. 22, but both are included in list C at s. 23. It follows that there is no statutory bar on their qualifying as plant.

HMRC specifically accept that silos for temporary storage can qualify for plant and machinery allowances, which will be given in the main pool.

It was reported in *Taxation* magazine back in January 1998 (8 January, in the Feedback section) that a silage clamp was held to be plant by general commissioners. This was on the basis that the silage clamp and an adjoining effluent tank were apparatus qualifying as plant, even though there was no extensive machinery.

Law: CAA 2001, s. 23 (list C, items 28, 29)
Guidance: R&C Brief 03/10 (see **Appendix 4**)

S17   Sinks

Sinks are included in list C at CAA 2001, s. 23. They will normally fall clearly within the definition of plant and machinery.

Taps, sinks, basins and drainers are specifically listed by HMRC as "building features" that can qualify for allowances at the standard rate. This is in the guidance issued in 2010 for the pig industry. The earlier *Football League* letter also mentioned that sinks would normally qualify for plant and machinery allowances.

Law: CAA 2001, s. 23 (list C, item 5)

Guidance: CA 21230 (see **Appendix 2**); R&C Brief 03/10 (see **Appendix 4**)

S18   Sleepers and ballast

Although the cost of roads, railways and tramways is caught by list B, there is an exemption in list C for "the provision of rails, sleepers and ballast for a railway or tramway".

It would be necessary to consider whether such expenditure would be treated as a long-life asset. A former exemption came to an end from the start of 2011.

Law: CAA 2001, s. 22 (list B, item 2), s. 23 (list C, item 31), s. 95

S19   Slurry and sludge dewatering equipment

"Small scale slurry and sludge dewatering equipment" is one of the technology classes specified in the water technology criteria list. Such equipment constitutes plant and machinery and will qualify for first-year allowances as **Environmentally beneficial technology** when all necessary conditions are met, as explained in that section.

According to the official website:

> "Mechanical slurry and sludge dewatering equipment is used to treat effluent streams and therefore improve water quality through the physical separation of the solid and liquid fractions of the effluent. Dewatering also leads to a reduction in waste volume and can contribute to significant waste disposal savings through reduced transportation and landfill costs."

Three types of equipment may qualify under this heading. In all cases, the specific item must be included on the water technology product list.

The three categories of equipment that can qualify are as follows:

- belt press equipment;
- centrifuge equipment;
- filter press equipment.

Where the criteria for first-year allowances are not satisfied, such equipment will still qualify for plant and machinery allowances, allocated to the main pool.

Law: CAA 2001, s. 45H; SI 2003/2076, art. 3(2)(k)

Guidance: wtl.defra.gov.uk/product_search_landing.asp; R&C Brief 03/10 (see **Appendix 4**)

S20   Slurry storage facilities

Slurry stores hold manure until it is ready to be used on a farm.

Typically the store is a building with sold walls and roof, but open at one end to allow machinery to enter and operate. However, slurry may also be stored in tanks or pits.

HMRC have indicated specifically that allowances can be given for the following:

- "Slurry storage systems, including, for example:
    - slurry storage tanks (whether above or below ground)
    - any reception pit &/or effluent tank &/or channels and pipes used in connection with the slurry storage tank
- Small scale slurry and sludge dewatering equipment."

HMRC have also given the following more extensive guidance:

"Our view is that slurry storage systems located anywhere in the UK, which are used for the temporary storage of slurry, qualify as plant or machinery for the purposes of the capital allowances legislation.

However, any building or structure which is part of a slurry storage facility does not qualify because it is specifically excluded by S21 CAA 2001 and does not constitute plant or machinery.

See, for example, the case of *Attwood v Anduff Car Wash Ltd* 69 TC 575, in which it was held that the structure housing a car wash was not part of a single item of plant and machinery. Justice Carnwath explained that: 'It remains necessary to apply the premises test in order to identify and exclude those parts of the complex which function simply as premises, and which are therefore not plant.'

For example, a slurry storage facility at a farm may include the following components:

- an above ground circular store
- a reception pit
- an open sided shed which provides shelter to the tank, preventing rainwater from falling into the store – the circular store is situated inside the shed

In this example the circular store and the reception pit are plant or machinery and qualify for capital allowances. Any channels or pipes associated with them also qualify. However, the shed is a structure and is therefore specifically excluded from being plant or machinery.

Officers of HMRC should, in general, accept claims for plant and machinery allowances in respect of slurry storage systems. Enquiries should be limited to significant claims for systems which appear to differ from the components described above, or facilities which include buildings or structures."

Law: CAA 2001, s. 23 (list C, item 29)

Guidance: HMRC Brief 66/08; R&C Brief 03/10 (see **Appendix 4**)

S21   Soap dispensers

These are a common item, not to be overlooked, in any new build, purchase or refurbishment of a commercial property with toilet facilities. They will qualify for standard rate plant and machinery allowances in all normal circumstances.

S22   Solar panels

Solar panels qualify for plant and machinery allowances, but writing-down allowances are given only at the slower rate applying for "**Special rate expenditure**". Solar panels are not, however, **Integral features**.

The HMRC view is that solar panels were special rate expenditure even before the matter was put beyond doubt in 2012:

> "Capital expenditure on solar panels, which include photovoltaic varieties, which generate electricity, and solar thermal systems, which provide hot water, has generally been treated as special rate expenditure on the basis that they are integral features of buildings or structures ... . In addition they generally have an economic life of over 25 years.
>
> From 1 April 2012 for corporation tax and 6 April 2012 for income tax all capital expenditure on solar panels is specifically designated as special rate."

AIAs are available for expenditure on solar panels.

See also Solar thermal collectors below.

Law: CAA 2001, s. 104A(1)(g)
Guidance: CA 22335; www.hmrc.gov.uk/tiin/tiin684.pdf

S23   Solar shading

External solar shading is included in the list of integral features. The costs will qualify as special rate expenditure.

There is no definition of what the term "external solar shading" covers so the expression must be interpreted normally. Such shading is typically seen on buildings that have large glass areas: the basic principle is that the shading can reduce both glare and air conditioning costs, but this must be balanced with the need to maintain levels of natural lighting where possible.

Numerous types of solar shading are available on the market. One of the simpler varieties is a fixed *brise soleil*; a horizontal protrusion from the building may prevent a direct hit from the sun when it is higher in the sky (i.e. in the summer months) while allowing the sun's rays to reach into the building at other times of year.

A fixed *brise soleil* is most likely to be used (in the UK) for south-facing façades. If the building faces east or west, the lower altitude of the sun may render such an approach ineffective and may instead necessitate a moveable shading system. Such a system may be anything from manually controlled shutters to sophisticated computer-controlled technologies that operate automatically to follow the path of the sun and to adjust the shading accordingly.

External shading can be made out of a variety of materials. Aluminium is typical but wooden louvres may also form part of the system, or it may be a composite of both materials. Translucent glass shading is also found.

Law: CAA 2001, s. 33A

S24   Solar thermal collectors

First-year allowances are available, where the conditions are met, for "solar thermal systems and collectors". See **Enhanced capital allowances** for a general overview of the issues.

According to the official guidelines, solar thermal systems:

> "are built around a solar collector that has a dark coloured absorbing surface, which traps solar radiation and converts it into heat. This heat is then transferred to a storage vessel by means of a circulating fluid, or in some instances, the solar collector could be directly connected into the heating circuit".

Allowances are available for both individual solar collectors ("for use in installer-assembled solar thermal systems") and for "complete, ready to install, fixed configuration, solar thermal systems". In each case, first-year allowances will be due only if the specific product is named on the energy technology product list.

Law: SI 2018/268, art. 3(2)(k)

Guidance: https://www.gov.uk/energy-technology-list

S25   Sound insulation

Sound insulation is included in list C at CAA 2001, s. 23, as long as it is provided mainly to meet the particular requirements of the qualifying activity (item 7).

There is an apparent contradiction between that provision, however, and s. 23(4) which excludes an item whose principal purpose is to insulate the interior of a building.

This is a difficult area to reconcile and the HMRC manuals do not provide any assistance. A claim for such costs would seem to be justified on the basis that item 7 must have some force, especially as item 7 is more specific in referring only to sound insulation and even then only where it is for the particular purposes of the trade.

This is one of many examples of circumstances where qualifying expenditure may be concealed within a general heading that would appear to be non-qualifying. So, for example, the cost of sound insulation may be within a general category of "Walls" (for example), and may need teasing out accordingly.

Law: CAA 2001, s. 23 (list C, item 7); s. 23(4)

S26   Spare parts

The cost of spare parts will normally be written off as revenue expenditure. Former HMRC guidance (in the old capital allowances manual) contained the following:

> "Treat the original item of machinery or plant and everything in it as one item qualifying for capital allowances. To the extent that later expenditure merely maintains that item of machinery or plant in full working order it is revenue expenditure and so does not qualify for capital allowances.

> Spare parts may be bought before a repair, they will be used for, is necessary. If they are merely held for the purpose of effecting repairs they will not qualify for capital allowances. The expenditure will not normally be capital expenditure.

> Spare parts may be held more or less permanently on standby for substitution as and when required while repairs are being carried out on the parts replaced to make those parts replaced either fit for return to the original machinery or plant, or to be

held on standby in their turn. You should treat the expenditure on the spare parts held on standby as capital expenditure qualifying for capital allowances. For example, where an aircraft is bought together with a spare engine and a set of spares as a package treat the whole cost as capital expenditure on the provision of plant."

This guidance has not been reproduced in the current version of the HMRC manual, but there is no obvious reason why the principles should have changed.

Guidance: former CA 1567

S27   Special rate expenditure

The following categories of expenditure are classified as "special rate" expenditure, attracting writing-down allowances at a lower rate than other assets. The costs of these items is normally taken to the special rate pool, the main exception being assets that have an element of private use (e.g. by a sole trader), where allowances will be calculated in a single asset pool:

- thermal insulation;
- integral features;
- long life assets;
- cars that are not main rate cars;
- cushion gas; and
- solar panels.

Law: CAA 2001, s. 104A
Guidance: CA 23220

S28   Splashbacks

Splashbacks, typically in the form of a relatively small tiled area, may be placed around a toilet, basin or sink. The treatment of these was considered in the *Wetherspoon* decision. This was in the context of the rules (at s. 25) for **Alterations to buildings**, where certain costs are allowable for an existing building only. Tiling would not be allowed other than under the s. 25 provisions.

The Upper Tribunal ruled that a small area of splashback tiling around a basin installed in an existing building would be allowed:

> "The splash-back tiling can be said however to be an alteration to the existing building, incidental to the installation on the basis that it was designed to enable the basin to be used without damaging the adjacent brickwork, and for no other purpose."

However, no allowances would be due if the splashback area was simply a notional part of a larger area of tiling:

> "There is ... a distinction between the specific splash-back tiling, created simply because of the installation of the sink, and the continuation of the entire tiling around the work areas of the kitchen for numerous reasons. In our view, neither such general tiling, nor any "fractional element" of it, would qualify under [what is now s. 25]."

Law: CAA 2001, s. 25

Case: *J D Wetherspoon plc v HMRC* [2012] UKUT 42 (TCC)

S29   Sports facilities

Sports apparatus used for the purposes of a qualifying activity will qualify as plant or machinery. More difficult issues arise with arenas etc.

A football stand is not plant. This is fairly clear from first principles (it is the place within which the activity is carried out rather than the apparatus used for that activity). The point was confirmed in the *Burnley Football* case, where the commissioners commented:

> "The stand is not plant functioning, whether passively or actively, in the actual processes which constitute the trade. The football matches take place and the spectators come to watch within, rather than by means of, the stadium."

Similarly, an all-weather race track costing nearly £3 million was held not to be plant in *Lingfield Park*. The commissioners' decision that allowances were due was overruled in the Chancery Division. The judge was:

"quite unable to see how, without doing violence to the way in which language is used, one can describe the [all-weather track] as being, or functioning, otherwise than as part of the premises on which the business was conducted".

Anchor International

In *Anchor International*, however, it was held (initially by the commissioners, but confirmed in the Court of Session) that expenditure on a five-a-side football pitch was on plant and machinery. The huge synthetic carpet:

> "was not merely part of the premises, but was the means whereby the operation of providing five-a-side football on a synthetic pitch was carried out".

Again, the court agreed with the commissioner that:

> "the carpet was the means by which the respondents generated profits rather than merely the setting, and that the carpet constituted plant".

The word "merely" is important here, as the court was saying that the carpet was able to function as plant even whilst also functioning as the setting. Furthermore, the works underneath fell into the category of "alteration of land for the purpose only of installing the plant". Those works included excavation, infilling and drainage.

Before these general principles could be applied, however, it was necessary for the court to consider whether there was any statutory bar to claiming allowances, under the provisions now at sections 21 and (more particularly) 22 of CAA 2001. If the costs were incurred on a fixed structure, no allowances could be claimed (unless they were somehow rescued by s. 23). To understand the reasoning of the court in this respect, it is necessary to start with an appreciation of how the artificial surface was formed.

The pitch was formed by excavation and then by building up various layers. First, a layer of "terram geotextile" was lain on the formed lower surface; next a layer of stone was added, of around 200 to 300mm; next came a further layer of terram geotextile "to provide a porous barrier over the stone, to protect the underside of the synthetic grass carpet and to keep it clean". The synthetic grass "carpet" (with a depth of some 25mm) was then lain onto this layer, in strips of no more than about four metres wide. This carpet was then covered with sand, the weight of which (up to around 30kg per square metre) anchors the synthetic grass carpet to the base and stops it from moving. The sand has a secondary purpose of filling the space between the tufts of synthetic grass "to keep the pile upright giving the surface its durability and playing characteristics".

The carpet had a life expectancy of between approximately five and ten years, depending on the level of use. In practice, some parts would need repair sooner than others, because of the nature of the game being played on the surface.

HMRC contended that it was necessary to consider the pitch as a whole, and that allowances were denied by what is now item 7 of list B at s. 22 (any other fixed structure). Even if the carpet was considered in isolation, "as a realistic matter it was fixed; it was weighed down by 22 metric tons of sand and could not be taken up as a whole and used elsewhere".

For the company, it was argued that the carpet was an asset in its own right, as it was replaceable without affecting the pitch as a whole. In any case, "the carpet was not fixed; it was resting on the prepared base weighed down by sand without any connection to what was underneath".

In reaching its decision in favour of the company, the court commented as follows:

> "It seems to me that the carpet has a separate identity; it will wear out in five years with frequent use, or eight or nine years with less use. If part of the carpet wears out before then, that part can be patched. When it is completely worn out, the works underneath are retained and merely rolled and filled in if there has been subsidence and another carpet is laid on top. A different supplier might supply the replacement carpet. This seems to me analogous to a heavy machine standing on a concrete base. The machine cannot be used without the base but the machine can be replaced and a new one put on the same base. The relevant item of plant is the machine which retains its separate identity. Here it is the carpet, not the pitch, even though the carpet cannot be used without the preparatory works to the ground on which the carpet is laid, just as the machine cannot be used without the base."

Furthermore, the court agreed with the company that the carpet was not fixed:

> "Whatever 'fixed' means in the context of the definition of structure, a carpet resting on the ground, however heavily weighed down with sand, is not fixed to anything. The fact that it cannot be moved as a whole or even in the same size rolls in which it was installed does not mean that it is fixed."

Furthermore, the court concluded that neither the carpet nor the pitch was a structure:

> "Looking at the meaning of 'structure' in the context of the [legislation] the carpet on its own is clearly not a structure. Having decided that the relevant item of plant is the carpet it is not necessary to decide whether the pitch is a structure but I would have decided that it was not. On the ordinary meaning of language, the pitch is not a 'fixed structure of any kind, other than a building.' Land has been dug out and filled in with stones and terram sheeting with a carpet resting on top. The examples of structures in [list B] are large civil engineering items, such as tunnels, roads, dams, docks and dikes. The pitch is not like any of them and is not constructed in the way one expects a structure to be constructed."

In practice, HMRC will seek to explore the distinction between premises and apparatus, based on the facts of each case. HMRC acknowledge that this is a difficult area, noting that "the contradictory judgements do not provide clarity as to how [all-weather and artificial] surfaces are to be regarded". That is obviously true, but the *Anchor International* case does provide some strong arguments supporting the claiming of allowances in similar cases. HMRC are overplaying their hand when they say that the case "was decided on its own particular facts as presented to the Special Commissioner and does not determine the matter for any other case, unless the facts are identical"; it is quite possible that there will be other cases where the facts are not identical but are similar enough for the same principles to be applied.

See also **Football grounds (equipment at)** and **Golf courses** above and **Sports grounds (safety), Squash courts** and **Tennis courts** below.

Cases: *Brown v Burnley Football & Athletic Co LTD* (1980) 53 TC 357; *Shove (HMIT) v Lingfield Park* [2003] BTC 422; *Anchor International Ltd v CIR* [2005] BTC 97

Guidance: CA 21260

S30   Sports grounds (safety)

In the 1970s and 1980s, special rules were introduced to give capital allowances in relation to expenditure on safety at sports grounds. It was announced at the end of 2011 that "the reliefs are no longer required as the Government considers that the stock of existing sports grounds have been brought up to the standards appropriate for their size and use".

The reliefs were repealed from April 2013.

Formerly, the legislation covered three different types of expenditure:

- safety expenditure incurred at sports grounds designated under the *Safety of Sports Grounds Act* 1975 (s. 30);
- safety expenditure incurred at sports grounds designated under the *Fire Safety and Safety of Places of Sport Act* 1987 (s. 31);
- other grounds not specifically covered by the *Safety of Sports Grounds Act* 1975, but capable of designation (s. 32).

The rationale for the withdrawal of these reliefs suggests that claims made under these rules were latterly of little value. Previously, extensive additional claims had been possible under these provisions. Just one example of this is illustrated by the following comment at CA 22240:

> "The construction of a building or structure does not normally qualify under Sections 30, 31 or 32. However, if a local authority requires the installation of a police control room,

the expenditure will qualify for capital allowances provided that the normal conditions of are satisfied."

Law: CAA 2001, s. 30 to 32

Guidance: CA 22240; www.hmrc.gov.uk/tiin/tiin820.pdf

S31   Sprinkler systems

Sprinkler systems are included in list C at s. 23 and will clearly qualify as plant and machinery in normal circumstances. Any associated wiring will likewise qualify, whether in a new building or an existing one.

HMRC guidance specifically states that "alarm and sprinkler systems" will be accepted as plant.

Law: CAA 2001, s. 23 (list C, item 10)
Guidance: CA 21200

S32   Squash courts

HMRC guidance to tax officers regarding squash courts reads as follows:

> "You may get a claim that the cost of constructing a squash court qualifies for PMAs as expenditure on the provision of plant.
>
> Do not accept the claim. You should apportion the expenditure.
>
> Accept that the playing surfaces including the plaster skim on the walls, the lines, the door and the 'special' floor of a squash court are plant, as are the spotlights, ventilators etc., and give PMAs on the expenditure incurred on them.
>
> Do not accept that the walls, foundations, roof, balcony and stairs are plant. Do not give PMAs on the part of the expenditure on the squash court incurred on them."

Guidance: CA 22130

S33   Staff accommodation

Some businesses provide living accommodation for staff, and the question arises of whether or not capital allowances can be claimed for fixtures or other plant or machinery in the accommodation. A number of different technical considerations can arise.

Restrictions are in some cases imposed for plant or machinery provided for use in a **Dwelling-house**. As considered under that heading, however, the restrictions apply to ordinary property businesses and to special leasing (as defined). They do not apply to furnished holiday letting businesses or to trades generally.

So the essential principle when considering the treatment of staff accommodation is to determine the nature of the qualifying activity for which the allowances are being claimed. If the activity is a property business then the restriction applies but if it is a trade then it does not.

If that hurdle is successfully negotiated, it should still be remembered that allowances are restricted if the plant or machinery is in use partly for "other purposes" – including private use. The legislation is quite messy here, in that it imposes separate rules for AIAs, WDAs and FYAs. For these purposes, private use by a sole proprietor or a business partner would constitute other use, but private use by an employee or director would not. (The employee benefits in kind rules would sort out the tax issues for the employee.)

Example

Jess and Phil run two pubs in neighbouring towns. They live in accommodation above one of the pubs and they employ a manager, Dave, who lives rent-free in accommodation above the other pub.

There is no property business here, as no rent is being received, so the restriction for plant in a dwelling-house is not an issue. The flat occupied by Jess and Phil is, however, used exclusively for private purposes, so no claim may be made for allowances for that flat. (If it can be shown, as a fact, that the accommodation is in fact used partly for business purposes then a partial claim may be possible.)

Dave's flat can in principle be the subject of a claim and there should be no problem claiming for the cost of any machinery and for any integral features. There is a possible argument here that some items are not plant, as plant is by definition used for the trade, whereas the items in question are used privately, albeit by an employee of the trade. It is not known whether HMRC would take this point in practice in this context, but see the last part of the section on **Pictures** above for a consideration of the issues.

If Dave paid rent for the flat, it would be necessary to decide as a question of fact whether Jess and Phil were using the flat for the purposes of the pub trade (no dwelling-house restriction) or for a separate property business (in which case the restriction would be applied).

Law: CAA 2001, s. 35

S34   Stairs

As a general principle, stairs do not qualify as plant (s. 21, list A, item 1). The restriction applies if the stairs are "in or connected with" a building, so there is no statutory bar on stairs that are not so connected. Stairs to climb up a slide at a funfair, for example, would not be barred from allowances by item 1.

In *Wimpy*, the company failed to convince the commissioners or the courts that a claim should be permitted for the cost of staircases in the restaurants.

Law: CAA 2001, s. 21 (list A, item 1)

Case: *Wimpy International Ltd. v Warland* [1989] BTC 58

S35   Stamp duty land tax

The purchase of chattels is not chargeable to SDLT, but SDLT is payable in respect of fixtures in a property. The SDLT is then treated as part of the purchase price for capital allowances purposes. It constitutes capital expenditure on the provision of the plant or machinery.

This, at least, is how the wording is interpreted in practice. The HMRC manuals appear to be silent on the matter, though the SDLT manual does provide some useful guidance on the distinction between chattels and fixtures.

Guidance: SDLTM 04010

S36   Steelwork

Steel structures that form the framework of a building will be caught on general principles and will not be allowable as plant or machinery.

Law: CAA 2001, s. 21

S37   Storage equipment and storage tanks

Storage equipment and storage tanks are both included in list C at CAA 2001, s. 23. As such, they may qualify as plant even though affixed to a building or constituting a fixed structure.

Whether such items will in fact qualify depends on the nature of the asset in question and on the use to which it is put. Numerous possible categories may apply, but see – in particular – **Animal feed systems, Boreholes, Buildings, Cold rooms/cold stores, Floors and flooring materials, Grain silos, Manure storage, Shelves, Silos and silage clamps, Slurry storage facilities, Strong rooms**.

Law: CAA 2001, s. 23 (list C, items 4, 28)

S38   Strong rooms

Strong rooms in a bank or building society are mentioned in list C at s. 23. The effect of this is that they are not automatically disqualified from being plant and machinery by virtue of being incorporated in a building or of being a structure.

This does not mean that strong rooms will automatically qualify as plant (and they are clearly not machinery). There are two reasons for this caution.

First, the protection of list C will not apply if the principal purpose of the strong room "is to insulate or enclose the interior of a building or to provide an interior wall, floor or ceiling which ... is intended to remain permanently in place".

More generally, the fact that a strong room is included in list C means simply that the treatment of the room must be considered on general principles. There is a passing reference to such assets in a case concerning dog kennels. In *Carr v Sayer*, the following comment was made by the judge:

"One of the functions of a building is to provide shelter and security for people using it and for goods inside it. That is a normal function of a building. A building used for those purposes is being used as a building. Thus a building does not partake of the character of plant simply, for example, because it is used for storage by a trader carrying on a storage business. This remains so even if the building has been built as a specially secure building for use in a safe-deposit business."

So does a strong room qualify? The matter may still need to be tested, but the author's view is that it must be able to do so in some circumstances, as there was otherwise no point in including it in list C. Perhaps the distinction needs to be made as follows: if part of a building has a particular strength, to act as a strong room, it may nevertheless fail to qualify, on the grounds that it is still the premises within which the business is operating. But if the strong room is clearly contained within the overall premises, it seems reasonable to argue that the room is effectively a large safe and that it should qualify.

When the current list C was introduced by FA 1994, it was put to the Revenue by the Institute of Taxation that strong rooms might be needed by solicitors or investment trust managers. The Revenue made the following comments in response to those representations:

"In practice, we have only accepted that strong rooms in banks or building societies can be plant (and not necessarily in every case). The precise facts are, as always, crucial, but, generally, we have not accepted that an ordinary room becomes plant because, say, better locks are fitted, bars are put on the windows and it is called a 'strong room'. Most claims for strong rooms outside the banking sector fall into this category and, for simplicity, the Clause focuses on this instead of attempting to define the ingredients of a qualifying strong room. You will note that 'safes' are protected in all cases."

Law: CAA 2001, s. 23 (list C, item 12)
Case: *Carr v Sayer* [1992] BTC 286
Guidance: CA 22030

S39   Structures (generally)

As a general principle, structures do not qualify as plant and machinery (s. 22). However, this is not as severe a restriction as it may appear.

Definition

First, the definition of structure is not clear cut. The following quotation, from the IBA part of the capital allowances manual, remains helpful in determining how the term "structure" is to be interpreted:

> "You should treat something as a structure if it has been artificially erected or constructed and is distinct from the earth surrounding it.

> Land which retains its character as land is not a structure, even if it has been cultivated or modified in some way. For example, grass tennis courts, grass football pitches, grass bowling greens and golf courses are not structures."

The guidance goes on to include the following quotation from Scrutton J's ruling in the early rating case of *CIR v Smyth*:

> "In my view it is a question of fact in each case; a gravel path though from repeated gravellings it is harder than the surrounding soil would not in my opinion be a structure, while the roads one is familiar with in Switzerland, the Tyrol, and Italy, in parts built up on mountain sides, in parts cut out of solid rock, would I think clearly be structures, as would the elaborate compositions of concrete, wood blocks, and tarmac used for heavy motor traffic at the present day. Between the two there is every variety of degree of solidity and permanence.

> Again, the modern earth banks of a reservoir, recently erected and continually repaired, may well be a structure, while the huge earthworks, long ago constructed and repaired, but now become part of the original earth and left to weather with it such as Maiden's Castle, Flower's Barrow and Badbury Rings in the county of Dorset, or Grim's Dyke, Offa's Dyke and Dane's Dyke, as they run through England, have, in my view,

long ceased to be structures, and become natural features of the earth.

I think a structure is something artificially erected, constructed, put together, of a certain degree of size and permanence, which is still maintained as an artificial erection, or which, though not so maintained, has not become indistinguishable in bounds from the natural earth surrounding. What degree of size and permanence will do is a question of fact in every case."

Fixed

Second, the term structure is defined to mean "a fixed structure of any kind, other than a building". It follows that the statutory restriction applies only to *fixed* structures.

The meaning of this term is not defined for capital allowances purposes and is not always clear cut. As HMRC have said (in relation to **Polytunnels**, but the guidance is of general application):

"Quite what the ordinary meaning of being 'fixed' amounts to is not entirely clear. There is a spectrum of potential definitions of 'fixed'. At one end of the spectrum 'fixed' could mean simply that the structure is set in place so that it does not move. At the other extreme it could mean that it is attached permanently in a certain place on the land such that it can never be moved intact.

Accordingly, it is necessary to look carefully at the facts of each case ... ."

As such, there will be cases where it can legitimately be argued that a particular asset is not a fixed structure.

Exceptions

Third, list B does not include all structures.

Although item 7 is a catch-all provision, it is subject to three important exceptions. See the commentary on **Water towers** for an exploration of the significance of these exceptions, including the references to industrial buildings, which remain valid for these purposes even since the abolition of the IBA rules from April 2011.

Furthermore, the whole of the statutory restriction for structures is subject to s. 23, which includes list C. Many of the later items in the list are structures that are nevertheless given the chance to qualify as plant or machinery. These include dry docks (item 23), certain jetties etc. (item 24), certain towers (item 26), and fixed zoo cages (item 33). The items just named are illustrative and not exhaustive.

It is quite clear from the case law that a structure can, in rare circumstances, qualify as plant or machinery. This was well summarised by Lowry CJ in *Schofield v Hall*, as follows:

> "I conclude, accepting Mr. Nolan's argument for the Company, (1) that the Commissioners were entitled to find that the silos, which were admittedly structures, were also plant, (2) that plant does not require to be mechanically active in its operation (although, to the extent that it is so, the distinction from a mere structure is easier to appreciate) and (3) that the question for decision must be considered in relation to the trading activities as a whole."

Despite all these observations, the general principle remains that most structures do not qualify for capital allowances. The distinction between plant and the structure housing for plant was brought out in the *Bowerswood* swimming pool case, considered in more detail at **S42** below.

Law: CAA 2001, s. 22, 23 (list C, various items)

Cases: *CIR v Smyth* 3 KB 406; *Schofield v R & H Hall Ltd* (1974) 49 TC 538; *Bowerswood House Retirement Home Ltd v HMRC* [2015] UKFTT 94 (TC)

Guidance: CA 22090, 31110

S40   Structures for amusement rides

There is a specific mention, in list C at s. 23, of "the provision of structures and other assets for providing the setting for any ride at an amusement park or exhibition". It does not follow that such items necessarily qualify as plant or machinery, but they can be freely considered on normal case law principles.

Law: CAA 2001, s. 23 (list C, item 32)

S41   Surveillance systems

Surveillance cameras and associated equipment will clearly qualify as plant and machinery in normal circumstances, together with any wiring costs directly associated with the equipment.

If the equipment is likely to be replaced within approximately eight years, consideration should be given to use of a short-life asset election.

See also **Burglar alarm systems.**

Law: CAA 2001, s. 23 (list C, item 8)

S42   Swimming pools, etc.

Swimming pools operated by hotels, leisure centres, etc. will normally qualify as plant and attract allowances at the standard rate.

Although it is probably correct to describe a swimming pool as either a structure or part of a building, any statutory bar on claiming allowances is removed by item 16 in list C, which covers "swimming pools (including diving boards, slides and structures on which such boards or slides are mounted)".

In *Beach Station Caravans*, Megarry J determined that the pools in question were "part of the apparatus used by the Company for carrying on its business as caravan park operators". As such, they were "part of the means whereby the trade is carried on, and not merely the place at which it is carried on". The purpose of the pool was "to provide and retain a suitable body of water which is circulated, cleansed and heated, and so will provide a medium in which the visitors to the caravan park can safely disport themselves, affording them a pleasurable and safe buoyancy".

Following that decision, HMRC instructions to tax staff are as follows:

> "Give plant or machinery allowances on swimming pools provided for the trades of hotelier, caravan park operator, holiday camp operator etc. The expenditure that qualifies includes the cost of excavation, pool construction and terracing. It does not include the cost of things like changing

rooms and sun lounges. If the pool is an indoor pool the building housing it is not plant."

The VAT case of *Boys' and Girls' Welfare Society*, though based on different legislation, may be of use if arguing about the housing of the pool. While it seems clear that the main structure of the building will not qualify as plant, there may be grey areas concerning the nature of the inner walls, for example. The case concerned a hydrotherapy pool for use by young people with disabilities. The view of the Tribunal was that:

> "the pool itself (including the adjacent pedestrian area used for access to the water) and the environmental control system form in our view an integral piece of equipment for use by the handicapped".

The Tribunal also commented on the building housing the pool:

> "We draw a distinction between on the one hand the structural walls of the building, with their cavity filling and on the other hand the applied thermal and acoustic lining round the walls of the pool room, which we regard as part of the pool installation itself."

More recently, the tax treatment of a large conservatory which housed a swimming pool was considered by a tax Tribunal in *Bowerswood*. The pool was in use for the residents of a nursing home. It was argued that the conservatory should be treated as part of the pool as it was an integral part of it and as – without the housing – the pool would be of no commercial utility. The Tribunal accepted, as a point of fact, that "an open air swimming pool would be of less utility to a nursing home than an indoor swimming pool" but did not accept that a pool would be of *no* utility for such a home. In the end, the decision was an easy one for the Tribunal:

> "We are satisfied therefore that the Conservatory is a building or fixed structure and is excluded from capital allowances by sections 21 or 22. Those sections are not disapplied by section 23 because the Conservatory does not fall within section 23(2) or list C. It is not necessary for the purposes of this decision for us to go on and consider whether the

Conservatory would otherwise fall within the normal meaning of the word plant."

Law: CAA 2001, s. 23 (list C, item 16)

Cases: *Cooke v Beach Station Caravans Ltd* (1974) 49 TC 514; *Boys' and Girls' Welfare Society* (MAN/96/1041 15274); *Bowerswood House Retirement Home Ltd v HMRC* [2015] UKFTT 94 (TC)

Guidance: CA 22060

T1   Taps

Taps, sinks, basins and drainers are specifically listed by HMRC as "building features" that can qualify for allowances at the standard rate.

"Efficient taps" are one of the technology classes specified in the water technology criteria list. As such, the equipment may qualify for first-year allowances as **Environmentally beneficial technology** when all necessary conditions are met, as explained in that section.

Four types of equipment may qualify under this heading. In all cases, the specific item must be included on the water technology product list.

The four categories of equipment that can qualify are as follows:

- automatic shut off taps;
- electronic taps;
- low flow screw-down / lever taps;
- spray taps.

Law: CAA 2001, s. 45H; SI 2003/2076, art. 3(2)(d)

Guidance: wtl.defra.gov.uk/product_search_landing.asp; R&C Brief 03/10 (see **Appendix 4**)

T2   Taxi licence plates

For taxi licence plates, as for personalised **Number plates**, it is necessary to distinguish the physical plate from the rights attaching thereto. The physical plate is an item of plant but the right to operate the taxi, which the plate represents, is not.

Guidance: CA 21250

T3   Taxis

The definition of "car" for capital allowances purposes is considered at the appropriate heading (**Cars**) above. Taxis are normally treated in the same way as any other cars, with the result that **Annual investment allowances** are denied for most taxis.

HMRC guidance is that "Hackney carriages (traditional 'London black cab' type vehicles)" should not be treated as cars for capital allowances purposes (so AIAs are available for such vehicles). No clues are given as to why this should be the case. In statutory terms, however, there are only certain options. Such vehicles are clearly not motorcycles, and it is surely impossible to argue that hackney cabs are primarily suited for carrying goods rather than people. The special treatment must therefore be on the basis that a London cab is "not commonly used as a private vehicle *and* unsuitable for such use" (emphasis added – both halves of the test must be met).

It is a question of fact whether the London cab, or indeed any other vehicle, can be said to have met these tests. Factors that may have influenced the HMRC treatment of London cabs would include the lack of a front seat, the unusual arrangement of the passenger seats, and the very small boot space.

Most taxis will clearly be cars for capital allowances purposes, and only writing-down allowances will be due (at the standard or "special" rate as appropriate, depending on emission levels).

Law: CAA 2001, s. 38B, 268A
Guidance: CA 23510

T4   Telecommunications systems

Telephones, faxes and similar equipment, together with any associated wiring, will clearly qualify as plant and machinery. Writing-down allowances will be given at the standard rate.

Consideration should be given to use of a short-life asset election unless the full cost of such equipment is covered by the **Annual investment allowance** for the year of purchase. Use of the election will generally accelerate the tax relief if the equipment in question is kept for no more than about eight years and is then scrapped or sold for a minimal amount.

If structures are used "for the purposes of a trade which consists in the provision of telecommunication, television or radio services" then they are not caught by the restrictions in s. 22 for most structures and they can therefore be considered on their own merits, applying normal case law principles.

See also **Underground ducts and tunnels for utility conduits.**

Law: CAA 2001, s. 22 (list B, item 7(c)), s. 23 (list C, item 8)

T5   Telephones and fax machines

These, and similar items, clearly qualify as plant or machinery. Even if they are incorporated into the building, there is a statutory exemption for "computer, telecommunication and surveillance systems (including their wiring or other links)".

In practice, the main issue since 2008 will be to determine whether any such costs need to be treated as integral features. The telephones and fax machines clearly do not, but the associated wiring is less clear cut.

HMRC guidance makes it clear, however, that the wiring should not be treated as part of the electrical system:

> "The cost of a ducting system within the building or structure follows the tax treatment of the system or systems that the ducting supports. So ducting which relates solely to the building's electrical system would be part of that system and would qualify for 10% WDAs, whereas ducting relating solely to a computer system could qualify for 20% WDAs. Where ducting supports two or more systems simultaneously, the relevant expenditure should be apportioned on a fair and reasonable basis, and capital allowances may be claimed on each portion of the total expenditure at the rate appropriate to that portion."

This is considered more fully under **Electrical installations and equipment** above.

Before the introduction of the rules relating to integral features, HMRC accepted as plant the trunking for the telephone system in *Cole Brothers*.

Law: CAA 2001, s. 23 (list C, item 8)
Case: *Cole Brothers Ltd v Phillips* [1982] BTC 208
Guidance: CA 22330

T6   Televisions

Televisions, and related equipment, used for the purposes of a qualifying activity will almost certainly be plant or machinery. Vinelott J was perhaps surprisingly cautious in *Cole Bros* when he commented that:

> "The courts may yet have to consider whether expenditure on the provision of enticing amenities – for instance, piped music or television to entertain customers whilst their cars are filled with petrol or washed, or a creche, or a children's playground in a department store can be said to be expenditure on the provision of plant. The question does not arise in this case."

Arguably, a television – with its sophisticated technology – is in any case a machine, within the broad definition given to that term by HMRC. See **Machinery** above.

HMRC specifically accept that "in television hire businesses television sets that are hired out are plant or machinery".

HMRC have also given the following guidance in relation to cabling systems:

> "If you receive a capital allowance claim for an underground cable system (including television, telecommunications, or electricity supply systems) the costs of installing the cables will include the costs of excavating the land and providing ducting that houses the cables. The cabling and the ducting may be recognised as separate components of the asset in the claimant's accounts (so that they are depreciated at different rates). Where the ducting is installed as a direct incident of the installation of the cabling, the costs of the ducting and the associated excavation are, for capital allowance purposes, part of the costs incurred on the provision of the cabling regardless of the treatment in the accounts. In these

circumstances, if the cabling is not itself a long-life asset, the long-life asset rules are not separately applicable to the ducting."

Although of relevance by analogy rather than specifically in relation to televisions, it may be noted that fibre optic cabling is part of a list of "typical examples of plant or machinery" in HMRC's guidance manual at CA 23084.

Case: *Cole Brothers Ltd v Phillips* (High Court) (1980) 55 TC 188
Guidance: CA 21200, 23084

T7   Tennis courts

A hotel, or a furnished holiday letting property, might offer a tennis court as a facility for guests. The question of whether a grass court, for example, could qualify has been raised on a number of occasions, but there is no clear cut answer.

A tennis court is obviously not a building. Furthermore, HMRC are on record as saying that a grass tennis court is not a structure, and indeed made that point in the *Family Golf Centres* case. So far so good, but there are other obstacles.

First, it would be necessary to negotiate s. 22(1)(b), which states that no allowances are given for "expenditure on ... any works involving the alteration of land". There is not a great deal of guidance on how HMRC would interpret this wording, though R&C Brief 03/10 contrasted the alteration of land generally with its alteration for the purposes of installing plant & machinery. The concept was also considered in the *McMillin* case, where an "earth bund" was denied relief partly on the basis of this section. The restriction would be subject to let-outs by virtue of s. 23 (list C) but in practice none of those would seem to apply.

Even if it can be argued that for some reason the creation of a tennis court does not constitute the alteration of land, it will be necessary to determine whether the court would qualify as plant on ordinary case law principles. This leads back to the issue of apparatus being contrasted to premises – is the court part of the apparatus with which the trade is carried on, or is it part of the setting in which that trade is carried on?

The *Lingfield Park* case concerned an all weather track (AWT) and the concluding words of Mummery LJ, as follows, would seem to cover a tennis court even more clearly than they did the track:

> "It was not open to the General Commissioners, on the facts found by them, to conclude that the AWT functioned as plant. The only reasonable conclusion, on the facts found by them and on a proper application of the premises test, is that the AWT functions as premises on which the trade of horse racing is carried on by Lingfield.
>
> The purpose, use, construction and nature of the AWT are such that the AWT functions as premises for horse racing, as does the grass racecourse running parallel with it. It is common ground that the grass track is not plant; nor is the construction of a replacement or additional grass track; nor is the construction of a building to cover in the grass track, so that it can be used for racing in all weathers. None of these are items of plant. It would be an inaccurate use of language to describe any of them as the means, apparatus, equipment or tool by which or with which Lingfield's trade is carried on. It is more accurate to describe them as a place or premises, or part of a place or premises, on or in which the trade of organising and promoting horse racing is carried on.
>
> In my judgment, the same is true of the AWT. I agree with Mr Milne that the AWT is not land in its natural state. It is synthetic in nature. It has a limited life, unlike land in its natural state. I also agree with him that the AWT is not a building affording shelter or security. Those features of the AWT do not, however, prevent the AWT from functioning as premises on or in which the trade of horse racing is conducted. The effect of the AWT is to enlarge the area of the racecourse space available to Lingfield to function as premises, on which more frequent horse racing can take place.
>
> As for the supposed separate identity of the AWT, it is no more separate from the premises in or on which Lingfield's trade is conducted than the grass racecourse or the other parts of the premises at Lingfield Park. Nor does the fact that the top surface can be dug up and carted away for

valuable re-sale give the AWT an identity separate from the premises. I agree with Hart J when he said ([2003] STC 1003 at [15]):

> 'For my part I am quite unable to see how, without doing violence to the way in which language is used, one can describe the AWT as being, or functioning, otherwise than as part of the premises on which the business was conducted. It was no doubt separately identifiable from other parts of the premises both as a matter of visual inspection and having regard to the way in which it had been constructed and maintained. I cannot, however, see that this made it lose its character as part of the premises for the purposes of the premises test.' "

So a claim for a tennis court appears to be problematic. However, the cost of any moveable equipment will in principle be allowed in full. So allowances would be due for the net and its supports, for any seats etc., and for equipment that is kept long term for use by visitors.

Cases: *Family Golf Centres Ltd v Thorne* (HMIT) (1998) Sp C 150; *Shove (HMIT) v Lingfield Park* [2003] BTC 422
Guidance: CA 21260, 31110

T8   Thermal insulation

There are specific provisions to provide tax relief, by way of plant or machinery allowances, where no relief would otherwise be available for the cost of thermal insulation of an existing building. The provisions do not apply to a dwelling-house used in a residential property business, but they are extended to cover landlords who add thermal insulation to properties other than a dwelling-house.

Formerly, the special treatment applied only to industrial buildings, but it was extended from April 2008. From the same date, however, expenditure qualifying under this heading is classed as being special rate expenditure, attracting writing-down allowances only at a slower rate.

The wording refers to "insulation against loss of heat [of] a building occupied ... for the purposes of the qualifying activity" (or, as the case may be, of a building "let ... in the course of the business"). The wording thus makes it clear that the provisions apply only to loss of heat and so they cannot be used to claim relief for, e.g., a cold store or temperature-controlled warehouse (but these are likely to qualify in their own right in any case).

The wording "insulation against loss of heat" is given a natural interpretation and HMRC have provided the following guidance:

> "Treat capital expenditure on things like roof lining, double-glazing, draught exclusion and cavity wall filling as expenditure on thermal insulation."

The guidance goes on to say how dual purpose expenditure will be treated:

> "Sometimes expenditure may be incurred for more than one reason. For example, double-glazing may be installed to insulate against both noise and loss of heat. The expenditure will qualify under Section 28 provided that it is clear that insulation against loss of heat is one of the main reasons why it was incurred."

The clear HMRC view is that the provisions do not apply to thermal insulation costs incurred during the original construction of a property. Presumably, this is on the grounds that the property that is still being built cannot yet meet the condition of being occupied for the purposes of the qualifying activity. Arguably, the point is not quite as clear cut as HMRC suggest.

If a claim is made under this heading, any subsequent disposal value is treated as being at a value of nil (s. 63(5)). One effect of this is that allowances claimed may not be passed on to a future owner.

If a landlord incurs expenditure on energy-saving materials, the question may arise of whether he should claim under these rules or under those found at ITTOIA 2005, s. 312 or (for corporation tax purposes) at CTA 2009, s. 251. The technical name for these other provisions is "Deduction for expenditure on energy-saving items" but they are often referred to as "Landlord's Energy Saving Allowance" (or "LESA").

The legislation makes it clear that the landlord's entitlement to the more favourable 100 per cent deduction is preserved by excluding such expenditure from a plant and machinery claim (see s. 28(2B)).

Law: CAA 2001, s. 27, 28, 104A
Guidance: CA 22220

T9   Toilet cubicles

The *Wetherspoon* case considered the question of whether allowances were available for the cost of creating cubicles (whether laminate or blockwork) around newly installed toilets.

The case law development was rather unusual. The First-tier Tribunal held that allowances were due, under the rules for **Alterations to buildings**, for the cost of the partitions, on the grounds that they were incidental to the installation of the toilets themselves. Furthermore, they specifically extended this treatment to blockwork partitions as much as to partitions of a less durable nature.

HMRC appealed in relation only to the blockwork partitions. As such, the treatment of the other partitions stood. Nevertheless, the Upper Tribunal questioned HMRC (the Respondents in the case) about this treatment, with the following rather odd result:

> "The Respondents did confirm, however, when asked by us, that they considered that allowances had wrongly been conceded in relation to the expenditure on the non block-work partitions, though they were not now seeking to overturn that decision."

The Upper Tribunal therefore had to let the decision stand, but indicated strongly that they believed that that was an incorrect application of the law. According to the Tribunal, allowances were not due either under general principles or under the special rules for building alterations, for the costs of constructing the toilet blocks in the former basement area:

> "The Appellant's contention starts with the sanitary ware. We are almost asked to visualise toilet bowls in an empty void, whereupon we are then asked to conclude that nobody would use the toilets, unless cubicles were created. Having created the partitions, and then naturally attached cubicle doors, floor

and wall tiling is then said to be incidental, as are the partitions to screen off the cisterns. The resultant position is that it is suggested that the entire building work on the toilet blocks is said to be expenditure on building alterations, incidental to the installation of the plant, namely the actual toilet bowls and cisterns.

We consider that description to be extremely unrealistic. The realistic summary is that the overall renovation involved the construction of luxurious toilet blocks, into which various items of plant were installed. Whatever the precise order of construction and installation, we consider that the Appellant's contention that the building works are all incidental to the installation of the toilet bowls and cisterns involves the tail wagging the dog."

Law: CAA 2001, s. 25
Case: *J D Wetherspoon plc v HMRC* [2012] UKUT 42 (TCC)

T10   Toilets and urinals

As regards toilets generally, see **Sanitary ware**. Toilets will qualify for plant and machinery allowances and the costs will be included in the main pool of expenditure.

HMRC do not accept that "the costs of making building alterations to toilets (for example, to widen a doorway to facilitate wheelchair access)" can qualify (see **Appendix 3**).

"Efficient toilets" are one of the technology classes specified in the water technology criteria list. As such, the equipment may qualify for first-year allowances as **Environmentally beneficial technology** when all necessary conditions are met, as explained in that section.

Three types of equipment may qualify under this heading. In all cases, the specific item must be included on the water technology product list.

The three categories that can qualify are as follows:

- low flush toilets;
- retrofit WC flushing devices;
- urinal controls.

See also **Toilet cubicles.**

Law: CAA 2001, s. 45H; SI 2003/2076, art. 3(2)(e)
Guidance: wtl.defra.gov.uk/product_search_landing.asp

T11   Tool boxes

The treatment of tool boxes bought by car mechanics is touched upon in the *Employment Income Manual.* These tool boxes can be expensive (several thousand pounds) so the question arises of whether capital allowances may be claimed.

HMRC guidance implies that the cost of an expensive tool box will be accepted where the normal conditions are met for employee claims. The primary condition is that the item in question must be necessarily provided for use in the performance of the duties.

In relation to tool boxes in particular, the guidance includes the following:

> "The cost of the equipment is not relevant to the 'necessarily' test. Do not argue that an employee who chose to purchase an expensive item could have made do with a cheaper version."

See also **Employee expenses**.

Guidance: EIM 36500, 50700

T12   Trade marks

No capital allowances are available for the cost of registering trade marks. Such costs are not incurred on plant or machinery, and do not fall within any of the other categories of expenditure for which allowances can be given.

Guidance: CA 10020

T13   Trading stock

Items that may be capital expenditure for one business will be trading stock for another. The office desk, for example, will be capitalised for most businesses but will normally be stock for the furniture retailer.

315

It is a fundamental principle that capital allowances are given for capital expenditure. It follows that items that qualify for plant and machinery allowances for one business may not do so for another.

The one case that has probably been quoted more than any other in discussions about what constitutes plant was heard back in 1887 under the *Employer's Liability Act* 1880. Lindley LJ commented in that case that plant:

> "includes whatever apparatus is used by a businessman for carrying on his business – not his stock-in-trade which he buys or makes for sale; but all goods and chattels, fixed or movable, live or dead, which he keeps for permanent employment in the business".

Case: *Yarmouth v France* [1887] 4 TRL 1
Guidance: CA 21100

T14   Trams and tramways

Tramways are included in list B at s. 22. As such, they are excluded from the definition of plant and machinery and no allowances are due.

HMRC guidance confirms that plant and machinery allowances will not be given "on the provision, construction or acquisition" of such assets.

Despite the general prohibition on allowances for tramways, there is an exception for "the provision of rails, sleepers and ballast for a railway or tramway". This does not mean that such items automatically qualify as plant but the statutory distinction must be deliberate and so such items will presumably qualify as plant if functioning as such within a qualifying business.

Trams themselves will clearly be plant and machinery if used for the conveyance of people (or goods) as part of a qualifying activity.

Law: CAA 2001, s. 22 (list B, item 2), s. 23 (list C, item 31)
Guidance: CA 22020

T15   Trap doors

The claim for the cost of a trap door and ladder was rejected by the commissioners in *Wimpy* and this view was upheld in the High

Court and then by all three judges in the Court of Appeal. Fox LJ commented as follows:

> "These were required by the fire regulations to provide an escape route from the basement to the ground floor. The commissioners held that the expenditure on these items was on an alteration to the premises which was not plant. This was essentially a matter of fact for the commissioners whose decision was upheld by the judge. I think he was right."

Case: *Wimpy International Ltd. v Warland* [1989] BTC 58

T16   Tunnels

Tunnels are included in list B at s. 22. As such, they are excluded from the definition of plant and machinery and no allowances are due.

HMRC guidance confirms that plant and machinery allowances will not be given "on the provision, construction or acquisition" of such assets.

There is an exception, however, for Underground ducts and tunnels for utility conduits.

Law: CAA 2001, s. 22 (list B, item 1), s. 23 (list C, item 25)
Guidance: CA 22020

T17   Turfing

The cost of land does not qualify for plant and machinery allowances. For the particular consideration of turf, however, see **Carpets** and **Golf courses.**

Law: CAA 2001, s. 24

T18   Turnstiles

CA 21230, based on the Revenue's earlier *Football League* letter (see **Appendix 2**), indicates that turnstiles (and spectator counting equipment) "would normally qualify as plant or machinery". Indeed, turnstiles are almost certainly within the definition of machinery, and thus qualify for allowances without complication.

Guidance: CA 21230

U1   Underground ducts and tunnels for utility conduits

Underground ducts for utility cables etc. are given an exemption from any statutory restriction on claiming allowances. More specifically, the saving provision applies to "the provision of pipelines or underground ducts or tunnels with a primary purpose of carrying utility conduits".

HMRC have given the following guidance to tax staff at CA 21200:

> "If you receive a capital allowance claim for an underground cable system (including television, telecommunications, or electricity supply systems) the costs of installing the cables will include the costs of excavating the land and providing ducting that houses the cables. The cabling and the ducting may be recognised as separate components of the asset in the claimant's accounts (so that they are depreciated at different rates).
>
> Where the ducting is installed as a direct incident of the installation of the cabling, the costs of the ducting and the associated excavation are, for capital allowance purposes, part of the costs incurred on the provision of the cabling regardless of the treatment in the accounts. In these circumstances, if the cabling is not itself a long-life asset, the long-life asset rules are not separately applicable to the ducting."

See also **Cabling**.

Law: CAA 2001, s. 23 (list C, item 25)
Guidance: CA 21200

U2   Uninterruptible power supplies

These are one of the technology classes specified in the energy technology criteria list. As such, they will qualify for first-year allowances as **Energy-saving technology** when all necessary conditions are met, as explained in that section.

According to the official website:

"Uninterruptible power supplies are products that are specifically designed to maintain the continuity and quality of a power supply to electrical appliances or electrically driven equipment in the case of input power failure. When the mains electricity supply is operating, they charge up an energy storage device, which can be used to provide electrical power for a defined period when the mains electricity supply is interrupted."

These are widely used in industry and commerce to protect computer and other power-sensitive equipment. The details of this sub-category were revised in 2018.

The qualifying technology includes both "static" and "rotary" power supply units or packages.

Expenditure under this heading only qualifies for first-year allowances if the specific product is included on the energy technology product list.

Law: CAA 2001, s. 45A; SI 2018/268, art. 3(2)(l)
Guidance: https://www.gov.uk/energy-technology-list

V1   Valeting bays

The treatment of "car valeting bays" was considered in a 2014 case that never had much chance of success. The decision concerned something that the taxpayer described as a "valeting bay" but that the Tribunal referred to from the outset as "the Building". (The wording chosen by the Tribunal is unfortunate as it seemed to pre-empt their decision from the outset. Nevertheless, they clearly reached the right decision on the facts.)

The taxpayer operated a Renault franchise and was required to apply "glasscoat finishes" to the cars it supplied to customers. The finishes were applied using hand-held buffing equipment and it was found that "the application of the product had to be made at a temperature of between 60 and 70 degrees Fahrenheit". It was argued for the company that the building where this took place was "a tool of the trade" and was "a necessary part of the process which enabled the glasscoat to be applied". With this starting point, it was argued that the legislation (beginning at s. 21) should be "interpreted to reflect and give effect to this".

HMRC were able to argue simply that it was a building, and that allowances were therefore not available. This was an easy argument to maintain, given the finding that it consisted of a concrete floor, walls of standard concrete block construction, and a flat roof set on wooden beams.

The Tribunal concluded that:

> "The Building keeps out the elements and some dust and similar matters and is like an office or workshop in the sense of being a place where people work. It is not a tool of the trade. It is a place of work which does not amount to plant."

As such, the appeal was rejected both on ordinary case law principles and also on the basis of the statutory restrictions in s. 21.

Law: CAA 2001, s. 21
Case: *Rogate Services Ltd v HMRC* [2014] UKFTT 312 (TC)

V2   Value added tax

The cost of items on which capital allowances are claimed will typically include VAT. Where the VAT paid on the acquisition of the asset is allowable as input tax for VAT purposes then capital allowances can only be claimed on the cost of the asset net of the VAT input tax reclaimed. In all other cases, the capital allowances claim can include the VAT as part of the qualifying expenditure.

There may be capital allowances implications when a person incurs an "additional VAT liability" or receives an "additional VAT rebate". The VAT Capital Goods Scheme (which applies to large capital items of capital expenditure) adjusts the VAT due if the use of an asset changes during the period of ownership.

The implications are discussed fully in *Capital Allowances* (available from Claritax Books). Broadly speaking, however, additional VAT paid by the owner of an asset is qualifying expenditure for capital allowances purposes – and the receipt of a VAT rebate is a disposal event – if the asset is still owned at some time in the chargeable period in question.

Law: CAA 2001, s. 234ff.
Guidance: CA 29230

V3   Vehicle wash water reclaim units

These are one of the technology classes specified in the water technology criteria list. As such, they will qualify for first-year allowances as **Environmentally beneficial technology** when all necessary conditions are met, as explained in that section.

According to the official website:

> "In a car wash dirty wash water flows from the gully in the wash bay into a below-ground three chamber sump tank, where heavy solids and sludge settle out and floating debris is prevented from flowing through the sump by an internal baffle arrangement. From the final chamber, the wash water is pumped through the reclaim unit (which removes particles down to a size of 15-20 microns) before being discharged into a 'clean' wash tank."

The qualifying technology includes both partial and full reclaim systems.

See also **Car wash apparatus.**

Law: CAA 2001, s. 45H; SI 2003/2076, art. 3(2)(l)
Guidance: wtl.defra.gov.uk/product_search_landing.asp

V4   Vehicles

Vehicles are machines, and therefore all qualify in principle for plant and machinery allowances.

This includes cars, vans, lorries, tractors, other agricultural vehicles, trucks, cranes, diggers, etc.

Special rules affect the way allowances are given for **Cars.**

Guidance: CA 23084

V5   Ventilation systems

Ventilation systems are one of the classes of asset that HMRC have explicitly stated should be accepted as plant.

The cost of such assets must now be classified as "special rate expenditure" and thus attracts allowances at a lower rate. Specifically, this treatment applies to (among other items) "a space or water heating system, a powered system of ventilation, air cooling or air purification, and any floor or ceiling comprised in such a system".

First-year allowances may be available where the relevant conditions are met. See **Heating, ventilation and air conditioning equipment**.

See also Air conditioning systems.

Law: CAA 2001, s. 33A(5)(c)
Guidance: CA 21200

V6   Viaducts

Viaducts are included in list B at s. 22. As such, they are excluded from the definition of plant and machinery and no allowances are due.

HMRC guidance confirms that plant and machinery allowances will not be given "on the provision, construction or acquisition" of such assets.

Law: CAA 2001, s. 22 (list B, item 1)
Guidance: CA 22020

W1   Wallpaper designs and pattern books

Wallpaper pattern books were held, in *Rose & Co*, not to be plant. The reason, however, was that they were not considered to be capital expenditure. If such items are held for permanent employment in the business, they will normally qualify as plant without any problem.

In *Arthur Sanderson*, designs were acquired or created for use in the manufacture of wallpaper. The costs were held to be on plant or machinery.

Cases: *Rose & Co. (Wallpaper & Paints) Ltd v Campbell* (1968) 44 TC 500; *McVeigh v Arthur Sanderson & Sons Limited* (1969) 45 TC 273

W2   Walls

Walls do not normally qualify as plant or machinery. This would already be true on ordinary case law principles but the prohibition is specifically reinforced in numerous ways, including:

- list A, item 2 (walls generally);
- list A, item 5 (lift shafts, etc.);
- list B, item 6 (sea walls only).

It is possible that a wall (or at least part of the cost of a wall) might be exempt under various items of list C, including sound insulation, moveable partitions, equipment for containing fires, strong rooms in a bank, though these exemptions do not apply for "any asset whose principal purpose is to insulate or enclose the interior of a building or to provide an interior wall [which] is intended to remain permanently in place".

In *Wimpy*, wall tiles were not accepted as plant, but wall panels were allowed.

A dental practice might have lead-lined walls to prevent radiation leakage. There is at least a possible argument that such walls – if their sole purpose is to counter the radiation – might qualify as an incidental part of the cost of the radiation machinery itself.

See also **Panelling, Partition walls, Personal security, Thermal insulation.**

Law: CAA 2001, s. 21 (list A, item 1), s. 23 (list C, various)
Case: *Wimpy International Ltd. v Warland* [1989] BTC 58

W3   Wash basins

Wash basins are included in list C at CAA 2001, s. 23. They will normally fall clearly within the definition of plant and machinery, attracting allowances at the standard rate. HMRC guidance specifically states that wash basins should be accepted as plant.

Law: CAA 2001, s. 23 (list C, item 5)
Guidance: CA 21200

W4   Washing machines

Washing machines are included in list C at CAA 2001, s. 23, both specifically and as falling within the general category of machinery. They clearly fall within the definition of plant and machinery if used in a normal way for the purposes of a qualifying activity.

"Efficient washing machines" are one of the technology classes specified in the water technology criteria list. As such, the machines may qualify for first-year allowances as **Environmentally beneficial technology** when all necessary conditions are met, as explained in that section.

Two types of equipment may qualify under this heading. In each case, the specific item must be included on the water technology product list.

The first category is for "efficient continuous tunnel washers", which are "designed to provide continuous processing of laundry on an individual batch basis".

The second category is for "efficient professional washer extractors", which "clean and rinse laundry using water, chemical, mechanical, and thermal means. Water is extracted by a spin extraction".

Law: CAA 2001, s. 23 (list C, item 1, 5), 45H; SI 2003/2076, art. 3(2)(j)
Guidance: wtl.defra.gov.uk/product_search_landing.asp

W5   Waste disposal systems

These are included in list A as items that do not qualify for plant and machinery allowances. There is no further HMRC guidance on how the term is to be interpreted.

See, however, **Sewerage and drainage systems** for a fuller discussion.

Law: CAA 2001, s. 21 (list A, item 3), s. 23 (list C, items 1, 2)

W6   Waste heat to electricity conversion equipment

This category of **Energy-saving technology** was added in 2015 to the list of categories qualifying for the scheme of enhanced capital allowances.

According to the official ECA guidance:

> "Waste heat to electricity conversion equipment (WHECE) covers products that are specifically designed to convert waste heat to electrical power by means of a closed thermodynamic power cycle that does not involve the internal combustion of fuel."

Two categories of product are covered, as below. In each case, the descriptive wording is taken from the energy technology criteria list.

Organic rankine cycle heat recovery equipment

This category, added in 2015 and updated in 2018, covers products that are specifically designed to convert waste heat to electrical power by means of a closed thermodynamic power cycle that does not involve the internal combustion of fuel. According to the criteria list, the equipment:

> "typically captures waste heat from exhaust stacks in manufacturing plants, or other waste heat from industrial processes, and uses it to generate electricity that is used on site."

Saturated steam to electricity conversion equipment

This category was added to the energy technology list in 2018. The equipment in question "is specifically designed to convert waste or excess saturated steam, from a specific process, into electrical power by means of a closed thermodynamic power cycle that does not involve the internal combustion of fuel".

The 2018 guidance lists two examples:

1. "Screw expanders – as wet steam passes through the product, it turns a screw rotor, which is connected to a generator. Energy is removed from the steam as the

pressure reduces, which is converted into rotational shaft energy and then electricity."

2. "Non-condensing or back pressure turbines – equipment which features rotary turbines where high pressure input steam is allowed to expand as it passes through the turbine. This releases energy and lowers the pressure of the steam at the outlet, without increasing the temperature ."

Guidance: http://tinyurl.com/oqskeeg (shortened link)

W7   Water management equipment

"Water management equipment for mechanical seals" is one of the technology classes specified in the water technology criteria list.

As such, the equipment may qualify for first-year allowances as **Environmentally beneficial technology** when all necessary conditions are met, as explained in that section.

According to the official website:

"Mechanical seals are used to prevent the escape of liquids and gases from rotating equipment, mixers, compressors and pumps. To allow seals to function correctly, clean water is injected to provide lubrication (this is termed 'seal water'), and although seal water flows are typically small, they are often continuous and result in high water usage over time.

Water can be conserved either by recycling seal water or by regulating internal flows (process fluid) by channelling particulates back into the product stream, thereby reducing the requirement for seal water. Creating a pressure gradient that prevents leakage may also reduce seal water requirements."

Three types of equipment may qualify under this heading. In all cases, the specific item must be included on the water technology product list.

The three categories of equipment that can qualify are as follows:

- seal water recycling units;
- internal flow regulators;
- monitoring and control units.

Where the criteria for first-year allowances are not satisfied, normal principles must be applied. Unless the circumstances are unusual, such equipment will no doubt qualify as plant and machinery and allowances will be given in the main pool.

Law: CAA 2001, s. 45H; SI 2003/2076, art. 3(2)(n)

Guidance: wtl.defra.gov.uk/product_search_landing.asp

W8   Water meters

"Meters and monitoring equipment" are one of the technology classes specified in the water technology criteria list. Such meters and equipment constitute plant and machinery and potentially qualify for enhanced capital allowances when all necessary conditions are met.

See **Meters** for further details.

Law: CAA 2001, s. 45H; SI 2003/2076, art. 3(2)(c)

Guidance: wtl.defra.gov.uk/product_search_landing.asp; R&C Brief 03/10 (see **Appendix 4**)

W9   Water re-use systems

"Water re-use systems" potentially qualify for enhanced capital allowances as **Environmentally beneficial technology**.

HMRC guidance has now been removed but the following former wording remains helpful:

> "Water reuse 'systems' are processed differently to 'products' on the WTL. ...
>
> Due to their bespoke nature, these technologies are both eligible for ECAs via a certification scheme for each individually installed system, rather than the standard product list used for other technologies on the WTL.
>
> Water reuse involves reusing suitably treated wastewater from one process for a different purpose. Water reuse technology reduces the demand on drinkable sources of

freshwater and reduces the volume of wastewater discharged to sewer. Water reuse can be an economical way to reduce your costs.

The business sectors that can benefit most from using water reuse systems include the following industries:

- food and drink
- printing
- chemicals
- construction
- electronics
- metal finishing."

The certificate is known as a "certificate of environmental benefit".

Law: CAA 2001, s. 45H; SI 2003/2076, art. 3(2)(g)

Guidance: wtl.defra.gov.uk/product_search_landing.asp; www.hmrc.gov.uk/budget2013/tiin-4016.pdf; R&C Brief 03/10 (see **Appendix 4**)

W10   Water supplies and water tanks

"Mains services, and systems, for water" are initially excluded from relief by virtue of item 2 at list A at s. 21.

However, a "cold water system" now falls into the category of integral features, attracting allowances at the lower "special rate".

In guidance that pre-dates the integral features rules, but that is still shown as current in the HMRC manual, the point is made that "most cold water systems etc. should not be looked at as a single entity and you should adopt a piecemeal approach to them".

See, generally, **Hot and cold water systems**. For first-year allowances available for specified forms of water technology, see **Environmentally beneficial technology**.

Law: CAA 2001, s. 21 (list A, item 2), s. 33A(5)(b)

W11   Water towers

The correct tax treatment of water towers is not clear cut.

In the *Lowestoft Water* case, a tower was held not to be plant, but this view was rejected by a majority in the House of Lords decision in *Barclay, Curle*, the majority view being that it did function as apparatus, harnessing gravity to perform a trade function.

Those cases both pre-dated the statutory rules now starting at s. 21 and it seems quite clear that a water tower would now have to be classed as a fixed structure. This will rule out classification as plant and machinery unless a statutory escape clause can be identified.

List C at s. 23 includes references to storage tanks and to certain reservoirs, but neither of these is an ideal description (though it could certainly be argued that a water tower is a large storage tank).

It may be that the let-out clause can be found in item 7(a) of list B at s. 22. This refers to structures, excluding those more specifically included in list B, "within Chapter 2 of Part 3" which provides or provided a partial definition of "industrial building" for the now repealed IBA rules. The effect of this is that a structure that falls within the definition of industrial building is not included in the list of fixed assets to which list B applies.

The next, obvious, problem is the repeal of the IBA legislation, but this is not an issue. FA 2008, Sch. 27, para. 33 reads as follows:

> "Despite the repeal of Part 3 of CAA 2001 by section 84, Chapter 2 of that Part continues to have effect for the purposes of paragraph (a) of item 7 in List B in section 22(1) of that Act (structures which are not plant and machinery)."

It may be noted in passing that Chapter 1 has not been reprieved for these purposes, so certain sections remain, but without any statutory anchor. Taken at face value, though, it does appear that Table B at s. 274 may provide the statutory key to allow a water tower to qualify as plant or machinery. Item 2 in that list refers to "water" and then to "an undertaking for the supply of water for public consumption". The statutory mechanism is clumsy and unclear but if that is not the effect of item 7(a) then it is difficult to see what role that part of the legislation does play.

If this statutory route is accepted as legitimate, it will be necessary to determine the treatment of a water tower on case law principles. As discussed above, these would seem to authorise a claim in normal circumstances.

Law: CAA 2001, s. 21, 22, 23, 274; FA 2008, Sch. 27, para. 33

Cases: *Margrett v Lowestoft Water & Gas Company* (1935) 19 TC 481; *CIR v Barclay, Curle & Co Ltd* (1969) 45 TC 221

W12   Ways

"Ways" are included in list B at s. 22 (alongside such related items as hard standings, roads, vehicle parks, etc.). As such, they are excluded from the definition of plant and machinery and no allowances are due.

HMRC guidance confirms that plant and machinery allowances will not be given "on the provision, construction or acquisition" of such assets.

Law: CAA 2001, s. 22 (list B, item 2)
Guidance: CA 22020

W13   Website creation

Tax relief will normally be due for the costs of developing a commercial website. HMRC take the view that the cost may need to be capitalised if the site "is capable of directly generating income".

More specifically, the HMRC guidance (from their "capital v revenue toolkit") is as follows:

> "Even though expenditure on website development may be shown in the accounts as advertising, marketing or IT costs, this does not necessarily mean that it is allowable as revenue expenditure. In order to identify the correct tax treatment the exact nature of the website costs should be examined.
>
> Application and infrastructure costs, including domain name, hardware and operating software that relates to the functionality of the website should normally be treated as capital expenditure. Design and content development costs should normally be treated as capital expenditure to the extent that an enduring asset is created. One such indication

may be an expectation that future revenues less attributable costs to be generated by the website will be no less than the amounts capitalised.

A website that will directly generate sales, subscriptions, advertising or other income will normally be regarded as creating an enduring asset and consideration should be given to treating the costs of developing, designing and publishing the website as capital expenditure.

Whilst a revenue deduction would not therefore be allowable, this capital expenditure will generally qualify as expenditure on plant and machinery for capital allowances purposes. Expenditure on initial research and planning, prior to deciding to proceed with development, is normally allowable as revenue expenditure."

At BIM 35870, HMRC seem to take a less generous line, arguing that "the cost of a web site is analogous to that of a shop window. The cost of constructing the window is capital; the cost of changing the display from time to time is revenue". However, it is thought that this is an unduly simplistic approach to the matter and is now superseded by the more recent *toolkit* guidance.

For many businesses the distinction will in practice be irrelevant, if the capitalised cost can be fully claimed by way of **Annual investment allowances**.

For companies within the intangible assets regime, HMRC guidance also contains the following (from the *Corporate Intangibles Research & Development Manual*):

> "Where expenditure on websites is recognised on the balance sheet under UK GAAP it is treated as expenditure on tangible assets; this is not the case under IAS. On adoption of IAS it may be necessary to recognise expenditure on the creation of a website (that has previously been recognised as expenditure on a tangible asset) as expenditure on an intangible asset.

> Where this occurs and an allowance was made to the company under Part 2 of the CAA01 when the asset was recognised as a tangible asset, the website expenditure of the company is excluded entirely from Schedule 29.

> Capital allowances will continue to be appropriate for further expenditure by the company on the website."

See also UITF abstract 29 (website development costs) if further information is required regarding the accounting treatment.

Guidance: www.hmrc.gov.uk/agents/toolkits/capital-v-revenue.pdf; BIM 35870; CIRD 25145;

W14   Wind turbines

Section 22 of CAA 2001 states that expenditure on the provision of a "structure" does not constitute expenditure on plant or machinery. The restriction is extended to include "any works involving the alteration of land". List B at that section includes a variety of specified structures, containing an exception for gas production but nothing for electricity production. A generic definition of "structure" is then given, which encompasses "a fixed structure of any kind, other than a building".

It seems clear that a wind turbine is a structure, so a statutory exemption is required to justify its treatment as plant and machinery.

The key element at list C (within s. 23) is item 1, which is for "machinery (including devices for providing motive power)". The meaning of "motive power" and indeed of "providing motive power" is a technical one and the former term seems to be used in somewhat different ways in different scientific contexts. The author would not wish to give a strong view on whether a wind turbine could be said to "provide motive power".

HMRC's definition of "machinery" only goes so far, but it seems entirely reasonable to classify a wind turbine as such. It contains the various moving elements that one expects to find in a machine and there really seems to be little reason to doubt that it falls within the definition. It is also possible that wind turbines will qualify as plant or machinery via the mostly repealed IBA legislation, if the qualifying activity is that of "an undertaking for the generation, transformation, conversion, transmission or distribution of electrical energy". The principles, still relevant since April 2011, are discussed under **Water towers** above.

It is understood that the small element of uncertainty is causing difficulties for PFI and other large scale engineering projects. The author's view is that all modern wind turbines, set on land or at sea to generate energy from the power of the wind, are structures but are also machinery. If that view is correct, the assets would therefore qualify for plant and machinery allowances. Some support for this view may now be found in HMRC's *Capital Allowances Manual* at CA 23084, which includes wind turbines in a list of "typical examples of plant or machinery".

The amounts of money at stake can be substantial. Quite apart from the cost of the turbines themselves, it will be necessary to consider what related installation costs will qualify. Those related costs, including the flattening of land and the creation of roads, may be large. The general principles are discussed further under **Alteration of land** above, but particular issues arise in relation to turbines. Typically, these may be installed in remote locations and it may be necessary to widen or even create roads to allow the turbines to be delivered. If newly created roads will be needed to service the turbines, and not merely to put them in place at the start, then they may fail the test of being "for the purpose only of installing plant or machinery". On the other hand, if the roads have to be widened purely to allow the turbines to be brought to site then it may well be possible to argue that allowances are due. If a new road is built, but it is wider than normal to accommodate the delivery loads, then it is at least arguable that a portion of the costs should qualify for allowances.

Another area of difficulty in relation to wind turbines is to determine whether there is a single asset (mast and turbine) or two separate assets. This can have an impact on the amount qualifying for relief and – in some circumstances – on whether the expenditure needs to be classified as long life expenditure, thus attracting writing-down allowances only at the slower "special" rate unless **Annual investment allowances** are available. It is possible, for example, that the mast will have a 40-year life but the turbine itself will need renewing after 20 years.

There are no easy answers to these issues, and it may be that official HMRC guidance (more robust than the passing reference at CA 23084) will be needed, or even a test case, before the correct treatment of such costs is definitively established.

Law: CAA 2001, s. 22, 23 (list C, item 1), s. 274; FA 2008, Sch. 27, para. 33
Guidance: CA 23084

W15   Windmills

This section is concerned with traditional windmills, perhaps now used as a tourist attraction rather than for grinding flour. For modern power-generating equipment, see **Wind turbines** above.

The question of whether a windmill is an item of plant or machinery is not entirely clear cut. Currently, there seems to be no HMRC guidance on the matter.

The statutory starting point is to be found in sections 22 and 23 of CAA 2001. The first of these two sections states that expenditure on the provision of a "structure" does not constitute expenditure on plant or machinery. The restriction is extended to include "any works involving the alteration of land". List B at that section includes a variety of specified structures. A generic definition of "structure" is then given, which encompasses "a fixed structure of any kind, other than a building".

This therefore raises two questions. Is a windmill a structure, and (if so) is there any statutory exemption to justify the treatment of a windmill as plant and machinery?

Structure

It seems fairly clear that a windmill is a structure, both from a commonsense point of view and from case law. Lord Denning confirmed this in the *Cardiff Rating Authority* case, where he defined a structure as:

> "something of substantial size which is built up from component parts and intended to remain permanently on a permanent foundation; but it is still a structure even though some of its parts may be moveable, as, for instance, about a pivot. Thus, a windmill or a turntable is a structure".

Machinery

If it is accepted that a windmill is a structure, it can only qualify for capital allowances if it is exempted by virtue of list C at s. 23 of CAA 2001.

The key element at list C is item 1, which is for "machinery (including devices for providing motive power)". So is a traditional windmill a machine? See the entry for **Machinery** above for a fuller discussion but, in brief, an item that is machinery qualifies for plant and machinery allowances in its own right, without any need to prove that it is also plant.

HMRC's definition of "machinery" only goes so far, but it seems entirely reasonable to classify a windmill as such. It contains the various moving elements that one expects to find in a machine and there really seems to be little reason to doubt that it falls within the definition.

A traditional windmill is arguably the premises within which any business is being carried on, rather than apparatus used for the trade. So it may not be plant. Nevertheless, if the whole mill can be considered to be a machine it will qualify for allowances in its own right, without any need to demonstrate that it is an item of plant.

Law: CAA 2001, s. 22, 23 (list C, item 1)

Case: *Cardiff Rating Authority v Guest Keen Baldwin's Iron and Steel Co Ltd* [1949] 1 All ER 27

W16   Windows

Windows are included in the definition of building, and so do not normally qualify as plant or machinery.

By contrast, the cost of double glazing, if added to an existing commercial property (but not when installed in a newly built property) will qualify for plant and machinery allowances if tax relief is not otherwise available. HMRC are quite explicit in allowing this:

> "Treat expenditure incurred on adding insulation against loss of heat to a building (other than a dwelling-house used in a residential property business) occupied by a person for the purposes of a qualifying activity, as capital expenditure

incurred on plant or machinery. This treatment also applies to a landlord who adds thermal insulation to a building (other than a dwelling-house) let by him in the course of his business.

[Plant and machinery allowances] are available for this expenditure if no relief (either an allowance or deduction) is otherwise available."

Expenditure on thermal insulation is classed as "special rate" expenditure, and writing-down allowances are therefore given at the slower rate.

An unsuccessful attempt was made in *McMillin* to claim allowances on the cost of windows in a so-called "eco" cottage. The argument was that the windows had a function beyond that of letting light in and excluding draughts. By analogy with the "solar shading" category of integral features, it was argued that the windows performed a similar function as they were filled with argon and they faced south. The argument was forcefully (and properly!) rejected.

HMRC have confirmed that, in principle, a reinforced window could qualify as a security asset under the special rules given at s. 33 (see **Personal security**).

Law: CAA 2001, s. 21 (list A, item 1)
Case: *McMillin v HMRC* [2011] UKFTT 65 (TC)
Guidance: CA 22220, 22270

W17   Writing-down allowances

These allowances (WDAs) are not a category of expenditure and are therefore not covered in this volume in depth. A very brief overview, however, is as follows.

The basic principle of the writing-down allowance is that tax relief for capital expenditure is given over a number of years, very roughly mirroring the accounting concept of depreciation.

Writing-down allowances for plant and machinery are calculated year by year on the reducing value rather than on the original cost of an asset. If a single asset costs £10,000 and is written off at 18 per cent per year, for example, it would attract allowances of £1,800 in year one, with the balance of £8,200 carried forward. In the second year, allowances would be calculated as £1,476 (£8,200 at 18 per cent) and so on.

In practice, allowances are rarely given for a single asset in isolation (the main exception being where an item is used partly for private purposes). Instead, the concept of pooling ensures that allowances are calculated collectively on a pool of assets, taking account of any additional purchases in the year, and also of any disposal proceeds.

In practice, the position is made more complicated as **Annual investment allowances** will often be available. Also, some expenditure is excluded from the main pool and is instead allocated to (for example) the "special rate" pool (attracting allowances at a lower rate) or to a single asset pool, where allowances for each item must be calculated separately.

See *Capital Allowances* 2018-19 for full, practical commentary on these allowances. *Capital Allowances* is written by the same authors as this volume and is also published by Claritax Books.

Law: CAA 2001, s. 53
Guidance: CA 23200

Z1   Zero-emission goods vehicles

Goods vehicles clearly qualify as plant and machinery.

Full (100%) first-year allowances are available for expenditure incurred in the period to April 2021 on certain zero-emission goods vehicles. The vehicle must be registered and must also be "unused and not second-hand".

A goods vehicle is usually a van, but is in fact defined to cover any "mechanically propelled road vehicle which is of a design primarily suited for the conveyance of goods or burden of any description".

The vehicle qualifies as having zero emissions if it cannot in any circumstances emit CO_2 by being driven.

Various exclusions apply. In particular, vans used for leasing do not qualify. There are also statutory exclusions for vehicles used for various specified activities, including fisheries, aquaculture and (where performed for third parties) certain waste management activities. First-year allowances will generally be denied if the cost is subsidised by "State aid" or certain other forms of aid.

Although relevant only for the largest enterprises, the total expenditure on zero-emission goods vehicles that can qualify for first-year allowances (over the entire period for which they are available) is capped at €85m per undertaking.

Law: CAA 2001, s. 45DA, 45DB (as amended)
Guidance: CA 23145ff.

Z2   Zoo cages

A zoo cage is likely to be a structure as long as it is fixed in place, and it is thus initially caught by s. 22. However, an exemption in list C (item 33) specifically applies to "fixed zoo cages".

It is not clear why that particular item is included in list C, and its inclusion does not guarantee that a fixed zoo cage will qualify as plant. But the fact that it is listed at all implies that a fixed zoo cage will be accepted as plant in at least some circumstances.

HMRC are at pains to point out that list C:

> "does not operate by analogy: for example item 33 which refers to fixed zoo cages does not apply to any other form of animal shelter such as kennels or stables."

It is understood that HMRC previously made a distinction between zoo cages and kennels by pointing out that zoo cages have the additional function of displaying animals safely to the public, rather than merely housing them. See also **Kennels** above.

Law: CAA 2001, s. 23 (list C, item 33)
Guidance: CA 22030

Appendices

Appendix 1: Buildings and structures: statutory rules

In determining what qualifies as plant or machinery, the key legislation is found at sections 21 to 23, reproduced below. Between them, these sections first create a distinction between "buildings" or "structures" (on the one hand) and "plant or machinery" (on the other). They then immediately blur that distinction by presenting a long list of items that may qualify as plant or machinery even though they may be (or may form a part of) a building or structure.

The key point to bear in mind about list C (at s. 23) is that the inclusion of an item does not necessarily mean that it will qualify as plant or machinery. If we take item 23 as an example, we see that dry docks may qualify as plant. This is because the courts had reached such a decision before the list was initially compiled for FA 1994. It is quite possible, however, that a dry dock might fail to qualify as plant in other circumstances. If an item is included in list C, it must be considered using the general principles that have emerged from case law decisions over many decades. Having said this, the inclusion of an item in list C may perhaps be taken as a presumption in favour of its qualification as plant or machinery in the absence of any strong reasons to the contrary. This is simply on the basis that items must all have been included in list C for a reason, and this arguably puts the onus on HMRC to show why an item mentioned in list C should not qualify.

Since 2008, s. 23(2) has included a reference to integral features, which can qualify as plant or machinery in their own right (see s. 33A). For these items (including, for example, electrical and general lighting systems) there is no longer any need to refer to case law precedents. They qualify for plant or machinery allowances in their own right "as if" the expenditure were capital expenditure on the provision of plant or machinery for the purposes of the qualifying activity.

21.   Buildings

21.1   For the purposes of this Act, expenditure on the provision of plant or machinery does not include expenditure on the provision of a building.

21.2 The provision of a building includes its construction or acquisition.

21.3 In this section, "**building**" includes an asset which–

a. is incorporated in the building,

b. although not incorporated in the building (whether because the asset is moveable or for any other reason), is in the building and is of a kind normally incorporated in a building, or

c. is in, or connected with, the building and is in list A.

List A – Assets treated as buildings

1. Walls, floors, ceilings, doors, gates, shutters, windows and stairs.

2. Mains services, and systems, for water, electricity and gas.

3. Waste disposal systems.

4 Sewerage and drainage systems.

5. Shafts or other structures in which lifts, hoists, escalators and moving walkways are installed.

6. Fire safety systems.

21.4 This section is subject to section 23.

22. Structures, assets and works

22.1 For the purposes of this Act, expenditure on the provision of plant or machinery does not include expenditure on–

a. the provision of a structure or other asset in list B, or

b. any works involving the alteration of land.

List B – Excluded structures and other assets

1. A tunnel, bridge, viaduct, aqueduct, embankment or cutting.

2. A way, hard standing (such as a pavement), road, railway, tramway, a park for vehicles or containers, or an airstrip or runway.

3. An inland navigation, including a canal or basin or a navigable river.

4. A dam, reservoir or barrage, including any sluices, gates, generators and other equipment associated with the dam, reservoir or barrage.

5. A dock, harbour, wharf, pier, marina or jetty or any other structure in or at which vessels may be kept, or merchandise or passengers may be shipped or unshipped.

6. A dike, sea wall, weir or drainage ditch.

7. Any structure not within items 1 to 6 other than–

   a. a structure (but not a building) within Chapter 2 of Part 3 (meaning of "industrial building"),

   b. structure in use for the purposes of an undertaking for the extraction, production, processing or distribution of gas, and

   c. a structure in use for the purposes of a trade which consists in the provision of telecommunication, television or radio services.

22.2 The provision of a structure or other asset includes its construction or acquisition.

22.3 In this section–

"(a) **structure**" means a fixed structure of any kind, other than a building (as defined by section 21(3)), and

"(b) **land**" does not include buildings or other structures, but otherwise has the meaning given in Schedule 1 to the Interpretation Act 1978.

22.4 This section is subject to section 23.

23. Expenditure unaffected by sections 21 and 22

23.1 Sections 21 and 22 do not apply to any expenditure to which any of the provisions listed in subsection (2) applies.

23.2 The provisions are–

section 28 (thermal insulation of buildings);
section 33 (personal security);
section 33A (integral features);
section 71 (software and rights to software);

section 143 of ITTOIA 2005 or section 40D of F(No.2)A 1992 (election relating to tax treatment of films expenditure).

23.3 Sections 21 and 22 also do not affect the question whether expenditure on any item described in list C is, for the purposes of this Act, expenditure on the provision of plant or machinery.

23.4 But items 1 to 16 of list C do not include any asset whose principal purpose is to insulate or enclose the interior of a building or to provide an interior wall, floor or ceiling which (in each case) is intended to remain permanently in place.

List C – Expenditure unaffected by sections 21 and 22

1. Machinery (including devices for providing motive power) not within any other item in this list.

2. Gas and sewerage systems provided mainly–

   a. to meet the particular requirements of the qualifying activity, or

   b. to serve particular plant or machinery used for the purposes of the qualifying activity.

3. [Omitted by FA 2008, s. 73(1)(b)(ii).]

4. Manufacturing or processing equipment; storage equipment (including cold rooms); display equipment; and counters, checkouts and similar equipment.

5. Cookers, washing machines, dishwashers, refrigerators and similar equipment; washbasins, sinks, baths, showers, sanitary ware and similar equipment; and furniture and furnishings.

6. Hoists.

7. Sound insulation provided mainly to meet the particular requirements of the qualifying activity.

8. Computer, telecommunication and surveillance systems (including their wiring or other links).

9. Refrigeration or cooling equipment.

10. Fire alarm systems; sprinkler and other equipment for extinguishing or containing fires.

11. Burglar alarm systems.

12. Strong rooms in bank or building society premises; safes.

13. Partition walls, where moveable and intended to be moved in the course of the qualifying activity.

14. Decorative assets provided for the enjoyment of the public in hotel, restaurant or similar trades.

15. Advertising hoardings; signs, displays and similar assets.

16. Swimming pools (including diving boards, slides and structures on which such boards or slides are mounted).

17. Any glasshouse constructed so that the required environment (namely, air, heat, light, irrigation and temperature) for the growing of plants is provided automatically by means of devices forming an integral part of its structure.

18. Cold stores.

19. Caravans provided mainly for holiday lettings.

20. Buildings provided for testing aircraft engines run within the buildings.

21. Moveable buildings intended to be moved in the course of the qualifying activity.

22. The alteration of land for the purpose only of installing plant or machinery.

23. The provision of dry docks.

24. The provision of any jetty or similar structure provided mainly to carry plant or machinery.

25. The provision of pipelines or underground ducts or tunnels with a primary purpose of carrying utility conduits.

26. The provision of towers to support floodlights.

27. The provision of–

    a. any reservoir incorporated into a water treatment works, or

    b. any service reservoir of treated water for supply within any housing estate or other particular locality.

28. The provision of–
    a. silos provided for temporary storage, or
    b. storage tanks.

29. The provision of slurry pits or silage clamps.

30. The provision of fish tanks or fish ponds.

31. The provision of rails, sleepers and ballast for a railway or tramway.

32. The provision of structures and other assets for providing the setting for any ride at an amusement park or exhibition.

33. The provision of fixed zoo cages.

23.5 In item 19 of list C, "**caravan**" includes, in relation to a holiday caravan site, anything that is treated as a caravan for the purposes of–

a. the Caravan Sites and Control of Development Act 1960, or

b. the Caravans Act (Northern Ireland) 1963.

Appendix 2: Football League letter

In 1991, HMRC wrote to the Football League indicating the types of expenditure likely to qualify for plant and machinery allowances. The list, and some introductory comments, are now included in HMRC's *Capital Allowances Manual* at CA 21230, as reproduced below.

The background was that the Taylor report was published at the start of 1990 following the Hillsborough disaster the previous year. The now repealed legislation of sections 29 to 32 was based on the legislation formerly at sections 69 and 70 of CAA 1990, enacted in March of that year.

The effect of the special legislation was (per s. 27, which is still there in shortened form) to apply the capital allowances legislation "as if" the expenditure were capital expenditure on plant and machinery. It is therefore quite possible that an asset would be excluded from the definition of plant and machinery by s. 21 (per the wording of s. 21(1)), would *not* be rescued by List C, but would nevertheless be brought back into play by s. 27 and following sections.

As such, HMRC may be able to argue that expenditure on some of the items listed below was only qualifying by virtue of the now repealed legislation at former sections 30 to 32.

In past years football clubs may have incurred expenditure on ground improvements in order to implement the recommendations of the Taylor report. The Inland Revenue had discussions with the Football League about what expenditure was likely to qualify for capital allowances. Following those discussions the Inland Revenue sent the Football League a letter on 25 January 1991 indicating what expenditure was likely to qualify. The letter listed as an appendix the sort of assets used by a football club in its trade that would normally qualify as plant or machinery. The list can be found below. Many but not all of the items listed qualify as plant under the current legislation, the rate of WDA will depend on the particular asset. As with all cases concerning the plant/premises divide and the question of whether or not an asset qualifies for PMAs the requirement is to identify the particular function of the particular asset in the particular trade and to then apply the statutory tests in Sections 21 to 23 CAA 2001.

This is the list:

1. Advertising hoardings and perimeter boards which are not simply part of a perimeter fence or other structure.

2. Air conditioning plant, fans and ventilation machinery.

3. Automatic exit doors and gates.

4. Bicycle holders.

5. Cameras, televisions, video recorders.

6. Cars, coaches and vans.

7. Computers, printers, photocopiers, typewriters and cash registers.

8. Cookers, fridges, freezers, microwaves, dishwashing machines.

9. Crush barriers securely fixed to the ground are not plant or machinery but they may come within the 1975 safety legislation and so qualify under CAA01/S32 CA22240.

10. Electric scoreboards and visual displays.

11. Fencing is not plant or machinery but it may come within the 1975 safety legislation and so qualify under CAA01/S32 CA22240.

12. Fire alarm systems, fire extinguishers, sprinkler systems.

13. Floodlighting.

14. Floor coverings that are not part of the building or structure; for example, carpets (but not tiles which are stuck down).

15. Goalposts and certain movable training equipment of a capital nature, for example, a vaulting horse (but not equipment which is part of the premises).

16. Heating installations, boilers and water heaters.

17. Lifts and hoists.

18. Public address equipment – microphones, amplifiers and loudspeakers.

19. Racking, shelving, cupboards and furniture.

20. Telephones and telephone equipment, for example, private exchanges.

21. Toilet sanitary ware, sinks and basins, baths and showers whether for staff or public (but not the mains water supply).

22. Turnstiles and spectator counting equipment.

The letter gave some guidance on seats. It said that most modern types of seats are likely to qualify as plant or machinery, both plain plastic tip-up seats and more luxurious types of seat. It makes it clear that seating which is no more than an integral part of the stand will not qualify.

It says that the incidental costs of installing seats, or any other type of plant or machinery, may qualify under CAA01/S25 CA21190. It says that expenditure will not qualify as incidental if it creates an essentially new asset such as a stand or a terrace with an entirely new rake. It also says that we would not expect expenditure to qualify as incidental if it is large in proportion to the cost of the plant or machinery being installed.

Remember that not all expenditure incurred by clubs to comply with the requirements of the Football Spectators Act 1989 will qualify for capital allowances. The normal rules will apply.

The letter states that expenditure on the fabric of a police control box will not qualify for capital allowances. We have now been advised that some local authorities take the view that they have the power under the Safety at Sports Grounds Act 1975 to require police control rooms to be installed. If that happens the expenditure will qualify under CAA01/S32 CA22240.

Appendix 3: Disability Discrimination Act

Under the terms of the *Disability Discrimination Act*, service providers are required to make "reasonable adjustments" to their premises to address any physical features that prevent disabled people from using their services. HMRC have issued guidelines in relation to the tax treatment of such expenditure. The guidance includes the following comments on capital allowances.

In the reorganisation of the HMRC website, and the gradual move of material to the Gov.UK site, this material appears to have been removed. Nevertheless, there is no reason to think that the underlying principles have changed.

Ramps

Expenditure on building or installing a permanent ramp to facilitate access by members of the public qualifies only if the work is carried out to an industrial or agricultural building or 'qualifying hotel'. Relief is given for the expenditure under the IBA code or agricultural buildings allowance ABA code.

Businesses that buy moveable ramps that are not permanently fixed to the building are able to claim PMAs on the cost of the ramp.

Toilets and washing facilities

Minor adjustments, such as changing doors on cubicles from opening inwards to opening outwards, would normally be wholly deductible for tax purposes as revenue expenditure.

The costs of making building alterations to toilets (for example, to widen a doorway to facilitate wheelchair access) are not allowable for tax purposes, unless the building is an industrial or agricultural building or qualifying hotel. In those circumstances, the alteration costs qualify for IBA or ABA capital allowances.

The cost of new sanitary ware installed to comply with DDA requirements qualifies for PMAs. So do the costs of installing the sanitary ware.

Signs

The costs of permanent signage qualify for PMAs.

Expenditure on, say, affixing warning transparencies on glass doors or similar surfaces qualifies for relief as a revenue expense. The use of coloured paint to make things easier to see (by, for instance, painting doors, step edges, or passages in contrasting colours) is allowable in full for tax purposes.

Hand rails

Where businesses replace existing handrails with special handrails to ease access for disabled people, the expenditure would normally be accepted as a repair and would be deductible in full.

Where new handrails are installed for the specific purpose of helping customers with mobility impairments, the cost would constitute capital expenditure but would qualify for PMAs.

Lighting and electrical systems

From 1 April 2008 new expenditure on lighting and electrical systems qualifies for a 10 per cent writing down allowance per annum as integral features. Electrical systems do not include computer, telecommunication, and surveillance systems (including their wiring), nor fire alarm or burglar alarm systems.

If the lighting appears on the Energy Technology Criteria List 100 per cent first-year allowances can be claimed. More guidance can be found in the Capital allowances manual.

Internal and external doors

Usually, doors are considered to be part of the premises and do not qualify for capital allowances. As such, no allowances are due on installing new doors.

But where a door is no longer fit for use, it is likely that the cost of replacing it would qualify for relief as a repair, and so is wholly deductible as a revenue expense.

Quite often simply replacing a traditional door handle with a D-shaped or similar handle enables service providers to provide improved access.

A door handle would normally be an integral part of the door to which it is affixed, with the result that it would not qualify for PMAs. Any replacement of the door handle, however, counts as a repair, and so is allowable as a revenue expense. Some mechanical door handles may not qualify as a repair, where they are actually an improvement over the previous handle, but they could qualify for PMAs as machinery.

Lifts

Where expenditure is incurred on constructing a new commercial building the cost of constructing the lift shaft is not allowable.

However, the cost of installing a lift or replacing an existing lift with a modern lift is considered to be expenditure on an integral feature and qualifies for a 10 per cent writing down allowance per annum. In addition, if incidental to the cost of installing the lift machinery, the costs of installing the lift shaft will also qualify for PMAs. More guidance can be found in the capital allowances manual.

Steps and stairs

Expenditure on knocking down steps and replacing them with ramps is not allowable. However, expenditure on adding fluorescent and coloured strips to the edges of steps, approaching and within business premises, to assist access by visually impaired people, is allowed as revenue expenditure on repairs and maintenance.

Alterations to walls and floors

Alterations to the fabric of a building are not normally allowable for tax purposes, unless the building is an industrial or agricultural building or qualifying hotel or unless the alterations are incidental to the installation of plant or machinery. So any expenditure on making new doorways or widening existing doorways would not normally qualify for relief.

However, repairs to floors, for example, to level out uneven surfacing due to wear and tear over time, is allowable as a revenue expense.

Also, HM Revenue & Customs (HMRC) accept that painting walls or floors in bright contrasting colours, to assist access by visually impaired people, is allowable as revenue expenditure on repairs and maintenance.

Car parks

HMRC accept that expenditure on, for example, redefining parking areas by repainting parking bays to provide wider, designated bays for disabled parking, is a revenue expense, which is allowable in full for tax purposes.

Where the work is more substantial, for example, to include car park resurfacing, then as long as there is no improvement element, the expenditure is allowable as normal revenue expenditure on repairs.

Paths

Normally expenditure on paths or land does not qualify for capital allowances. However there is a distinction between improving and repairing property. While expenditure on improvements generally counts as capital expenditure (which does not normally qualify for allowances) expenditure on repairs is a revenue expense, which is allowable in full for tax purposes.

Thus, where a business incurs expenditure on its paths in order to remove obstacles that could present a danger to the disabled, for example on:

- replacing cracked or uneven paving slabs;
- cutting back protruding or overhanging objects, grass or other vegetation,

the expenditure is revenue expenditure and is allowable in full.

Appendix 4: R&C Brief 03/10: Guidance on plant and machinery capital allowances for the pig industry

Early in 2010, HMRC Brief 03/10 was published, entitled "Guidance on plant and machinery capital allowances for the pig industry".

The document includes lists that are of primary interest to farmers but that are also relevant for other businesses. The declared aim of the document was to "illustrate the range of assets on which the pig industry might claim plant and machinery capital allowances". A quick review will show that the lists are far from comprehensive but they still provide a helpful summary of HMRC's views on the correct tax treatment of a wide range of assets.

The HMRC document has not been updated, at the time of publishing this edition of this book, with regard to changing rates and allowances. For example, the reference to annual investment allowances of £50,000 is now incorrect. Care should therefore be taken with how this document is used. The principles remain valuable, however.

Readership:

This Revenue & Customs Brief will be of particular interest to businesses involved in the pig industry and their tax advisers.

Background:

Following the Government's decision to phase-out agricultural buildings allowances by April 2011, the Department for Environment, Food and Rural Affairs (DEFRA) approached HM Revenue and Customs (HMRC) to discuss the implications of this change for certain agricultural sectors that are particularly heavy investors in buildings and structures with very short economic lives. A prominent example of such a sector is the pig industry. As a result of these discussions, HMRC agreed to prepare some additional guidance, to illustrate the range of assets on which the pig industry might claim plant and machinery capital allowances (including the new £50,000 Annual Investment Allowance). This guidance is reproduced below.

The Pig Industry – guidance on plant & machinery capital allowances (PMAs)

Introduction

This special guidance is intended to help the pig industry make claims for plant & machinery capital allowances (PMAs) by providing examples of some of the main types of expenditure that can qualify for PMAs. PMAs allow capital expenditure to be deducted from business profits. The main PMAs are:

Enhanced capital allowances (ECAs): rate 100 per cent

ECAs enable a business to claim 100 per cent of its expenditure on certain energy-saving or environmentally beneficial plant & machinery (P&M) in the year the expenditure is incurred. [Some types of equipment that may be covered are mentioned below, but whether any particular item will qualify depends on whether it falls within the precise eligibility criteria. Please check the ECA website for more precise details.]

Annual Investment Allowance (AIA): rate 100 per cent for expenditure on P&M up to £50,000 each year.

The AIA applies to both main rate (20 per cent) and 'special rate' (10 per cent) expenditure on P&M. The expenditure must be incurred on or after 1 April 2008 (companies) or 6 April 2008 (sole traders & partnerships).

Temporary 40 per cent First-year allowance (FYA) for 2009-10:

This extra encouragement to invest was announced by the Chancellor at Budget 2009, and applies to most expenditure on P&M incurred in the year 2009-2010 (not otherwise wholly relieved by the 100 per cent ECAs or AIA).

Writing-down allowances (WDAs) at 20 per cent or 10 per cent a year for 'main rate' or 'special rate' P&M expenditure respectively.

'Special rate' expenditure includes expenditure on the new classification of 'integral features' of a building or structure, incurred on or after 1 April 2008 (companies) or 6 April 2008 (sole traders & partnerships). But most expenditure on P&M qualifies at the main rate of 20 per cent.

Small pools allowance:

This is an alternative WDA, applying to accounting periods beginning on or after 1 April 2008 (companies) or 6 April 2008 (sole traders & partnerships), which allows the whole balance in the (10 per cent) 'special rate', and/or main (20 per cent) rate pools to be written-off at once, where the balance in either or both of those pools is £1,000 or less.

Notes:

1. These PMAs apply only to capital expenditure on 'plant and machinery' (P&M). This means that:

Buildings & structures

2. Although certain fixtures in buildings & structures may qualify as P&M (please see the examples that follow) – the shell of the building itself (for example, walls, floors, ceilings, doors, windows and stairs) does not generally qualify. And fixed structures (such as bridges, aqueducts, roads, hard standings and car parks) do not qualify for PMAs.

Revenue expenditure

3. Expenditure on routine maintenance & repairs normally constitutes a revenue deduction, deductible from the business's revenue account for tax purposes. As revenue, rather than capital expenditure, it cannot qualify for PMAs. However, one exception is expenditure on replacing the whole or more than 50 per cent of an 'integral feature' (such as an electrical or cold water system, heating system or lift) which, if incurred after 1/6 April 2008, is deemed to be capital expenditure in all cases, and which will generally qualify for WDAs at 10 per cent.

Double allowances

4. Double or allowances on the same amount of expenditure are not permitted. For example if:
   - in the year 2009-2010, a business spent (say) £75,000 on a new slurry storage system, it could claim a 100 per cent AIA on £50,000 of that cost, and a 40 per cent temporary FYA on the balance of £25,000, that is, total allowances of £50,000 + £10,000 = £60,000 in the year 2009-2010. This would leave £15,000 to be written down at 20 per cent a year in 2010-2011 and in later years;

- a 100 per cent ECA is claimed on (say) a piece of equipment costing £100,000, then that cost is wholly relieved and an AIA may not be claimed on that same piece of equipment to give more than 100 per cent relief.

General

5. Expenditure on the provision of P&M (for example, transportation & on site installation costs) and alteration of land for the purpose only of installing P&M, can qualify for PMAs at the rate applicable to the P&M being installed. However, expenditure on works involving the alteration of land more generally do not qualify. For example, the cost of levelling land in order to provide a stable base for a heavy machine would qualify, but the cost of levelling land in order to lay a hard standing or a foundation for a building would not qualify.

Examples of P&M

1. Outdoor items

Expenditure on the following can qualify for the AIA, FYA, WDAs and, in some cases * ECAs-

- Slurry storage systems, including, for example:
    - slurry storage tanks (whether above or below ground),
    - any reception pit &/or effluent tank &/or channels and pipes used in connection with the slurry storage tank;
- Small scale slurry and sludge dewatering equipment (*may qualify for 100 per cent ECA);
- Rainwater harvesting and filtration equipment (*may qualify for 100 per cent ECA);
- Gutters and associated piping for carrying rain water harvested for business uses;
- Sewerage systems designed to meet the particular requirements of the business;
- Silos for temporary storage;
- Concrete pad surrounded by low-level barriers for temporary storage of manure;

357

- Storage tanks;
- Moveable pig tents or pig arks;
- See also under '**general plant & machinery**' and '**cars**' at 3 and 4 below for the treatment of vehicles, etc.

2. Fixtures in buildings or structures

Expenditure on the following can qualify for the AIA, FYA, WDAs and, in certain cases* ECAs.

In the case of WDAs, certain fixtures attract WDAs at 20 per cent & others at 10 per cent – as shown separately at (a) and (b) below-

(a) Building features that can qualify for WDAs at 20 per cent

- Monitoring systems (including telemetry) for monitoring temperature, humidity, lighting, water and food levels;
- Water meters and monitoring equipment, including flow meters and water management software (*may qualify for 100 per cent ECA);
- Computer & telecommunications systems (including their wiring or other links);
- Fire alarm, burglar alarm & surveillance systems (including their wiring or other links);
- Feed systems (whether or not automated);
- Slatted flooring areas (as internal parts of a slurry system);
- Farrowing crates;
- Moveable, adjustable pen dividers;
- Taps, sinks, basins and drinkers (certain water efficient taps *may qualify for 100 per cent ECA);
- Fitted bathrooms, toilets, showers, kitchens & furnishings in office and staff accommodation used in the business (certain water efficient taps, toilets and showers *may qualify for 100 per cent ECA).

(b) Building features that can qualify for WDAs at 10per cent

- All parts of a general electrical system (whether providing mains power or a lighting system) irrespective of whether or not the system is designed to be 'trade specific';

- Certain lighting controls and Automatic Monitoring & Targeting (AMT) equipment designed to save energy, *may qualify for 100 per cent ECAs, if certified by the Department for Energy and Climate Change (DECC);

- All parts of air conditioning systems including, for example:
  - Ventilation shafts,
  - ACNV (automatically controlled natural ventilation) shutters,
  - Metal mesh & curtain arrangements for controlling airflow;

- Cold water, hot water and heating systems, including pipes, pumps, boilers, valves, etc. (but not sinks or basins that are plumbed into the system that can qualify for WDAs at 20 per cent – see above);

- Thermal insulation added to existing buildings or structures. (Certain pipe work insulation *may qualify for 100 per cent ECA.)

3. Non-fixtures: general plant & machinery (20 per cent) apart from cars

Expenditure on the following can qualify for the AIA, FYA, WDAs and, in certain cases* ECAs-

- Any agricultural or other machinery used for the purposes of the business. For example:
  - Specialist equipment for the production storage, handling & distribution of pig feed,
  - Pig transportation crates,
  - Pig weighing and handling equipment;

- Lorries, vans, tractors, trailers, fork-lift trucks and other agricultural vehicles & machines;

- Computers & computerised equipment;
- Free-standing heaters & air conditioning units (certain radiant heaters *may qualify for ECAs);
- Office equipment & furnishings.

4. Other P&M: Cars

Expenditure on cars used for business purposes does not qualify for the AIA or temporary 40 per cent FYA, but can qualify for:

- 100 per cent FYA if the car is electrically propelled or its CO_2 emissions do not exceed 110 grams per kilometre driven (g/km),
- 20 per cent WDA if the car's CO_2 emissions exceed 110 g/km, but do not exceed 160g/km, or
- 10 per cent WDA if the car's CO_2 emissions exceed 160g/km.

These environmentally based rules, to tie the rate of WDA to a car's CO_2 emissions, apply to expenditure on cars purchased on or after 1 April 2009 (companies) or 6 April 2009 (sole traders and partnerships).

Further information
CT VAT
Reliefs Incentives & Capital Allowances Team
3rd Floor
Mail Station A
100 Parliament Street
London
SW1A 2BQ
Phone: 020 7147 2610
Email: Joy Guthrie

Issued February 2010.

Footnotes

PMAs – more detailed, general guidance on capital allowances is contained in HMRC's Capital Allowances Manual.

*ECAs – In all cases where 100 per cent ECAs are mentioned in this note, please check the ECA website for the precise eligibility criteria.

Table of legislation

Note: there are general references to sections 21 to 23 throughout this book. Such general references are included only sparingly in the table below. However, full coverage is included below of references to particular subsections and of the items in lists A to C.

Sections 21 to 23 are reproduced in full at Appendix 1.

Capital Allowances Act 2001

Safety of Sports Grounds Act 1975

Index of cases

General index

372

378

Printed and bound in Great Britain by
Marston Book Services Limited, Oxfordshire